The Appearance of Equality

Recent Titles in
Contributions in Legal Studies

The Appearance of Equality

Racial Gerrymandering, Redistricting, and the Supreme Court

Christopher M. Burke

Contributions in Legal Studies, Number 89

GREENWOOD PRESS
Westport, Connecticut • London

Library of Congress Cataloging-in-Publication Data

Burke, Christopher Matthew, 1963–
    The appearance of equality : racial gerrymandering, redistricting,
and the Supreme Court / Christopher M. Burke.
      p. cm.—(Contributions in legal studies, ISSN 0147–1074 ;
no. 89)
    Includes bibliographical references and index.
    ISBN 0–313–30751–2 (alk. paper)
    1. Apportionment (Election law)—United States.   2. Representative
government and representation—United States.   3. Law and politics.
4. United States—Race relations.   I. Title.   II. Series.
KF4905.B87   1999
342.73′053—dc21   98–41416

British Library Cataloguing in Publication Data is available.

Library of Congress Catalog Card Number: 98–41416
ISBN: 0–313–30751–2
ISSN: 0147–1074

First published in 1999

Greenwood Press, 88 Post Road West, Westport, CT 06881
An imprint of Greenwood Publishing Group, Inc.
www.greenwood.com

Printed in the United States of America

The paper used in this book complies with the
Permanent Paper Standard issued by the National
Information Standards Organization (Z39.48–1984).

10 9 8 7 6 5 4 3 2 1

Contents

Preface

Words of caution to the reader. Do not expect to find, in the pages that follow, an answer as to what constitutes fair representation; how to arrive at its measure; or concrete suggestions as to how to remedy its lack. From the words and appearances of Supreme Court opinions, I have culled philosophical narratives or strategies of justification that give fleeting structure to debates over what constitutes fair representation in Voting Rights Act and reapportionment cases. However, there is very little new in the law and even less certainty. To this paradox, the subject of fair representation presents no exception.

Although I may claim that there is no such thing as fair representation, nothing that I write will dissuade those who believe ardently in a particular standard from thinking otherwise. It may be that capturing the essence of fair representation is as futile as trying to collect fog in a mason jar. The thing or its practice alters as we collect and examine it. Yet, the absence of fair representation seems to increase the urgency for arguments asserting its presence.

Several people whom I will not mention assisted me in this enterprise through time, opinion, and support. Though I do not acknowledge you by name, please accept my heartfelt appreciation. I would be remiss if I did not recognize Lawrence Burke, Dorothy Burke, Michael Hull, Jacquelynn Nikolaus, and Andrew Burke who offered material and personal support without which it would have been impossible to see this enterprise to its conclusion. Peter Carstensen graciously extended to me access to the University of Wisconsin Law School library. Heather Staines of Greenwood Publishing Group extended to me this publishing opportunity, and to her I owe my gratitude. Elizabeth Meagher, production editor at Greenwood Publishing Group, patiently guided me through various preparations of this manuscript. Copyeditor Beth Wilson had the thankless task of reworking the manuscript into a readable form. Finally, I acknowledge my personal and professional debt to Lisa Nelson who reviewed and critiqued the pages that follow in many different drafts and forms, from the beginning to the end.

Introduction: The Evolving Discourse on Fair Representation

This book attempts to describe and undo various liberal and communitarian strategies of justification that structure United States Supreme Court opinions in the area of political representation. The interpretive method employed herein introduces a means by which to situate opinions and illustrate that no conception of representation is legally unassailable or inherently politically liberal or conservative. This book tells the uncertain story of the creation of political fairness by the Supreme Court and warns against relying upon legal institutions at the expense of the democratic process in the quest for fair representation.

With the evolution of the Voting Rights Act (VRA) from 1965 through the present, legal and political standards of fair representation have undergone vast change as previously excluded minorities have asserted a greater political presence. Enlarging the number of groups covered under the VRA (1975) and changing the standard of proof necessary to make out a claim of vote dilution (1982) have changed the way we think about what is representative and fair. The language used to characterize what is fair and representative and the political designs that the rhetoric reflects allow us to formulate arguments for and against different concepts of fair representation as legal standards change. The practice of deliberation, within and outside formal politico-legal institutions, creates the standard of fair representation rather than finding it beyond politics. We must argue and persuade others in the political community of the veracity of our views, and the formal law is a necessary part of the argument—but not, perhaps, the entire solution.

The practice of law is paradoxical in the area of fair representation. The law demands that we hold explicit conceptions of the good regarding the legal mechanisms for ensuring fair representation, but truncates debate over differing conceptions of the good by placing certain options off limits (*e.g., de jure* proportional representation). The result is that the current debate over fair representation is incredibly polarized. Effective articulations of fair representation present courts with compelling choices and seemingly allow little room for debate. For an example, race-conscious communitarianism, which welds race and the practice of representation to the ideal of fair representation, must be reckoned with in any debate over the propriety of using the law to promote a greater minority presence in electoral bodies.

Reflecting politics in this area, United States Supreme Court decisions reveal the rich language and competing theories of fair representation. The textual diversity of Supreme Court discourse in fair representation was recently illustrated by such decisions as *Bush* v. *Vera, Shaw* v. *Reno, Shaw* v. *Hunt, Miller* v. *Johnson* and *Abrams* v. *Johnson*.[1] These decisions illustrate the dynamic measure of political representation and point to the limits of using the Supreme Court to promote a standard of fair representation as conservatives and liberals trade philosophical justifications of fair representation from case to case.

By placing the debate over fair representation into not only political and legal but also philosophical terms, I believe we are better able to understand the inevitable tensions that drive debates over representation into contentious political debates and ill-defined areas of the law. I employ such philosophical narratives as libertarian liberalism, egalitarian liberalism, liberal communitarianism, and conservative communitarianism to help explain the process that forms the practice and concept of fair representation. The evolution of fair representation depends upon creating new languages out of familiar vocabularies, and it may present an area in which the Supreme Court has, for the present, exhausted its competency.

The conflict over the meaning of fair political representation intensified in the early 1960's when the Supreme Court entered into reapportionment with *Baker* v. *Carr, Wesberry* v. *Sanders*, and *Reynolds* v. *Sims*.[2] The propriety of reapportionment and redistricting became a legal as opposed to a solely political determination. This invited legal challenges to apportionment schemes in nearly every state.

The Supreme Court's presence in the area of representation expanded rapidly after the passage of the VRA of 1965. New statutory causes of action proved less cumbersome and more effective than constitutional claims. Not surprisingly, the meaning of the VRA became a source of litigation. A consequence of the Court's decision to enter the apportionment arena, as well as of the passage of the VRA with a concomitant explosion of statutory challenges to apportionment and redistricting plans over the last thirty years, was an increased awareness of the lack of political power wielded by racial and language minorities. Government recognition of group claims in the context of interpreting the Constitution and the VRA intensified a fundamental legal debate over the political construction of fair representation.[3] This debate predates the Federalist and Anti-Federalist dispute over the contours of our political framework. It is an argument grown more complex and not likely one best dealt with by court pronouncements.

In Chapter 1, I explore the concept of fair representation. The legal discourse on fair representation in the United States has had to contend with the underrepresentation of minority groups, in particular blacks. The response by the political community to this malady has been, in part, to pass laws that, if enforced, promise to regulate if not remedy the problem. For example, Congress passed the 15th Amendment and the VRA to confront bars to the right to vote and the persistence of underrepresentation of blacks in electoral bodies. The framers and ratifiers of the VRA explicitly intended to get at the causes of low black political participation. The scope of the VRA has broadened to include a concern for the ability of racial and language minorities to elect candidates of their own choice. I argue that a consideration of fair representation must account for the underrepresentation of racial and language minorities. There may not be apparent legal or political solutions, but the question of the representation of racial and language minorities must be addressed in a serious contemplation of fair representation.

Commentators on fair political representation, with some exceptions such as Hannah Pitkin, do not give enough importance to the consideration of the elements of representation. By "elements" I mean those special terms used by an interpretive community concerned with writing on issues of fair representation. This is ironic since many commentators are lawyers, judges, and law professors, people for whom the ability to distinguish between the multiple meanings of a word or term is part of a craft over which they exercise mastery. Judges, theorists, and advocates adopt terms to characterize representation such as "representative," "governor," "candidate," "elector," and "political agent." It is important to look closely at these terms because they are fundamental to the discourse on representation. Exploring the disparate meanings attached to these terms enhances an appreciation of the complex nature of representation.

I next address the development of different theories of representation. I start with Hannah Pitkin's *The Concept of Representation,* which is basic to understanding contemporary debates over representation and the contributions of earlier philosophers on the subject.[4] I then explore various theories of representation in terms of communitarianism and liberalism. For instance, many aspects of the communitarian theory of representation developed by Edmund Burke are espoused in different forms in identity politics by contemporary race-conscious communitarians.[5] The liberal concept of representation is traced from Madison and John Adams through modern liberal theorists. As Pitkin demonstrates, certain aspects of representation such as authorization, accountability and the behavior and description of the representative recur in different forms and with different expectations in the historical development of the concept of representation. I discuss aspects of representation in terms of liberalism and communitarianism, and argue that liberal and communitarian conceptions of fair representation are not mutually exclusive.

Subsequently, I introduce a theory of minority representation advanced by Kathryn Abrams, Pamela Karlan, Melissa Williams, and other scholars that I characterize as race-conscious communitarianism. Race-conscious communitarian theories of representation critique liberal conceptions of the unencumbered self, rule of law, and procedural neutrality. They promote minority presence in representative bodies within a politico-historical understanding of group situatedness. Members of minorities are authorized to speak for their groups by virtue of their perspective. This perspective reflects the history and oppression of past and present group members. For race-conscious communitarians, the measure of fair representation takes the form of descriptive representation whereby the legislature is a picture of society. The representative's actions are legitimated by his or her particularities. This is a type of descriptive representation and finds its analog in Burke's discussion of the need for the direct representation of the American colonies and Irish Catholics in Parliament. However, no view of the political community is self-explanatory, and not all interests and individuals will be represented. Race-conscious communitarian theories of representation may replicate their criticisms of liberal theory by diminishing group solidarities that constitute political identity in order to promote the representation of particular groups. Nonetheless, race-conscious communitarian criticisms of representation may enrich liberal conceptions of what constitutes legitimate and fair representation.

I inquire as to whether race-conscious communitarian theories of representation are consistent with current liberal practice and argue that liberal practice does accommodate race-conscious communitarianism. However, race-conscious communitarian claims that circumscribe the political good threaten the ability of individuals, whether they are a part of a minority or of the majority, to articulate competing versions of fair representation, since to do so would entail compromising the solidarity of the minority group. This aspect of race-conscious communitarianism creates a dilemma for liberal legal institutions such as the Supreme Court.

I argue that liberal political practice, including the courts, accommodates competing liberal and communitarian theories of representation. For example, liberal practice forces race-conscious communitarians to argue why descriptive theories of representation ought to be promoted by such liberal institutions as the courts. In liberal practice, the exercise of representation is informed less by an *a priori* sense of the good than by a pragmatic and constant reevaluation of the political community of which one is a part. Theories of representation reflect partial views of what does, could, or should constitute the political community. Hence, representation is deliberation and is informed not by theories of how the representative ought to act or look but by the knowledge gained from practice. Representatives may possess a clear image of the good, but this cannot replace judgment gained from participating in the deliberative process. It may be at the expense of judgment that we look to legal fixes for minority representation.

In Chapter 2, I interpret the politics of fair representation as a rhetorical performance and introduce the method I employ to discover the motives driving reapportionment and VRA cases. Describing the rights discourse of fair representation as rhetorical does not mean that there is something real or objective with which it compares. Nor does it mean that our rhetorical practice is not in some sense objective. Our narratives are part of the reality we experience and describe. Describing a particular rights discourse as rhetorical merely means that language is the instrument we use to describe and convince. It is a dynamic, historical instrument. The meanings of words and the contexts within which they are employed change.[6] The rhetoric of this process is highly charged, and the stakes are high. The debate over fair representation questions some of the core tenets of representative democracy.

This chapter also considers the tone and substance of some of the secondary literature surrounding the politics of fair representation. The debate over fair representation brings into question race relations, the legitimacy of government practices and institutions, and the distribution of political power. As such, the opinions expressed in court decisions, newspaper articles, and law reviews tend to be strong, hyperbolic, and polemic. There is the sense in some of the writings that if the wrong course is taken with respect, for example, to setting Justice Department policy or interpreting the VRA, then all is lost for minority groups. Others are afraid that the Republic is heading toward an irreparable schism along racial and ethnic lines, and that race-based redistricting pursuant to the VRA hastens this process. These predictions are overwrought. No opinion, law, or policy directive is an unbridgeable crevasse. No concept of political representation stands in the way of debate as an immovable monolith. Ideas, decisions, and laws are open to interpretation, and interpretation is political. Maintaining that the debate over fair representation is rhetorical does not demean the stakes or the reality of the event. It only means that what will eventually become the standard for fair representation remains unclear. But there are answers with regard to representation that we assert to persuade others of the veracity of our position. The rhetoric of representation invokes both law and politics. Politics in this area is not likely to subside, and the legal standard of fair representation will continue to be litigated and debated, and to evolve.

For example, I discuss the discursive tools employed on behalf of those who espouse a theory of representation based on a physical and psychological correspondence between the representative and his or her constituency. The perspective defines the group, and the attributes of the group legitimate the perspectival representative. I discuss the political and legal implications of this for race-conscious communitarians. Race-conscious communitarians, no less than any other group of theorists, are dependent upon practices that authorize and inform their ability to convince their audience. One needs to be a part of an interpretive community for that individual to be comprehended. Reducing dissent within this group for the sake of making a coherent, concise legal argument is unfortunate for the articulation of the political good and forecloses the possibility of markedly different political consequences. The normalization of the perspectival candidate *via* the law lays the groundwork for the maintenance of a race-conscious communitarian orthodoxy that may be at odds with the contingency of liberal discourse.

I end this chapter by discussing the role of rhetoric in legal taxonomy. Because the law is also the play of words and the rememberance of phrases, its meaning changes. For example, the liberal theme of a case that yielded a politically liberal result may be appropriated at a later date by conservative justices. The law may also change because a statute, for instance, does not explicate itself, and its interpretations will differ and multiply. Likewise our reading of a statute may change because the meaning of cases seminal to understanding that statute have changed. When I discuss particular cases such as *Shaw* v. *Reno* and *Reynolds* v. *Sims*, it is with the knowledge that I cannot get to the bottom of these cases or glean a "bright line" rule despite attempts to ground my interpretation within a specific conception of the good. The result is that the legal debate over fair representation is contingent and does not lend itself to providing a long-term remedy for the persistent underrepresentation of minority groups.

Chapter 3 surveys the opinions of the United States Supreme Court and illustrates the rhetoric of what is fair representation prior to the landmark decision of *Shaw* v. *Reno* (1993). The opinions of various Supreme Court justices articulate and modify the standard of fair representation in specific fact situations at different times. For instance, enforcement of the VRA struck down practices such as poll taxes, literacy tests, and intimidation that denied the right to vote to blacks. In the late 1960's and the 1970's, the Court found that the use of racial gerrymandering and multi-member districts diluted minority voting strength and kept blacks from electing the candidates of their choice. By the 1980's, the Court refined the concept of vote dilution and minority representation to include the remedy of majority-minority districting.

Reynolds v. *Sims,* announced in 1964, is the historical starting point for my case analyses.[7] I argue that Supreme Court opinions form a body of representation jurisprudence, and express explicit and coherent liberal and communitarian versions of fair representation. These visions, sometimes contradictory, are just as often complementary. I maintain that whether a particular justice is politically liberal or conservative has very little to do with what rhetorical strategy he or she employs. For instance, politically liberal justices persuade us with communitarian rhetoric and with liberal rhetoric. The same is true of conservative justices. Thus, philosophical liberals on the Court are not necessarily politically conservative nor are communitarians necessarily politically liberal.[8] Furthermore, the same justice may employ both liberal and communitarian justifications in her opinion. The two theoretical frameworks are not mutually exclusive though they may be presented in opposition. Instead, communitarian and liberal frameworks project an ongoing dialectic in representation jurisprudence.

Reynolds v. *Sims* provided the Court with the different themes and basic vocabulary it would use to resolve VRA and 14th Amendment representation cases over the next thirty-five years. Of particular interest to my interpretation of *Reynolds* is Chief Justice Warren's use of philosophically liberal rhetoric to justify finding that Alabama's apportionment scheme, which weighted the votes of individuals differently, depending upon where they lived, violated the Equal Protection Clause. Voting, for Warren, was an individual right prior to any conception of how the political community of Alabama ought to be structured. At the time *Reynolds* was decided, Warren's opinion was considered politically liberal. Hence, the majority opinion in *Reynolds* was philosophically and politically liberal and explicated a form of egalitarian liberalism. By finding Alabama's plan dilutive of the urban voter's ballot, the majority articulated a result aimed at equality of political opportunity for the individual. Justice Harlan voiced a communitarian dissent with a politically conservative sensibility. He implored the majority to respect the various historical, economic, geographic, and occupational solidarities around which groups of Alabamans expressed their political desires. He sought to conserve Alabama's communities of interest, and a bicameral structure represented not only individuals but also associative interests. Harlan's warning against the impending intrusiveness of the federal courts in state reapportionment, and a subsequent dependence on the courts for political change, was prescient, to say the least. He distrusted the ability of the courts to adjudicate these types of political conflicts. This distrust eerily foreshadowed liberal dissenters in 1990's VRA cases such as Justices Ginsburg, Breyer, and Stevens, who warned against the Supreme Court's imposition of a theory of color-blind political equality at the expense of the political process.

The advent of the VRA supplied different types of issues to the Court than did cases brought pursuant to the Equal Protection Clause (*e.g.*, *Reynolds* v. *Sims* and *Baker* v. *Carr*). Early VRA cases dealt with physical access to the ballot, but those cases soon gave way to the consideration of vote dilution claims. In vote dilution cases, the plaintiff does not argue that his or her vote is not weighted as much as another's, nor that she or he is denied the right to vote. Instead, plaintiffs argue that the practices and procedures for selecting representatives deprive them individually, and as part of a minority, of the ability to participate in the electoral process and elect representatives of their choice. Various schemes, including multi-member districting, at-large elections, the changing of city boundaries, and the racial gerrymandering of single-member districts diluted the black vote. In these cases, black plaintiffs did not argue that they suffered a *Reynolds* v. *Sims* type of deprivation or that they were denied the right to vote. The claim of vote dilution was analytically distinct from earlier types of cases brought under the VRA and the 14th and 15th Amendments. The conclusion one draws from vote dilution claims under the VRA is that supposedly equal access to the ballot and equal weighting of votes are not enough to guarantee that minority voters will be equal participants in the political process.

As amended in 1975 and 1982, the VRA grew increasingly complex. The 1975 amendments to the VRA expanded coverage to additional minority groups. Hispanics, Asians, Native Americans, and Aleuts were brought under the umbrella of the VRA. Expansion of coverage was controversial. Originally, the VRA protected only blacks, and for good reason. Except for a few short years following the Civil War during Reconstruction, blacks as a group suffered comprehensive, institutional discrimination. Expanding the VRA to cover other groups whose claims for protection were tenuous in comparison with those of blacks may have diluted the law's moral and political force.

Gradually the egalitarian liberal ideal of representation articulated in *Reynolds* gave way to a politically liberal race-conscious communitarian theory of fair representation whereby the VRA was used to promote as far as possible the proportional representation of particular ethnic and racial groups. Section 2 of the 1982 amendments to the VRA dispensed with the necessity of proving purposive discrimination in order to make out a vote dilution claim. Instead, the plaintiff made a *prima facie* showing that the results of the electoral process did not produce as many minority representatives as would be indicated by their percentage of the population. Individual access to the ballot was not the issue; of importance was the electoral success of a particular minority. This led to measuring the propriety of a redistricting or reapportionment plan by the number of minority candidates elected. In practical and in legal terms, the idea of a group right to representation gradually supplanted the liberal theme of the right to representation pertaining to the individual prior to a notion of the good informed by communal associations.

By the mid-1980's, the VRA promoted the representation of minorities through the creation of majority-minority districts in vote dilution cases where plaintiffs proved that voting practices were discriminatory under a totality of the circumstances. The Court in *Thornburg* v. *Gingles* exhibited a preference for creating majority-minority districts where plaintiffs demonstrated racially polarized voting, whites consistently defeated black candidates, and a compact majority-black district could be formed. As a result of *Gingles* and the 1982 VRA amendments, voting rights activists and the Department of Justice pursued a policy of maximizing the number of majority-minority districts, at the state and congressional levels, with proportional representation of racial and ethnic groups as the unwritten goal. A possible consequence of majority-minority districting was an increase in the number of Republican officeholders at the state and federal levels as the remaining majority districts lost minority voters. The harm and the remedy in vote dilution cases brought pursuant to the VRA were seen in communitarian terms. Groups claimed representation rights and articulated a discernment of the political good whereby groups covered under the VRA were represented in rough proportion to their percentage of the population.

I criticize the use of majority-minority districts to the exclusion of other alternatives that may result in better representation for minority interests. For instance, proportionate influence districting, whereby blacks and other minorities are not packed into single-member districts but are spread into districts with sympathetic majority voters may result in increased minority influence in the legislature in comparison to the use of majority-minority districts. This alternative was explicitly not recognized as a remedy under the VRA in *Voinovich* v. *Quilter.*[9] Unhappily, the use of majority-minority districting segregated voters according to race. Districts became associated with particular groups through the force of law. Without incentives to cater to minority concerns, majority politicians could afford to ignore political programs perceived to benefit minority groups. At the same time, minority incumbents with safe seats had less inducement to engage in horse-trading with their majority counterparts. The political landscape was perceived by some to reflect a racial spoils system whereby groups were entitled to a certain level of success. These developments led to a new round of cases brought pursuant to the VRA and the Equal Protection Clause.

In Chapter 4, I continue the analysis by reconstructing in a philosophical framework the opinions in *Shaw* v. *Reno* and succeeding cases. These cases mediate the tension between treating all citizens in a neutral fashion and accounting for the historical underrepresentation of minorities in laws that distinguish among different racial groups. This discussion of fair representation is carried out in liberal and communitarian narratives. I argue that a liberal and communitarian dialectic in Supreme Court opinions sustains a vigorous and relevant contention over the formation of fair representation within a politico-historical rights discourse. Liberal and communitarian frameworks bend and expand to account for different fact situations. Philosophically liberal arguments that yielded politically liberal results in the 1960's may result in politically conservative outcomes in the 1990's. Likewise, the communitarian rhetoric employed by politically liberal dissenters such as Justices Stevens and Ginsburg in recent VRA and reapportionment cases is strikingly similar to that adopted by the conservative Justice Harlan in *Reynolds*.

I ask what *Shaw* v. *Reno* means, does not mean, and why. In *Shaw* a combination of Democrats eager to save their seats, blacks desirous of majority-minority districts, and a Department of Justice intent on maintaining its influence in the districting process in states covered by Section 5 of the VRA created two majority-minority districts where there had been none. As a result, North Carolina sent its first two black representatives to Congress in this century. This was accomplished by drawing bizarrely shaped districts. The impropriety of the districting process in North Carolina spoke for itself. The Supreme Court articulated an "I know it when I see it" standard for describing the North Carolina redistricting plan similar to Justice Stewart's identification of obscenity in *Jacobellis*. The North Carolina plan was political segregation at best and apartheid at worst.

Shaw was also a case about partisan consequences and had North Carolina not been intent on protecting Democratic incumbents, the resulting majority-minority districts would not have looked so odd. I also ask what those who criticize the Shaw majority for relying on appearances rather than reality leave out of the analysis. To assert that there is a reality out there that must be taken into account is a profoundly rhetorical contention. Maintaining that there must be something other than mere appearances upon which to base a 14th Amendment claim diminishes the real political and legal power that appearances possess.

My discernment of *Shaw* reveals a pattern of justification based on philosophically liberal terms by the politically conservative majority. This may be mildly ironic for those who remember that the politically liberal majorities in *Baker* v. *Carr* and *Reynolds* v. *Sims* used similar philosophically liberal strategies of justification. However, though the rhetorical strategy in *Shaw* is in many ways similar to that used in *Reynolds*, important differences may be apprehended. The shift from *Reynolds* to *Shaw* was not only from politically liberal to politically conservative but also from egalitarian liberal to libertarian liberal rhetoric. Likewise, the relatively liberal dissenters in *Shaw* frame the contest in liberal, race-conscious communitarian terms. Again, this may seem incongruous for those who recall that the conservative Justice Harlan's dissent in *Reynolds* employed a rhetorical strategy similar to the dissent authored by the liberal Justice Stevens in *Shaw*. Both articulated an explicit notion of the political good circumscribed by communal associations. These communal concerns included race, religion, occupation, history, geography, and partisanship. The pattern of rhetorical strategies in *Shaw* effectively transposed the pattern in *Reynolds*, where the liberal majority employed philosophical liberalism and were countered by Harlan, who appealed to the historical and communal nature of state politics in Alabama and across the country. The lesson to be learned is that particular strategies of justification are not inherently conservative or liberal. The same sentences may be appropriated for diametrically opposed political ends. This is the irony of representation jurisprudence and of using the law to evoke change.

Several important cases followed *Shaw* such as *Miller* v. *Johnson, Bush* v. *Vera, Shaw* v. *Hunt* (*Shaw II*), and *Abrams* v. *Johnson* (the progeny of *Miller* v. *Johnson*). One could read these cases as extending the logic of *Shaw* to the merits of Equal Protection Clause challenges to majority-minority districting. I believe this is the case, but that the logic of *Shaw* is neither Delphic nor self-explicating. The shape of things to come, a question so important to the *Shaw* majority, is a shape whose final form has yet to appear. Certainly, the mixture of race, politics, Justice Department meddling, and the text of the VRA is volatile and may result in the loss of further majority-minority districts. But this does not mean that the VRA is unconstitutional or that means other than majority-minority districting cannot be used to promote minority representation and avoid *Shaw*'s criticisms of state-sponsored racial separatism. It may mean that we have reached, for the time being, the limits of Court competence in reapportionment and redistricting, and that those seeking to promote fair representation should target institutions other than the Court.

An interesting trend revealed in post-*Shaw* cases is the ease with which conservative and liberal justices trade strategies of justification. For example, the conservative Justice Kennedy in *Miller* uses a libertarian liberal rhetoric to carry his message of color-blind legal neutrality in the Georgia redistricting process. The right to vote and participate in the political process pertains to the individual prior to his or her membership in a racial group. Amazingly, Justice Kennedy then shifts to a conservative, communitarian rhetoric to criticize the Justice Department for creating black communities, and majority-minority districts, at the expense of traditional or natural black communities. In *Abrams* v. *Johnson*, Justice Breyer matched the ease with which Justice Kennedy moved from a liberal to a communitarian argument. Considering, the same Georgia redistricting process two years later, Justice Breyer in dissent argued a familiar liberal, race-conscious communitarian concern for promoting the interests of a politically underrepresented minority group. However, Breyer then chided the Court for imposing its notion of good on a Georgia political process that produced two majority-minority districts. His concern that an explicit notion of the good could compromise political deliberation is consistent with Justice O'Connor's opinion in *Shaw* and Justice Kennedy's opinion in *Miller*. Finally, his fear of Court involvement in the political process conjures up similar jurisprudential worries by Justice Harlan in *Reynolds* and Justice Frankfurter in *Baker* v. *Carr*.

In sum, the evolution of the legal standard of fair representation facilitated, and was affected by, changing interpretations of the 14th Amendment and the VRA, a law that is applied to a multitude of rights claims in vastly different parts of the country.[10] In the 1990's, a politically conservative Supreme Court expressed its uneasiness with the use of some, but not all, majority-minority districts as a means to increase minority representation. Some members of the Court felt that the use of race as the predominant factor in districting sent the message that racial groups had exclusive interests and that representatives represented groups rather than individuals. Because of their shape and the purported predominant use of race in determining boundaries, some majority-minority districts implicated the protections afforded by the Equal Protection Clause, as the Court noted explicitly in *Shaw* and later cases such as *Miller*.[11] As a result, some majority-minority districts were invalidated. It is less clear, however, how these Court decisions will affect the number of minority representatives or the quality of representation for minority groups.[12]

Debates over the standard of fair representation in the academic literature commenting on *Shaw* and other VRA cases tend to reflect strong opinions. This should not be surprising, given the stakes involved. There is a longing to establish once and for all what is fair, what is an unconstitutional gerrymander, and what is representative. Some advocate models that, we are told, take self-dealing out of the apportionment and districting process. In other words, we must de-politicize politics to make it fair. Others argue that we must discern which oppressed groups to represent proportionally, and that we can do so by a careful examination of present and past claims of discrimination. No position is unassailable. Fair representation remains contingent. The academic literature and Supreme Court opinions reflect constant contention over the standard of fair representation. This is a fortunate, if uncomfortable, state of affairs for the political community. There is not, nor can there ever be, an absolute standard of fair representation unless the dialogue over what is fair and unfair stops. A deliberative process leaves long-term solutions open-ended, hopefully within reason, and with due respect for the concerns of those whose views did not carry the day. Liberal discourse allows us to keep asking questions and refining the extent of representation. Halting the discourse and imposing a solution outside of politics, beyond deliberation, leaves us with a much different type of political community than that comprised by our institutions and practices. Halting the debate and imposing a solution based on an extra-political understanding of fair representation is what is asserted by some race-conscious communitarians. However, the debate has not been halted by race-conscious communitarian critiques of liberal theory. Rather, it has been enriched. Race-conscious communitarian critiques of liberal theory in the area of representation inform and are informed by liberal practices that accommodate particular collective claims for representation without removing them from political contention.

I conclude by noting that just as the VRA underwent significant revision, so has our concept of representation as it relates to the legal standards that regulate it. What is fair representation for particular minority groups will not be settled by statute or by the Constitution. However, the politics of fair representation will persist and continue to be mediated by constitutional and statutory standards.

The discussion in Chapter 5 adopts liberal and communitarian frameworks within which to understand and justify rights claims affecting political representation. Supreme Court opinions interpreting the VRA and the constitutionality of reapportionment schemes grasp liberal and communitarian conceptions. I place the discussion into a theoretical context that includes, at the one end, libertarian liberal understandings of the political community and, at the other, liberal communitarian responses to the failure of libertarian liberal and egalitarian liberal theories to articulate a coherent notion of the good within which rights pertain to the individual. For instance, in liberal theory, the right to vote and the right to political representation belong to the individual, absent a conception of the political good within which the individual exercises his or her rights. Communitarians argue for the recognition of group solidarities, including race, religion, and place, that make possible rights claims and inform our notion of the good.

Liberal and communitarian understandings of representation need not oppose, although in the debate over fair representation, liberal and communitarian frameworks are presented as exclusive choices. Aristotle is a philosopher invoked by both communitarians and liberals as authoritative. I discuss the relevance of Aristotle's *Politics* and *Nichomachean Ethics* to the liberal and communitarian debate. I argue that to the extent that both liberals and communitarians invoke Aristotle to legitimate their competing theories of the political community, Aristotle remains relevant to our consideration of political representation. I also argue that because of the confusion surrounding terms used by Aristotle, including "community" and "communion," it is not necessary to view liberal and communitarian conceptions of the political community as mutually exclusive. The practice of liberalism incorporates many of the communitarian critiques of liberal theory. Procedural neutrality, a cornerstone of liberal practice, ultimately may enhance rather than hinder the development of legal solutions to the problem of minority underrepresentation by not privileging particular minority claims at the expense of others and by protecting the legal status of minority individuals. Communitarian critiques erect a strawman in the form of an extreme version of liberal theory—a strawman whose artificiality is belied by liberal legal practices such as Equal Protection Clause and VRA claims that articulate a notion of the political good, more or less defined, by which group rights reinforce communal solidarity.

Race-conscious communitarianism may be at odds with libertarian liberal notions of fair representation voiced by Justices O'Connor and Kennedy and Chief Justice Rehnquist. These justices oppose a race-conscious communitarian conception of representation because they believe it circumscribes the relevant political solidarity that informs an individual's political actions, diminishes racial group diversity, and reduces politics to a single factor, race, that has rended the political community.

I conclude by arguing that liberal practice accommodates communitarian critiques of fair representation without adopting so specific a formula that the discourse over fair representation halts. This is important because the measure of representation remains historically contingent. What was equitable once may not be equitable now, but we can still learn from the prior standard. However, the tolerance for alternative versions of the political good that inheres in liberal practice does not mean that liberal practice does not exert some pressure on race-conscious communitarians to modify their strategy for increased representation. It is likely that the demands made by race-conscious communitarians for fair representation will change radically as the structure of the political community changes along with attitudes held about fairness and the constitution of groups. Certainly, representation is not presently fair for all individuals and groups. This means that deliberation over the standard of fair representation must continue in order to benefit excluded minorities and for our concept of representation to remain relevant.

In the end, I find that different discursive strategies, broadly identified as liberal and communitarian, are used by the Supreme Court to justify the outcomes of various cases brought pursuant to the VRA and the Equal Protection Clause. However, no particular strategy of justification is inherently politically conservative or liberal. Moreover, it is unlikely that the Supreme Court will articulate a stable measure of fair representation. The law may not be the most fertile medium within which to articulate and pursue greater political inclusion. The greatest challenge facing liberal practice in the area of fair representation will be to discover new responses to the challenges facing marginalized groups who desire more effective participation in the political process and a less tenuous place in the political community. The Supreme Court offers one more forum in the deliberation over what is fair representation but is unlikely to provide minority communities with legal or political answers to the problem of political underrepresentation. It may be the case that the Supreme Court, and courts in general, are institutions incapable of articulating and sustaining a standard of fair representation. Such a view invites caution with investing a particular institution, such as the Supreme Court, with the authority to determine once and for all what is fair. Rather, it accepts the limit of the Court in the framework of this deliberation.

Chapter 1

Assessing Representation

This chapter considers the dimensions of political representation. Take, for example, the measure of fair representation. Some forms of representation are perceived to be equitable or fair, and others are not. This is especially the case in the United States as particular ethnic and racial groups are underrepresented persistently in proportion to their percentage of the population.[1] Thus far, the most effective legal mechanism to ensure equal access to representation of minority groups, after guaranteeing the right to vote, is the majority-minority district. In majority-minority districting, electoral districts are reconfigured so that minority voters comprise a majority of the district and elect a minority candidate. The underlying premise is that members of racial minorities more effectively and legitimately represent minority communities. To some extent, the communal identity of the representative informs and delimits the representative function. Operating on this limited set of premises, proportional representation of ethnic and racial groups becomes the *sine qua non* of fair representation. However, such a conception may omit important issues of representational practice that bear directly on effective representation even if they are not so easily summed up and measured.

I argue that a consideration of the concept of representation, let alone equal or fair representation, is premature without first undertaking an enumeration of its terms. The nomenclature includes "representative," "governor," "elector," "candidate," and "political agent." These terms have varied meanings and are used in dissimilar fashions by different authors. The meanings of these terms, the building blocks of the concept of representation, are highly contextual. Employing the relatively ambiguous and indeterminate elements of representation, I discuss its various theories. For instance, Hannah Pitkin and Edmund Burke emphasize the behavior of the representative. The discretion of the representative, once democratically authorized, is primary. Burke, Pitkin, and John Adams criticize theories of descriptive representation whereby the legislature ought to be a miniature of the nation. This may be contrasted with Iris Marion Young, Lani Guinier, and Kathryn Abrams, who in different ways argue for a descriptive correspondence of the representative and the electors.[2] Young, Guinier, and Abrams articulate a race-conscious communitarian understanding of the political community and the function of the representative.[3]

I also contemplate the role of groups in theories of representation. The presence of factions or interest groups was central to James Madison's view of representation and how to structure the Republic. Liberty was to faction as air was to fire. Factions were an inevitable by-product of political liberty and promoted robust debate. Yet, Madison wished to moderate the effect of factions. Left to pursue narrow, self-interested agendas, factions could have a deleterious effect on the health of the political community by delimiting individual choice and choking off deliberation on public issues. In particular, Madison feared tyranny by a majority faction over minority factions.[4] Similarly, Lani Guinier fears tyranny by a white majority over racial minorities. For different reasons than Madison's, she wishes to structure politics to prevent a tyranny of the majority. Guinier and others such as Iris Marion Young and Melissa Williams argue that certain factional interests, such as racial minorities, demand protection in the area of political representation because of their historical exclusion from political office. Many of the same terms and tensions that consumed the framers and ratifiers of the Constitution recur in contemporary debates, though the latter are informed by much different historical and political considerations.

UNDERREPRESENTATION AND THE VOTING RIGHTS ACT

A consideration of fair representation in the United States must acknowledge the persistent history of underrepresentation of particular groups. Underrepresentation is a widespread phenomenon. If underrepresentation is contrary to fair representation, then political representation has rarely been fair. In the context of urban and rural interests, underrepresentation was due to a faulty apportionment that overvalued rural votes. In the context of women, and racial and language minorities, underrepresentation found its origins in law and practices that forbade these groups from voting. Even with the spread of the franchise, various devices such as poll taxes, literacy tests, and blatant intimidation kept blacks and Hispanics underrepresented in state and national legislatures. Finally, after securing the vote and equalizing the apportionment process, the gerrymandering of district lines and various electoral practices prolonged minority group underrepresentation.

Current academic and political literature on representation concentrates on the persistent problem of the underrepresentation of racial minorities. The most apparent reason to privilege race in the area of representation is history: slavery, the Civil War Amendments, Jim Crow, and the Voting Rights Act. States denied blacks the right to vote and political representation in a systematic way unique in American history.[5] In the United States, judicial intervention in the area of fair representation began fitfully. With few exceptions, such as "white primaries," the area of representation was thought to involve nonjusticiable "political questions" that courts avoided. This changed in the early 1960's with such landmark cases as *Baker* v. *Carr* and *Reynolds* v. *Sims*.[6] Changes in society and the law, especially the Civil Rights Movement and the Voting Rights Act of 1965 (VRA), led the Court into areas that implicated more than the right to vote and apportionment on a population basis. As the VRA evolved, the Court debated the significance of the correlation between the description of the representative and the represented.[7] The VRA, originally designed to protect the right of blacks in the South to vote, gradually expanded to include five racial and language minorities.[8]

Changes in the VRA redefined the legal and political standard of representation. The liberal ideal of representation, whereby individual voters defined themselves in terms of fluid groups and evolving if parochial interests, was replaced by a statutory model linking voters' descriptive characteristics to the descriptive characteristics of their representatives.[9] This process integrated minorities into the institutions of government by creating majority-minority, single-member districts, and breaking up discriminatory multi-member districts.[10] Majority-minority districts contain a majority of minority voters, which increases the likelihood that they will elect the candidate of their choice. The creation of majority-minority districts was necessary to combat practices that tended to minimize the political strength of blacks and other minorities.[11] Majority-minority districts exploit the political power of racial factions. The ability of factions to control the deliberative process, and concomitant efforts to check them, have been a concern since this country's founding.[12] The VRA was designed to ensure equal access to the ballot and minority representation by forcing the majority faction, whites, to give up some power. In this sense, the VRA promotes racial diversity among elected officials.

In practice, the VRA may not be consistent with the Madison's effort to control the power of factions. It may exacerbate factional conflict. Ensuring the representation of underrepresented groups by single-member districting results in racial and ethnic enclaves. This may validate a sense of factional difference through federal law. Certainly racial interests have value apart from the law, but these interests are actionable under the VRA.

DIFFERENT ELEMENTS OF REPRESENTATION

To speak about representation, we need to be familiar with some of its core elements. Terms such as "representative," "governor," "political agent," "candidate," and "elector" are fundamental to discussions about fair representation. However, identifying the essential terms of representation is not enough because words such as "governor," "candidate," and "elector" carry multiple and inconsistent connotations.

Consider the term "governor." We might take this to mean a governor of a state, such as Governor Tommy Thompson of Wisconsin. But our notion of governor is not so crabbed as to be delimited solely by state governors. We go to the polls for more reasons than to elect a state governor. We elect all sorts of public officials who to a greater or lesser extent govern by exercising state authority or administering the laws: for instance, county executives, councilpersons, alderpersons, and judges. This is not nearly an exhaustive list of governors or of public officials whom electors elect. I further assume that a governor is a public official and that this public official governs. Of course, not all governors or public officials are directly answerable to electors.

One could argue that the Secretary of Defense or the head of the Federal Reserve is a governor; each is certainly a public official. Yet, neither is voted into office, although at one time they may have been candidates for their respective positions. In another sense, they were probably elected to their jobs; they were selected for the job from a list of candidates.[13] Depending upon one's understanding of governing, we might then acknowledge that not all officials we elect govern and that not all governors are elected to office through a popular vote.

Could we agree that governing is at first glance a task associated with the executive branch? When we vote for county or circuit court judges, do we say we are voting for our governors? Not usually. The extent to which some candidates—for instance those who wish to win a seat in the United States House of Representatives—are governors is unclear. Certainly, the administrative duties of the Speaker of the House make him a governor of the House. But what of the new Representative with little or no committee influence? It might be better to say that we vote for representatives who sometimes govern. Finally, governors are sometimes electors, though most commonly we think of governors as elected by electors. For instance, districting is part of the apportionment process, and it is highly political.[14] Districting involves the drawing of boundaries between electoral districts. It turns the election process upside down because "the purpose of voting is to allow electors to select their governors," but in the context of redistricting, it is the governors who pick the electors.[15]

The connotations that the term "governor" evokes are varied. Equally imprecise is the term "representative." Of primary concern to the adequacy of representation is the behavior of the representative. The task of representing is not generic. The representative function of a judge is different from that of a Senator or an alderman.[16] Nonetheless, there are similarities that cut across the category of representative no matter what the office. For instance, the ritual of voting is roughly the same. Within any particular jurisdiction, the franchise is just as limited for those voting for an alderperson as it is for those voting for a state supreme court justice or the President of the United States. Perhaps, then, the term "representative" and the concept of representation can be further defined by inquiry into how the representative is authorized. In a democracy, electors confer the representative's authority.[17]

An elector makes a choice. The restrictions on the elector's range of choices may or may not be apparent.[18] The act of politically electing in our society is constituted by specific institutions, rules, campaigning, and voting. I choose between candidate A and B through the ballot. By gaining more votes than her challenger, the winner can claim victory or even a mandate. Participating in an election is a legitimization ritual. It legitimates the winning candidate. However, perhaps most important it legitimates the institutions and practices of government.[19]

Elections determine winners and assure some change within the practices and political institutions we recognize as legitimate through our participation. Elections involve choosing among alternatives. The voter can compare the descriptive characteristics, the rhetoric on explosive issues like abortion or affirmative action, and the party affiliations of competing candidates.[20] Given their interests and the promises made by the candidates, electors make a choice as to which they perceive will best represent them.[21] In the United States, because of racially polarized electorates, this may turn on racial group affiliation.[22]

In general, before one can govern or represent, or continue to govern or represent, one must be elected. At this juncture, the present or potential representative is a candidate. Let us now consider the concept of a "candidate." A candidate for something, whether for a job or a political office, is one who aspires to be preferred.[23] Indeed, a candidate may hold an office and run for another office or for reelection. As such, candidates can represent and govern. Certainly the President or an alderman can be a candidate and continue to govern and represent. However, not all candidates are representatives or governors, as one may seek a preferment yet not hold an office.

Who is a viable candidate is to some extent delimited by the law. There are age restrictions for those wishing to serve as President or in Congress. The legal standard of fair representation further informs the ability of some candidates to run against other candidates.[24] This is especially true if a candidate is a member of a racial or ethnic community whose members do not attain office in proportion to their percentage of the population. In some cases, what is contested is not merely the candidate but the candidate's race or ethnicity. This is of particular importance when issues of race cleave the political community or where race identifies the particular electoral district.

DEFINING "REPRESENTATIVE": THE SUPREME COURT

One of the practices that affect our expectation of representation is voting. I previously argued that electors chose representatives, and occasionally their governors. In some instances, it is more precise to say that electors choose some of their representatives and governors from among candidates by the process of voting.   Voting is a fundamental legitimating ritual of representative democracies. As previously mentioned, this process is sometimes turned upside down. In redistricting and reapportionment, "officeholders and their political agents" decide upon their electorate.[25]   The composition of the electorate, in turn, influences the eventual choice of representative.

As mentioned above, the term "representative" is elemental to the consideration of representation. But this is not a term whose definition is self-evident. The law, our expectation of the law, and the fact situation in which we place it influence the breadth or narrowness of the term. For example, is an elected judge considered to be a representative? This question was of immense importance in the election of state supreme court justices in Louisiana.

The categorization of elected state judges was clarified recently by the United States Supreme Court. The question presented was whether elected judges were considered "representatives" for purposes of Section 2 of the VRA as amended in 1982.   The Supreme Court answered this question in the affirmative in *Chisom* v. *Roemer*.[26] The judges at issue were members of the Louisiana Supreme Court. No black had ever been elected to the Louisiana Supreme Court. The use of a multi-member district in an area of Louisiana populated substantially with blacks, but with a majority of whites, diluted black voting strength.[27]   If the multi-member district were split into two single-member districts, black voters would form a majority in one of the two districts. Black voters could then elect a candidate of their own choice.

Louisiana could have avoided litigation over how it elected its justices and continued its discriminatory practices. If Louisiana appointed its justices rather than elected them, the selection of Louisiana Supreme Court justices would not be subject to the limitations of the VRA. In practice, not all judges are elected. For instance, United States Supreme Court justices are appointed rather than elected, though they were candidates during their nomination process. Nonetheless, for a majority of the United States Supreme Court, the practice of electing justices in Louisiana placed judges in the category of representatives as that term was used in Section 2 of the VRA.

The Court reasoned that the VRA meant to increase the political success of racial and language minorities. The Court's interpretation, that a state supreme court justice was a representative, was consistent with a broad interpretation of the VRA.[28] The Court noted,

[I]f executive officers, such as prosecutors, sheriffs, state attorneys general, and state treasurers, can be considered representatives simply because they are chosen by popular election, then the same reasoning should apply to elected judges.[29]

Not surprisingly, Justice Stevens's determination that judges were representatives did not carry a unanimous Court.[30] Justice Scalia, joined by Chief Justice Rehnquist and Justice Kennedy, argued that Stevens's decision that a judge was a representative was driven by the majority's well-meaning if misguided determination to extend the powerful and plaintiff-friendly vote dilution test of Section 2 of the VRA to the election of judges. Scalia noted bluntly:

The Voting Rights Act is not some all-purpose weapon for well intentioned judges to wield as they please in the battle against discrimination. . . .In my view, sec. 2 extends to vote dilution claims for the elections of representatives only, and judges are not representatives. . . . In reality, it is the Court rather than Congress that leads us—quite unnecessarily and indeed with stubborn persistence—into this morass of unguided and perhaps unguidable judicial interference in democratic elections.[31]

The *Chisom* decision enlarged the scope of election practices that fell within the ambit of the VRA.[32] Some asserted that minority judges experienced a different representative relationship with the minority voters who elected them.[33] This relationship reflects the social and political meaning that race evokes in a given context. Direct representation rather than a virtual substitute occurred if blacks elected a black to sit on the Louisiana Supreme Court. In Louisiana, a minority justice would represent for the first time a previously unrepresented minority community.[34]

Chisom allows a look at how the Supreme Court renders the legal discourse of representation. Certainly one could argue that a judge is not a representative. Judges are part of the judicial branch, and representatives are part of the legislative branch. Judges have a special duty to interpret the law. Representatives make the law. Judges are not, in theory, swayed by public opinion. Representatives follow the polls. Nevertheless, these objections miss the mark. "Representative" as used in the VRA is a legal term with a meaning apart from its everyday and political usage. It is a term of art. Theories of representation should consider how the concept, and its elements, vary with context. *Chisom* is just such an example. The context of the dispute, a lawsuit under the VRA, influenced the interpretation of the term "representative" and the practice of representing in Louisiana.

THEORIES OF REPRESENTATION: PITKIN

Thus far we have introduced and briefly considered the interrelated terms "candidate," "elector," "governor," and "representative." They have no precise definition, yet we understand them, and they are elements for our consideration of representation. The fact that because we lack determinate meanings for these terms does not mean we cannot employ them. It means we must spell out the context within which these terms are used. Their connotations are informed by the variety of their usage. Given the wide array of commentators on representation, and their different institutional and historical locations, we should be surprised to find disagreement over the concept of representation abating.

Let us now consider Hannah Pitkin's view of representation, since her work is foundational for current debates on the subject.[35] Pitkin claims that the meaning of representation is historically contingent; it is inseparable from our political practices and institutions. For example, we link representation "to democracy, liberty and justice" though previous political communities did not.[36] How we authorize a representative is a primary consideration. Authorization is a means to conceptualize how members of a community are chosen to act for the group, perhaps through appointment or election. But Pitkin reminds us that this view of representation does not tell us what the representative ought to do, only that he may do it. It does not tell us what representation is or consists of.[37] The focus is on how the representative gains power, not what his or her function will be.

Likewise, the principle of accountability addresses the representative's relationship to his constituents. Pitkin notes that for accountability theorists, there is genuine representation if their representative is "held to account so that he will be responsive to the needs and claims of his constituents."[38] Still, being held accountable does not tell us how the representative acts so as to represent. The specific behavior that passes for accountability remains undefined. Even holding representatives accountable by various types of elections does not get at what type of behavior fulfills the representative's duties.

Alternatively, there are descriptive theories of representation. According to one view, representation corresponds in part to a representative's possessing physical traits in common with his constituents.[39] Pitkin finds the descriptive theory of representation incomplete. "Here, representation depends on the representative's characteristics, on what he is or is like, on being something rather than doing."[40] Under this view of representation, a legitimate government should mirror the nation.[41]

Is it the case that a representative who resembles her constituency is necessarily also effective? Pitkin doubts this is so. Yet "in political terms, what seems important is less what the legislature does than how it is composed."[42] However, the search for direct correspondence is chimerical. Representation involves standing in for; there will always be a lapse in resemblance between the legislature and the electorate as they undergo change in between elections.

Perfect accuracy of correspondence is impossible. This is true not only of political representation but also of representational art, maps, mirror images, samples, and miniatures. So it is always a matter of what information we need, what features are to be reproduced and what will be significant. . . . In a general sense, we are very much aware that politically significant characteristics vary with time and place, and that the doctrines about them vary as well—consider religious affiliation. . . . Descriptive representation is obviously relevant to political life, yet it is again only a partial view, and therefore deceptive in areas where it does not apply. We need only remind ourselves of some of the things it cannot do, aspects of political and other representation which it neglects.[43]

The perfect copy or reproduction is impossible, if for no other reason than that it is a question whose framing is intensely political. This is troublesome if we wish to establish a descriptive standard of fair representation, since "representation means the making present of something which is nevertheless not literally present."[44]

Just as the description of a representative changes according to one's concept of representation, so does the task of the representative.[45] There is no single thing that the representative must or must not do in order to represent. Instead, it is an evolving activity. For Pitkin, the behavior of the representative is central to her concept of representation.[46] Pitkin groups theorists of representative behavior into two camps: mandate and independence theorists. Mandate theorists believe the representative stands in for and articulates the views of those who sent him to the assembly. The independence theorist believes that the representative does his own work, and that his expert judgment best represents the constituency. This is particularly the case since a constituency rarely speaks with one voice. Is it possible that the representative performs both functions? Can he exercise his independent judgment in a manner consistent with the wishes of his constituency? Of course. The fact that the representative exercises judgment does not preclude listening to the wishes of his constituency. Likewise, it is not a failure of representation to exercise independent judgment over issues about which the constituency knows little or nothing.[47]

THEORIES OF REPRESENTATION: BURKE

Pitkin believes the behavior of the representative to be the most important facet of representation. Yet, she describes few specific things that the representative must do. If the representative's actions are paramount, what informs the representative so that he effectively represents? Edmund Burke's theory of representation is a case in point. Burke felt that the representative must exercise his judgment even if this meant opposing the wishes of a majority of his constituency.[48] In forming judgment, there was no substitute for experience. The able representative was not necessarily endowed with great intellect, but possessed wisdom distilled from deliberation. For Burke, "there are morally right answers in politics, and they can be found through the exercise of reason and judgment."[49]

Burke believed that a representative guided by experience and sensitive to the needs of his constituency could directly represent its interests and virtually represent others to whom he was not electorally accountable. A city that shared an interest with another city—for instance a mercantile interest—but that did not elect a representative, while the latter did, was virtually represented. The city that elected the representative was directly represented. In many cases, Burke believed that virtual representation was as effective as direct representation.[50]

Much contemporary literature denigrates the concept of virtual representation.[51] However, Burke believed that virtual representation could be preferable to direct representation because the virtual representative did not have to appeal to the passions of the people. He could exercise his judgment and represent their true interests. For Lani Guinier, the lack of democratic accountability dooms Burke's conception of virtual representation. Moreover, if we conflate racially descriptive representation with "actual" representation, as does Guinier, white officials elected by blacks are neither direct nor virtual.

For Burke, the difference between direct and virtual representation depends on whether or not the representative is electorally accountable to a particular constituency. Guinier's analysis is somewhat more complicated. On the one hand, she criticizes virtual representation because the representative is not democratically accountable to part of what she labels an interest constituency. In this case, the interest is that of blacks. On the other hand, a white representative who is elected in a jurisdiction with blacks may not actually or directly represent blacks because he cannot advance their distinct interests. They remain virtually represented, if represented at all, by a black elected elsewhere. Actual representation of black interests requires that the representative be electorally accountable and that she be black.

Guinier argues that the black interest is distinct from that of the majority. This is important for our consideration of what comprises representation. Certainly the distinct interests of a large minority must be represented. Actual representation of black interests is a democratic imperative because "it is unreasonable to expect blacks to allow others to name their reality, especially in the absence of visible reciprocity."[52] We need not accept Guinier's articulation of black reality or black interest to acknowledge her contribution to the debate over the constitution of representation.

Burke, as does Guinier, conceived of the nation as comprised of distinct interests, though he placed more importance on the process of deliberation than on the assertion of an interest. Deliberation flushed out the content of the interest. Therefore, it was essential that political deliberation consider the different interests of the political community. The types of interests we perceive may influence our concept of representation. Guinier conceives of interests chiefly along racial and ethnic, but also gender and political, lines, whereas Burke conceived of the political community in terms of corporate interests: mercantile, agricultural, professional, and colonial.[53]

For representation to be just, according to Burke, it was not necessary that every city or town be represented in Parliament. What was indispensable for effective representation was that each interest be represented in Parliament. This did not mean that the representative was a mouthpiece for those individuals whose interests he articulated—quite the contrary.[54] The constitution of interests (mercantile, agricultural, colonial, professional) was such that they were long-lived and fairly unchanging. In the contemporary United States, long-lived interests would include racial and language minorities. For

Parliament to be representative, it must account for the various interests of the community.   Parliament was not representative when some interests went unarticulated.   Burke cited Irish Catholics and the American colonies as examples.   In Burke's day, the colonies and the Irish did not elect representatives to Parliament nor were their interests represented.[55] Their position was roughly analogous to that of blacks in the United States prior to the passage of the VRA.   There were almost no blacks in Congress, and there was little likelihood that this would change.   Hence, blacks were not descriptively, directly, virtually, or actually represented.

For Burke, interests were stable but evolving.   There were certain long-standing interests for which the political community had to account.   Failure to do so denied those interests representation.   This has obvious analogs to contemporary criticism of the underrepesentation of racial and language minorities.   According to Burke, the representative must represent long-standing interests and account for the feelings of his constituency.   Feelings reflected the constituency's daily needs and wants.   The representative participates in deliberations with other Members of Parliament and listens to the plaints of the constituency to determine their sentiments.[56] The difficulty came in maintaining a proper distance between the people and the representative.   The representative did his constituency a disservice when he was unduly swayed by their opinions.   It was his charge to determine when their feelings appropriately informed his actions as a representative.[57] This was when their feelings coincided with the articulation of the national interest.

How does the representative determine the political good?   For Burke, the practice of representation shaped the good.   The representative represents interests and advances the general good.   "He must discover and enact the national interest. If he is a member of the natural aristocracy, he will be able to do so."[58]   The interests of the community were there to be found and articulated.[59]

THEORIES OF REPRESENTATION: MADISON

Burke advanced a civic republican theory of representation.   He envisioned a specific notion of the good, the national interest, defined by the interchange of particular corporate interests as articulated by their representatives within the institutions of government.   James Madison articulated a liberal theory of representation.   For the liberal, representation focused on the individual rather than the group prior to an explicit naming of the good.[60] Nonetheless, corporate interests remained important.[61] Certainly, Burke and Madison had different ideas about representation but they were not mutually exclusive.

Madison used the concept of "faction" to discuss the political pressure group.   Factions are, under the best of circumstances, shifting and temporary.[62] Factions defined political life for Madison.   The causes of faction lie in the natural diversity of political opinions.[63] The preferable course of action was to moderate the dangerous tendencies of faction. The self-interestedness of factions could disrupt and destabilize the political community.[64] Liberals such as Madison eschewed the rigid corporate boundaries that informed politics of the Old World. Although class and factional divisions remained important, particularly among religious groups, the relevant unit of analysis was the individual who shifted from faction to faction, depending on the political context.[65] The individual had political interests; political rights pertained to the individual.

Elections meant different things for Burke and Madison, and this was reflected in how they viewed representation. For Burke, the representative determined and advanced class interests while working toward the national interest.[66] For Madison, representation functioned well if it moderated the ruinous effects of faction and prevented one faction from dominating the assembly.[67] Tyranny of the majority, among the worst by-products of democracy, could be avoided through the representative mechanisms of a republican form of government.[68] Thoughtful action was the prescription for Burke; cautious inaction, except in extraordinary times, suited Madison.[69]

Liberals such as Madison, Adams, and Hamilton understood representation to be linked inextricably with democratic authorization.[70] Elections provided a means to join the representative to the represented. The representative function is essential to government in large countries like the United States where direct democracy is impractical. Madison favorably compared the republican form of government with direct democracy.[71] Direct democracy collapsed the distinction between an elector and a representative. For Madison and Burke, direct democracy was dangerous because it did not distinguish between the capacities of men. The superior judgment of better men was not taken into account. In direct democracy, the best were diluted by the worst; whose numbers were far greater. Direct democracy compromised the interests of the nation to the rapacity of the multitude. Of course, at this stage in history, the poor, women, and blacks seldom acted as political representatives so the benefits of representation were spread unevenly.[72] Nonetheless, some citizens were viewed as more fit than others to be representatives. Representation moderated the extremes of direct democracy and harnessed the democratic spirit within institutions less susceptible to public passions.[73]

To varying degrees, Madison and Hamilton embraced an elitist Burkean notion concerning the type of superior men who served as representatives.[74] This is no reason to condemn these thinkers, though by the standards of our time, they held politically untenable views. By the standards of their time, they were not antidemocratic. Nobody, or almost nobody, at that time espoused anything close to a contemporary standard of democracy as a measure of political morality. Fittingly, the democratic standard is a political or a historical one.[75] The views of Madison, Burke, and Adams remain relevant because we are their political progeny and also because we wrestle with many of the same problems they articulated and tried to solve. Madison's views on the dangers of factions reflect a wisdom we can apply analogously when racial groups make claims for greater representation.

For Burke and Madison, the representative was authorized to represent through elections. We also employ elections to elect any number and kind of representatives. For instance, we elect legislators to Congress and state legislatures. We also elect judges, prosecutors, county commissioners, school board members, mayors, governors, and the President. All on this list are representatives. Moreover, with the expansion of the VRA, which attempts to impose a baseline standard of fair representation, and constitutional protections such as the 14th and 15th Amendments, elections are thoroughly legalized and politicized.[76]

A problem transpires when the pool of voters seems, according to contemporary political fashion, exclusionary. The franchise extended gradually to include blacks, Native Americans, and women. With each step, the enlarged group of electors helped reestablish the legitimacy of the authorization process and of the government. Enlarging the franchise was the fair thing to do. It made democracy more inclusive. A determination that enlarging the franchise resulted in substantively better representatives cannot be separated from an election process that was regarded as more equitable because it embraced a broader cross section of society. Democracy meant inclusion. The more inclusion, the better democracy functioned.[77] But does greater inclusion result in better representation?

If the legitimacy of the authorization process depends on the election, then the legitimacy of the representative is dependent upon his authorization. A representative who is not authorized legitimately—for instance by some illegal electoral practice—falls short of what we now recognize as an actual or direct representative.[78] Both "actual" and "direct" refer to the link between the electors and the representative.[79] The representative must be authorized and subjected to some form of recall. This generally takes the form of a popular election. Ordinarily, she must be authorized by a majority of the pool of participating electors in any particular jurisdiction.[80]

The task of representing is multifaceted and not rigidly defined. It includes authorizing and accountability practices. It entails articulating and advocating the interests of the constituency. For the liberal, this may mean harboring distrust of those who advance a strong vision of the good whereby complex problems are reduced to a specific framework and exclude other possibilities. But what can inform the representative who remains skeptical of specific political frameworks, and cannot know all of the interests of her constituency? The institutional practices that produce her and that she helps transform.[81] The process of representation represents particular historical expectations about the representative.[82]

THE POLITICAL AGENT

As noted above in the *Chisom* case, "representative" is one of the most contentious elements in the discourse of fair representation. Another term at issue is "political agent." One of the problems of representation is that it is thought to be overly politicized.[83]   The whole representative process, purportedly, is manipulated by the powerful to remain in power.[84] Implicit in such criticisms is an ideal of fair representation where the current distribution of power among groups is altered to reflect an equitable arrangement. So whom are we to blame for our inability to construct a system of fair representation? We can accuse the "political agent." Awareness of the multifarious nature of "political agent" is necessary if we are to understand those who disapprove of a redistricting process infected with political agents. The process is "politics pure, fraught with the capacity for self-dealing and cynical manipulation."[85]   Of course, this is not a cause for despair. Could the process of political redistricting be otherwise?[86]

It may be reasonable to interpret "political agent" to include not only an aide to the officeholder but also those federal officials, lawyers, judges, and lobbyists who are a part of the redistricting process ordered by the VRA.[87] Our sense of political agent remains vague but inclusive. It is not necessarily pejorative.[88] Political agents are necessary to the political process. Given the ubiquity of political agents, it is difficult to conceive of the redistricting process as anything but political. This is the case unless one believes there is a means to order the political that is not political, self-dealing, and manipulative.[89] We might call this a belief in extra-political aspects of social diversity that, in turn, represent democracy, liberty, and justice.[90] How we recognize such a state of affairs or verify its existence requires persuasion. The fact that such a vision is open to manipulation does not make it any less real. It does, however, open it up for disagreement. This should not dissuade us from believing in and searching for those practices and institutions that produce our ideals of representation.

Such a vision of genuine representation presupposes a discernment that views the political community outside of the politics that constitute it.[91] Ironically, difference politics, which hopes to repair malrepresentation, claims to be informed by community practices.[92] Such criticisms invariably invoke extra-political standards of fair representation and replicate the same marginalizing practices they purport to critique by foreclosing other bases of identity, which inform representation.

A vision of the political good is inevitably a partial view. To be partial means one prefers something as opposed to other things.[93]   This is a fundamental prerequisite of politics. Even those who propose apolitical means of districting by invoking a standard in which a computer proportionally represents various groups advocate a specific political community and marginalize other alternatives. They decide how districting should occur.[94] This understanding of districting may not be democratic, but it is political.[95]

THE MINORITY REPRESENTATIVE

Race-conscious communitarianism reduces politically relevant group solidarity to race. Moreover, the good is defined in terms of social and political equality whereby historically informed patterns of domination and subordination among racial groups are transformed.[96] Racial communities that engage in more or less intense racial factionalism comprise the political community. Race-conscious communitarians argue that liberal practice, not simply liberal theory, ignores the primacy of the social context, particularly the racial or ethnic group, to informing and constructing the political good.[97] The challenge is to focus on those group attachments that inform political and social life.[98] Embracing a particular vision of the good does not lead one to hold conservative, as opposed to liberal, political values, although among members of a particular group, one type of politics may be preferred.[99]

For race-conscious communitarians, political interests are informed predominantly by membership in a racial or ethnic group. The community authorizes its representative to relate the interest of the community in the assembly.[100] This is the minority representative. I choose the term "minority representative" to describe the special perspective with which this particular representative is endowed. The perspective of the community is voiced by her presence in the legislature.

The minority representative's ability to represent the interests of the group is not authorized only at the ballot.[101] Rather, that ability is also ascribed. It produces and reflects her communal membership.[102] Racial identity, in this context, displaces the formation of other communities and diminishes particularities such as class, religion, and sex. Racial identity is objectified. It is the interest of the community and the lodestar of the representative.[103] Another aspect of the minority representative is her invulnerability to attacks on her judgment (her politics) by members of the majority. Members of the majority lack the political authority to critique; otherwise, they could actually represent members of the minority community. They lack the requisite social capital, historical memory, and ascriptive characteristics to criticize the minority representative because they lack her special perspective.

Political perspective is delineated by a person's membership in a racial community. The minority community identifies history, traits, and experiences that distinguish it from other communities. The state may invest social characteristics with political and legal properties. For instance, membership in one racial community rather than another results in different legal status under the VRA. As such, the minority representative's membership in a racial or language minority invests her with political and legal authority.[104] By definition, the minority representative's perspective is not shared with the majority by dint of experiencing a different social reality. Even if the majority takes up issues favoring the marginalized, it cannot actually represent minority interests. In practice, the minority seldom authorizes a majority member if there is a viable minority candidate.[105] The extent to which the authority of the minority representative originates in her membership in a minority group diminishes the importance of what the representative does. The political and legal value of the minority representative may lie less in representative behavior than in manufacturing a concept to authorize descriptive representation.

PROPORTIONAL REPRESENTATION, DESCRIPTION, AND MINORITY PERSPECTIVE

As elucidated earlier, Pitkin problematizes the concept of descriptive representation.[106] Some proponents of proportional representation claim Pitkin is enamored of a descriptive theory of representation. They cite her use of John Adams, who at one time said that legislatures should be "an exact portrait, in miniature, of the people at large."[107] Polsby and Popper believe Adams proposes, and Pitkin supports, descriptive proportional representation. Ironically, Pitkin argues that what Adams had in mind when he discussed representation is far different from what modern proponents of proportional representation have in mind. Adams made it clear that no representative body could ever perfectly correspond to the nation. Nor was it clear that he wished it would. Adams believed that power should be assigned "from the many to the few of the most wise and good."[108] Besides, as Pitkin reminds us, even portraits have to be interpreted.[109] Adams did not describe a portrait emphasizing equally the importance of all interests, but those interests he thought necessary to do justice. This requires civic education. Through education, we learn to recognize political significance. Most often, participating in the politics of a particular community does this. Likewise, Burke stressed the importance of representing interests, but felt that the political system ought to represent only those interests central to the realization of the national interest.[110] It is not apparent what interests are to be represented by proportional representation even if some interests seem transparent, because what is clear to one person may be less so to another.

No matter what electoral system we use—single-member district, multi-member district, or proportional representation—we will be represented proportionally. Those who espouse proportional representation advocate a specific electoral result in accord with their interests. Therefore, the real question is how proportions are meted out. Recent supporters of proportional representation advance it as a remedy for excluded interests. It promises more minority, female and social democratic officeholders.[111] However, the expectations of theory are not necessarily borne out in practice. For example, the use of single-member, majority-minority districts has had unexpected consequences. Political conservatives made gains as a by-product of packing black voters to create majority-minority districts.[112] One wonders whether proportional representation might also produce surprising results. Is one electoral system inherently more fair to minority groups? In the end, it is a question of what type of proportion we espouse. That is one measure of fairness.

Let us be more specific and introduce a few of the common pros and cons thought to characterize the single-member district as opposed to proportional representation. At the national level, the United States uses the single-member district system exclusively. This system is also the most common at the state and local levels. Single-member systems promote stable, two-party systems. Marginal or extreme interests rarely gain a voice in the legislature. Candidates advancing moderate or middle-of-the-road views tend to get elected. In the single-member district system, the winner must ordinarily amass at least 50 percent of the vote plus one in order to win election. This first-past-the-post system results in clear winners who obtain an outright majority. Single member districts focus an electorate's attention on a single representative. Electors identify with a single representative rather than several. The United States Supreme Court favors single-member districts over multi-member districts, in part, because multi-member districts were used to underrepresent racial minorities.[113]

The single-member district has its critics. It is the current system, and it is not working for many Americans, particularly members of racial minorities and women, who are not represented in proportion to their percentage in the population. The threshold for election is high, and it submerges legitimate but politically marginal interests. As a result, the votes of many voters are wasted. Alternative parties cannot break the stranglehold of the two major parties. In consequence, there may be low voter turnout. Finally, single-member districts reduce the electors' choice of candidates for any particular office.[114]

Let us turn now to the advantages of proportional representation. It encourages high voter participation; most Western democracies using proportional representation have voter turnout greater than in the United States. Variations of this system result in a wide variety of candidates across the political spectrum. As a result, third party alternatives become politically viable. With more choices and more winners, fewer voters "waste" votes. Political campaigns become issue- rather than personality-driven as political parties gain in importance. In Western democracies that employ proportional representation, women and ethnic minorities are represented in greater numbers than is the case in the United States. It is further asserted that political and racial gerrymandering abates as district boundaries wane in importance.[115]

Proportional representation is not without its critics. It is a strange system to most Americans, though proportional representation was prominent in various cities throughout United States history. It can lead to a Byzantine vote-counting system. Perhaps the most elaborate is the single transferable vote used in Ireland, where one's vote shifts from candidate to candidate, depending on the election threshold, and ballot counting is a drawn-out process. Proportional representation leads to coalition governments that may be unstable or beholden to small extremist parties. Two examples of this phenomenon are Italy and

Israel, where coalition governments have been unstable or beset by stagnation. Some commentators argue that proportional representation results in more winners and fewer wasted votes. But more winners devalue victory. Election results become harder to read. Confusion may encourage the formation of extremist parties that espouse antidemocratic tenets or encourage racial and ethnic intolerance.[116]

Proportional representation results in large geographic districts that sever the link between the individual legislator and his or her constituents. One of the advantages of the single-member district is the link between legislator and citizen. If the legislator is effective, she is intimately aware of local interests peculiar to her constituency. Proportional representation, to some extent, severs this link. This may place too much emphasis on party membership and political parties. The question for many voters is not a party's agenda but a candidate's personality and competence. If proportional representation is unlikely to be adopted on a wide scale in the United States, the single-member system may be employed to promote minority representation. But no electoral mechanism inherently offers representation that is more equitable. This is a function of the representative's behavior. Different electoral systems do, however, allow different types of representative behavior to flourish. A question to pose may be, given our prevailing social and political practices, which type(s) of electoral system best harness(es) the competing self-interestedness of groups and individuals. This is neither a new question nor one likely to be answered definitively. However, in its asking we assert an intergenerational link from Madison and Adams to contemporary critics of representation in the United States who argue that different electoral mechanisms are needed to account for underrepresented interests. One of the newest and most controversial changes in electoral practice is the state-sponsored use of single-member districts to increase the number of representatives from groups covered by the VRA.

PROPORTIONAL REPRESENTATION AND
MAJORITY-MINORITY DISTRICTS

The liberal, Madisonian practices encouraging fluid interest group formation and centrist political parties fail to work as effectively with single-member, majority-minority districts created by the VRA. Factional interests are promoted rather than mediated by the VRA.[117] It is a form of proportional representation of racial and language minorities within a single-member district framework. Despite its real and imagined failings, the single-member district system predominates in the United States. And despite criticism from both the political left and the political right, majority-minority districts effectively increase minority electoral success as measured by the number of minority officeholders. What are the consequences of using the majority-minority district as a device to increase the representation of one race as opposed to another? Racial polarization, notably absent in many districts not covered by the VRA, is routine in majority-minority districts, where the race of the candidate is the authorizing attribute of the eventual officeholder.[118]   Ironically, racial polarization is one of the factors the federal courts identify when remedying vote dilution by creating single-member, majority-majority districts.[119] Creating majority-minority districts may increase racial polarization in already polarized areas.

Supposedly, votes are wasted in single-member districts for those who are members of a permanent minority and cannot hope to elect the candidate of their choice.[120] Wasting votes is an inescapable occurrence; it is an attribute of all electoral systems.[121] The only question is to what degree votes are "wasted." Every time we vote and back the losing minority candidate, we in some sense waste our vote. We might use the term "wasted" if the expectation is that our vote will gain us more than participation in an election. Perhaps voters should have some say in governance beyond electing their representatives.[122] If we expect to elect the winning candidate rather than to participate in the election of a representative, and it turns out that we back the losing candidate on a regular basis, it makes sense to use the term "wasted" to describe our vote. For race-conscious communitarians, votes are "wasted" if a member of their racial community is not elected despite the fact that they participate in the election. Not wasting a vote becomes coterminous with electoral success.[123] In current VRA jargon, this is known as allowing voters to elect the candidates of their choice.[124]   The single-member district is thought to be consistent with Madisonian principles because it promotes compromise and two-party systems, which in turn impels factions to moderate their views.[125] This may not be the case with representatives who represent majority-minority districts. These are self-constituting factions whose political durability defines the measure of authenticity that the representative must attain. In practice, this sort of system adapts itself to bringing forth authentic representatives of the minority community only by the verbal trick of defining authenticity as counter-Madisonian racial politics.[126] The same types of permanent and exclusive factions that Madison wished to prevent are promoted by majority-minority districting.   Liberal practice accommodates race-conscious communitarian politics, including majority-minority districting.   But because of the supermajority of minority voters in their districts, these representatives have little incentive to advance interests other than those of the district.[127] Moreover, their guaranteed supermajority attenuates the accountability they have to voters in the district. The VRA legalized the factional distribution of legislative power along racial lines in covered jurisdictions. Separating voters according to their race was seen as a necessary means to accomplish one of the primary goals of the VRA: allowing members of minority groups to elect representatives of their own choice.

IDENTITY POLITICS AND JUST RECOGNITION

The preceding section linked fair representation with the proportional representation of blacks and other minorities. The minority group possesses a particular interest. The majority neglects this interest. Iris Marion Young also advocates the political recognition of oppressed communities because failure to do so extends oppression.[128] For Young, justice is political. She claims that the political discourse of liberal institutions expresses the needs of the unencumbered individual, and is at odds with a communal discourse that explores group oppression.[129] Injustice involves the unequal treatment of social groups. Cultural forms and practices such as skin color, common history, and self-identification inform social groups.[130] Young offers a theoretical basis for the arguments made by race-conscious communitarians for group representation in the context of fair representation. Minority representatives are needed to represent the perspectives of minority groups. Refusal to accommodate demands for communal representation on the grounds that this sacrifices legal neutrality reproduces dominant forms of political discourse and normalizes minority underrepresentation.[131]

Using Young's standard, fair representation implies institutions that promote the participation of marginalized social groups. This might take the form of an expansive reading of the protection afforded by the VRA and the construction of single-member, majority-minority districts.[132] Nonetheless, Young is uncomfortable with rule-of-law, procedural neutrality because it reproduces dominant group practices. She attacks the integrationist ideal through which groups like Native Americans and blacks are oppressed within an official discourse of color-blindness.[133] The politics of difference is to some extent the politics of particularities, but only a few particularities such as race or sex. Group identity is starkly opposed to the unencumbered individual as postulated in liberal theory.[134] But the politics of the particular informs one's sense of the individual to the exclusion of other particularities. This may also, ironically, replicate the criticism of liberal theory as eviscerating the notion of the individual by diminishing the universe of communal solidarities. According to Young, segregation on the marginalized groups' terms is necessary for that group to empower itself.[135] Group separateness allows members of these groups to practice solidarity.[136] As such, "specific representation for oppressed groups in the decision-making procedures of a democratic public promotes justice better than a homogeneous public."[137] However, in practice societies must promote some notion of commonality and balance this with recognition of different communal groups' demands. Young assures us that fears of group conflict are unwarranted because we should not have trouble deciding which groups the politics of difference ought to benefit.

It is important to remember that the [difference] principle calls for specific representation only of oppressed or disadvantaged groups. Privileged groups are already represented in the sense that their voice, experience, values and priorities are heard and acted upon.

Once we are clear that the principle of group representation refers only to oppressed social groups, then the fear of an unworkable proliferation of group representation should dissipate.[138]

Let us consider some general criticisms of Young's politics of difference and how they apply to representation. Her sense of group constitution is limited. Historical bases of identity are reduced unproblematically and applied *en masse* to group members. The core experience of the group is reproduced in the individual. Actual political representation requires that a fellow group member represent group members.[139] In this sense, Young subscribes to what Pitkin termed descriptive representation.

Young's theory of representation is based on a comparatively simplistic notion of minority identity. Yet, there may be difficulty discerning what it means to be black or who is black.[140] K. Anthony Appiah's notion of black identity is inextricably linked to white identity, undergoes continuous change, and is characterized by solidarities emphasizing class, gender, and sexuality.[141] Appiah's multi-dimensional idea of black identity does not fit within the clearly defined social categories used by Young. Group edges blur. White and black are not distinct and separate categories. They interact and define themselves with respect to one another. Moreover, the physical constitution of the group changes. Appiah is less optimistic than Young about embracing a politics of difference that promotes justice based on an uncritical sense of group differences.

Young notes that the normative ideals we use to comment on society necessarily reflect that society.[142] Yet, if our criticism of society is that domination and oppression characterize it, the same is true of our ideals. We are unable to conceive of a just society not characterized by domination or oppression. Rather, we conceive of a society composed of unequal communal relationships that we approve. Because Young's vision is a political evaluation, there will in all likelihood be some who disagree with her determination of oppressive as opposed to tolerant communal relationships.

THE IDENTITY OF REPRESENTATION

Relying on parts of Young's theory of difference, and sharing many of the perspectives on minority representation voiced by Abrams, Guinier, and Karlan, Melissa Williams tells us that particular minority groups have a special claim to representation.[143] Williams considers the efficacy of descriptive representation for minority groups. She argues against the overbreadth of some but not all theories of descriptive representation. Descriptive representation "appears absurd without some specification of which attributes of the citizenry are relevant for the purposes of political decision-making."[144] It collapses the functions of representative and elector. The representative no longer acts; the representative represents by being there.

The descriptive representative does not represent a constituency but is representative of a constituency. Williams delimits the representative's authority by those traits or experiences he has in common with his electors. By specifying what groups are important in the context of political representation, we are able to alter how we view fair representation and the representative function within a theory of descriptive representation.[145] According to Williams, representatives who share that race best represent factions founded upon a racial correlation. Those representatives can establish trust between themselves and the faction. Factions expect representatives to advance their interests against the interests of other factions or the nation as a whole.

Madison envisioned a political structure in which no single faction could dominate the institutions of the state for very long.[146] Opposed to Madison's view of faction, the politics of difference embraced by Williams views society as characterized by more or less permanent racial divides in which the majority race dominates the minority.[147] Absent government intervention, the minority has little incentive to trust the system of representation. Consequently, Williams argues, we cannot discuss fair representation absent an appreciation of the social groups and representative institutions that affect representation, and the common good we hope to realize.[148]

LIBERAL PRACTICE, IDENTITY POLITICS, AND MINORITY REPRESENTATION

Providing group preferences for historically oppressed groups challenges the liberal notion of equality.[149] Nonetheless, liberal practice may accommodate ascriptive groups' claims to representation at the expense of legal neutrality.[150] The VRA does not treat groups equally. It protects only five racial and language minorities. In this sense, liberal practice facilitates deviations from legal neutrality to account for social inequalities. The VRA causes some tension in liberal institutions, and this is reflected in the way it is litigated and interpreted. The individual may demand equality of opportunity from the liberal state. Each individual should possess an equal opportunity to elect a representative without state-sponsored racial gerrymandering.[151] However, those who argue that equality of opportunity reinforces racial and ethnic inequalities challenge this conception.[152] Liberal theory stresses fair procedure as opposed to equality of outcome. If the procedure of a particular law treats each applicant equally, then we need not determine what constitutes a fair outcome. Procedural fairness does not require us to possess a specific conception of the good by which to judge the outcome.[153] However, liberal theory does not accurately reflect liberal practice in representation jurisprudence. As mentioned earlier, Section 2 of the VRA contains a results test whereby the outcomes of elections are considered in terms of racial group proportionality.

Race-conscious communitarians link substantive equality and participation by members of marginalized groups.[154] The one person, one vote standard may establish procedural fairness, but it may not lead to increasing racial diversity in the legislature.[155] Ascriptive group demands for representation challenge the liberal ideal of the fluidity of group competition for political power. Williams and Guinier believe that single-member district systems underrepresent minority groups and facilitate a tyranny of the majority.[156] While race-conscious communitarians advance an ideal of representative bodies that reflects historically oppressed groups, there is no formula by which to recognize the diversity of the politically subordinated without slighting *bona fide* disadvantaged groups.[157] The law discriminates and privileges particular oppressed groups. It does not end the debate over who should be represented.

Historically there is a vital connection between identity and recognition.[158] Charles Taylor elegantly, if elusively, historicizes the notion of identity when he describes it as "where we are coming from."[159] Some groups were historically unrecognized in electoral bodies and remain proportionately underrepresented. This may reinforce oppressive practices.[160] Yet, if we recognize a particular diversity, we may stigmatize or hinder a group by emphasizing the very characteristics upon which it was excluded. We may also rule out other aspects of diversity, that inform political and legal marginality. Maintaining the *status quo* underrepresents blacks and Hispanics in political office. Yet, the *status quo* is historically contingent. With the increased representation of racial and language minorities, the degree to which the state is perceived to intervene or stigmatize changes.

Creating the perception of a just society is a matter of constructing a vision of society where certain practices and institutions are demonstrated to be virtuous and others are not. A just society maximizes the virtue of its hierarchies. Within this situation, promoting racial diversity in the legislature links self-fulfillment with self-realization.[161] How this occurs without reinforcing frameworks of oppression is the dilemma of difference.[162] Merely asserting the need to promote diverse representative bodies is not enough. Diversity requires that we discriminate. The voices we choose to hear are those of politically adept groups. They convince us, perhaps through litigation, that their voices should join the public chorus. The paradox is that only the politically powerful among those excluded groups are included. The marginalized remain silent. The marginalized are not represented by the marginal but by those possessing certain traits of marginality.

So what do we know about identity? It depends on social context.[163] Identity depends on its recognition by others.[164] Withholding recognition can oppress those who feel solidarity based on shared particularities.[165] The politics of difference emphasizes equal rights and entitlements such as voting rights and political participation.[166] Yet, it also may require us to treat different groups differently.[167] This is a shift from a color-blind neutral application of the laws to one that explicitly takes difference into account.[168] Charles Taylor notes:

Where the politics of universal dignity fought for forms of nondiscrimination that were quite "blind" to the ways in which citizens differ, the politics of difference often redefines nondiscrimination as requiring that we make these distinctions the basis of differential treatment.[169]

Treating different people differently may assume the form of affirmative action. The disadvantaged group that suffers from institutional discrimination requires preferential treatment.[170] Politically, such measures are presented as temporary remedies to level the playing field. This may be at odds with a group whose goal is not to be treated equally or assimilated but wishes to maintain its difference.[171] How, then, is the quest for the recognition of difference squared with liberal rule-of-law, procedural neutrality in the area of representation?[172] It may undermine the liberal view that requires us to assess the ability of the individual apart from the community to determine the common good. Privileging certain groups means that the state does not deal with all citizens equally. Color-blind, legal neutrality may be inconsistent with the politics of difference.[173] Groups in our society that struggle for increased political representation may restrict the behavior of group members. They "provide loose norms or models, which play a role in shaping the life plans of those who make these collective identities central to their individual identities."[174] These groups reinforce solidarity as they sanction aberrant behavior; they provide a standard to which all members of the community can attain in some form. In turn, the law promotes a marginalized group's political significance. The role the state plays in promoting collective identity is complex but partial. K. Anthony Appiah notes that state standards of diversity fail to capture the contingency of existence, but they do influence the categories we use to conceptualize others.[175]

There may be an authentic self, but there is not an authentic self removed from politics. Identity is manufactured with the tools we find in the social space we inhabit. Perceptions of equality and inequality mirror social practice. Inequalities are not natural in the sense that they exist *a priori* to the community, but neither are claims for justice based on this or that attribute of difference. In the context of representation, this is one reason to be wary of those who reduce individual and collective identity to specific group solidarity, such as race, shorn of the contingency that informs existence.[176] We should be equally wary of those who invoke the dominant discourse of legal neutrality to apologize for institutionalized inequalities.[177]

CONCLUSION: DELIBERATING ON REPRESENTATION

Commentators such as Guinier, Williams, and Young believe the cure for political underrepresentation is to reconceptualize the legal structure regulating representation and to increase the representation of the underrepresented groups. In short, contemporary criticisms of our system of political representation are criticisms of the political outcome of representation. By contrast, Pitkin did not dwell on the political consequences of changing the current means of ensuring representation, assuming the process of election was democratic. She, as well as Burke, stressed the representative role rather than the outcome of elections. The representative must listen to the views of his constituency. The representative acts in the interest of his constituency, but he is not a mere mouthpiece. The representative must exercise discretion and sometimes act independently or at odds with what the constituency desires.[178] Williams, like Young and Guinier, argues that race-conscious communitarianism leads toward a measure of fair representation based on the proportional presence of minority groups. In contrast, liberal theory promotes the image of state neutrality and treating individuals alike, without regard to race. Basing claims to representation predominantly on race violates this liberal tenet.[179] On the other hand, liberal institutions legalized group claims for fair representation. Liberal practice is hardly race-neutral or difference-blind. The categories of the VRA delineate racial and language minority difference.

The determination of fair representation turns on one's politics. Debates over fair representation are unlikely to settle the question once and for all. What is fair representation is a search for justice where there exist inequalities of political power among groups.[180] There have always been disparities of political power among different social groups. The debate over political inclusion is reinterpreted constantly. Critics such as Young, Guinier, and Williams are an important part of this debate. Criticisms of the inability of liberal institutions to accommodate different group claims for recognition reflect weaknesses in liberal theory. Indeed, difference politics are institutionalized through VRA litigation. The race-conscious communitarian critique of liberal practice calls for increased minority representation. Liberal practices can promote this end. The VRA recognizes that particular minority communities ought to have the ability to elect the representative of their choice.[181] It is inaccurate to argue that because this end is not a reality, liberal practices do not adequately promote diversity. To the contrary, liberal practices allow more diversity than we can describe.

I have emphasized the importance of different theories of representation. Certainly, Hannah Pitkin, Edmund Burke, and Lani Guinier are an unlikely trio. Yet, they share to a large degree a common vocabulary with regard to representation. They use terms like "representative," "elector," and "governor." They are all aware of the power of interests or groups in society. They are all interested in how these interests, group and individual, are represented. But their use of common terms and concepts does not yield common theories of representation. The meanings of terms change. The use of particular concepts, such as virtual representation, comes into and goes out of favor. Madison's concern with factions is heard in identity politics criticism wherein a majority faction silences minorities. Consequently, the theory as well as the practice of representation undergoes change as the elements of representation endure.

The terms and concepts we use to describe representation remain similar to those used by Burke and Madison in the 18th century. But our political reality is much different from theirs. We have different historical expectations as to the makeup of the legislature and the behavior of the representative. Contemporary theories of representation reflect the political pressures of the moment, which demand recognition and a recollection of things past. How we convince each other of the power of our forms of representation is a political event accomplished through language. The next chapter continues this review by exploring how the rhetoric of representation convinces others of the power of our views.

Chapter 2

Rhetoric and the Appearances of Representation

This chapter discusses the function of rhetoric in judicial opinions and in the general discursive practices that characterize the legal community.[1] Rhetoric not only persuades others of a characterization of a particular event, it becomes that event. Through rhetoric we may categorize a decision as politically conservative or liberal. It allows for both opposition and change in the debate over fair representation. The process of rhetoric may explain why particular theories of representation provide for different outcomes and why no theory of representation necessarily leads to a particular political or legal result. In practice, the strategies of justification in Supreme Court opinions are not inherently politically liberal or conservative.

I describe rhetoric in this chapter to explicate its pervasiveness in things legal. For instance, I oppose rhetoric to the law and explain why rhetoric is an integral part of the law. As an example, a court may be accused of fixating on mere appearances as opposed to reality when adjudicating racial gerrymanding cases. We are told that the court ignores the law only to be swayed by political rhetoric. However, in many cases involving the VRA and the use of majority-minority districting, the rhetoric of the Court could hardly express anything but the overtly political. I also employ the term "rhetoric" to refer to the persuasive moment in language when meaning is imparted but remains unsettled. Rhetoric allows for the simultaneous assertion of reality and appearances. We rely on the rhetoric of objective appearances to express what is real and what is merely apparent. We commit to a different persuasive strategy to establish what is not real. Reality need not oppose rhetoric. Rather, reality is a particular type of rhetorical event.

In this chapter, I establish the relationship of rhetoric to legal and political concepts of fair representation. First, I dissect the argument that members of a minority race ought to represent that race because they speak in a privileged voice. I call this the rhetoric of difference and argue that it is perceived to oppose majority discourse. I believe this opposition is powerful but false because difference rhetoric makes use of the conceptual categories of majority discourse. For example, minority speakers do not criticize the prevailing political hierarchy through such means as storytelling, though they may purport to do so.[2] Rather, they criticize the prevailing political hierarchy, using the logic of the latter. They publish in law reviews and social science journals. They argue cases employing a discourse familiar to judges. In short, the rhetoric of difference is majority discourse.

Second, I question whether the rhetoric of the minority group as expressed in myth and passion opposes rational argumentation. Rational argumentation is the discourse of the prevailing political hierarchy. Yet, it is hard to conceive how the minority group is understood in a court of law except through rational argumentation. Moreover, it is not clear that forms of rational argumentation, for example, legal forensics, exclude myth and passion.[3] Indeed, it is often by invoking beliefs of almost mythical proportions, such as the intent of the Founding Fathers,[4] and deploying passion, such as comparing a reapportionment plan to political apartheid, that legal syllogisms are most effective.[5]

Third, I examine how the rhetoric of community is opposed to that of individualism. Communitarianism imparts a rhetoric of interdependence. This opposes liberalism that purportedly expresses the rhetoric of a radical, abstract individualism. The problem with this communitarian and liberal opposition is that it fails to hold up under close scrutiny. In practice, liberal, rule-of-law institutions such as the courts, legislatures, and administrative bodies accommodate claims from different types of communities. For instance, black and Hispanic groups sue successfully for greater public representation under the VRA.[6]

Fourth, I skeptically appraise how appearance opposes reality in the determination of whether or not a particular district is a gerrymander. Commonly pilloried, gerrymanders are not necessarily good or bad things. The mistake is believing that we can take into account different historical and political claims, and employ some qualitative and quantitative standards for compact districting, to discern whether or not a district is a legal gerrymander. Instead, we rely on rhetoric, that is, appearances, to determine objective standards by which to define a gerrymander. We define a gerrymander by accepting a particular appearance as reality.

Finally, I consider how legal categories sustain the discourse they profess to explicate. Politics sustain the conservation of legal categories. These concepts are accepted as natural or legal, like property or contract, though there may be different views as to what legally constitutes a contract or property. Other categories are more or less in play. One of the most controversial of these is the general category of affirmative action, and it includes cases brought pursuant to the VRA.[7]

TROPES, REPRESENTATION, AND THE PERSPECTIVAL REPRESENTATIVE

How a VRA dispute is presented influences not only the outcome of the case but also how the law is read subsequently.[8] With respect to fair political representation, rhetoric compartmentalizes reality with terms like "liberty," "equality," "autonomy," "individual," "group," "race," and "ethnicity." These terms function as tropes.[9] They disguise and articulate liberal and communitarian assumptions; they announce the perspective of the representative; and they allow for a persuasive commentary on what is real as opposed to what is apparent.[10] These figures of speech permit the manufacture of a persuasive legal story about fair representation and a simultaneous commentary on the story, thus disposing of the need for prepolitical, prelegal grounds on which to establish the veracity of the narrative.[11] These terms self-define; their usages play on our expectations.[12] They allow for the circumstances by which their meanings are authenticated,[13] but they do not always yield for others the story we intend.[14] They set the stage for those political arguments we find convincing. Within these legal language games, there is no need to develop a theory of representation abstracted from the practice that allows the contemplation of such a theory. This is no way to talk about representation and inform legal debate exterior to the legal debate. There exists no such metalanguage.[15]

"Justice," "fairness," and "representation," all terms common to representation jurisprudence, are practices we objectify as goals or results. We describe what we do, or hope to do, as the standard by which to measure our actions. Descriptions are invariably rhetorical and compel through the use of tropes.[16] Tropes are hinge words that invite the reader to peer past the veneer of a surface-level reading, commonly called a literal reading, into the metaphorical meaning or subtext.[17] It should come as no surprise that when we read a story—for instance, a judicial opinion—each of us takes away a different message. Indeed, some of us take away many messages. We enrich our interpretation by recognizing the existence of subtexts: texts, that either are "discovered" upon a closer reading or are pointed out to us by someone with different insights. We may speak of a text, a story, as having different levels of meaning. We may also say that a particular text speaks to us, though this is a mischaracterization. We hardly ever say we speak with texts; rather, we read and interpret them. The text remains dormant until interpretation brings it alive.

Likewise, we may speak of texts as narratives.[18] They are stories that describe stories. Of course, different types of narratives tell different stories. So "narratives" can be read any number of ways. As such, it is useful to ask which assumptions are woven into a story. Assumptions may be expressed in terms of oppositions. For example, nature is opposed to civilization, the raw is opposed to the cooked, and the sacred is opposed to the profane. In commentaries on the VRA, the political is opposed to the legal, and white is opposed to black. Tropes, such as characterizing a particular district as "racially polarized," reveal oppositions as well as the foundations upon which the oppositions are based. They link the oppositions that give structure to the narrative and believability to the story.

A narrative persuades; else it would not narrate.[19] We would not know what not to hear. How persuasively the oppositions in the narrative are resolved—for instance, by declaring category A good and B abhorrent—depends in large part on how effectively the writer presents the opposition of A to B. If the narrator is successful, he or she manages to narrate intelligibly. In doing so, subjective forms of social organization such as race and ethnicity appear objective. An uncontested social format reproduces itself and blinds us to the possibility of a reality in which race and ethnicity go unrecognized.[20] Race and ethnicity project as natural categories rather than politico-historical artifacts. This facilitates the recognition of race as an ascriptive trait and the promotion of racial and ethnic equality as a transcendent truth.[21]

The reordering of a particular sentence may render it understandable, ironic, or incomprehensible. Likewise, interpretation depends not only on that which we choose to observe but also on the play of our words. Consider the assertion that this or that phenomenon, such as culture or race, is socially constructed.[22] What is meant is that social conventions intervene in our perception. So, the sign "white" refers to a person we learn to recognize as white. The historical and political implications of this insight cannot be separated from the signing. "White" is a metaphor for the referent. "White" also corresponds to conditions that permit the metaphorical relation between the sign and the referent. Even assuming that the political or the contingent could be banished from the metaphorical, rendering a grammatical relationship objective, inquiry into the social text cannot be rendered scientific or determinable in any apolitical sense.[23] Why is this? Contingency or politics cannot be banished from our inquiry. The play among words makes comprehension possible.[24]

DIVERSITY OF A SPECIAL SORT

Rhetoric is especially relevant to lawyers and judges because they labor with language. It is the subject of legal inquiry and the object, a legal decision, is the presence of legal desire. Simply, lawyers and judges want the text that is not present, and this desire brings the text, the decision, into being and defers its ultimate form. The language of previous opinions and relevant statutes is parsed to conjure the legal argument. Descriptions of legal conflicts offer their own explanations but they cannot, except in a noncontroversial sense, be used to inform others or us about the essence of our perceptions. This is important, though not unique, to the context of voting rights because it means that we cannot articulate a just representation outside of what we are able to describe. A just representation is socially constructed, and a political representation is inevitably socially constructed. The difference between the two is a political determination.[25] We cannot employ a language that is not infected by politics or rhetoric.[26]

What does rhetoric reveal about the politics of representation? In the context of representation, race-conscious communitarians promote "diversity" among officeholders as a good. Diversity is a code word.[27] It signifies to the listeners that the speaker is "one of us." In the name of diversity, we recognize racial and ethnic communities.[28] Recognizing diversity means taking into account those particularities that inform us of the individual's social and political existence. Accounting for diversity entails some retreat from the neutral application of the law.[29] We make political choices as to which particularities we embrace. Recognizing diversity carries a political price. It excludes as it includes.[30]

Of course, this is characteristic of all categories. But the difference is that the politics of difference presents diversity as crossing boundaries and making connections.[31] However, there is no categorical structure that is not diverse if we understand "diverse" to mean an appreciation for and recognition of the different traits upon which categories are constructed. So the difference is that "diversity" means more than diversity. "Diversity" means variety or distinction of a particular sort and reflects political choices. Recognizing diversity is part of current liberal practice.[32] The problem, then, is one of definition: Whose claims for diversity do we recognize, and whose do we ignore?

Perhaps we should recognize actual or authentic claims. Rhetoric that reflects true claims ought to be privileged over that of unauthentic claims. Unauthentic rhetoric can obfuscate justice, and therefore ought not to be heard by the law. But how does one establish authenticity?[33] Perhaps authenticity pertains to the individual.[34] The individual is prior to such collective categories as gender, ethnicity, nationality, and race. Yet, there does not seem to be any inherent reason why authenticity could not pertain to the collective. Indeed, the authenticity of an individual calls out for recognition of the individual's collective solidarity. "My being, say, an African-American among other things, shapes the authentic self that I seek to express."[35] The tension of collective oppositions such as white and black informs claims to recognition and authenticity. After all, the recognition of black identity is, in part, facilitated by "white society." American society and institutions centrally shape African-American identity; it cannot be seen as constructed solely within African-American communities.[36] The term "African-American identity" defines a group. This group may voice claims under the VRA, which in turn is used as a means to air communal grievances.

Liberal rhetoric—for example, stressing the primacy of the individual over the group or that rights pertain to an individual prior to an explicit conception of the good—has dominated recent Supreme Court decisions in VRA cases. Opposed to the assumptions underlying the liberal rhetoric used by Justice O'Connor in *Shaw I*, and elsewhere, are those who subscribe to critical race theory and/or race-conscious communitarianism.[37] For race-conscious communitarians, race is the paramount political and legal characteristic. Communitarianism has theoretical relevance and political power if it is informed by recognition of the claims to equality made by a minority race in the context of majority domination. As mentioned in Chapter 1, under the VRA, race is presumed to authorize representation. It furnishes the unique perspective that the majority cannot replicate. It deauthorizes criticism by those who are not so endowed.[38]

The minority representative speaks for the group.[39] The rhetoric of minority representation conserves the minority group by reproducing its history, needs, and concerns. Tenets central for the minority group include a particular interpretation of a history of oppression and struggle. Holding these beliefs and sharing their history helps establish authenticity. Those who have the political and racial capital to authorize, authenticate group members. This is politics, as is asserting group solidarity *vis-à-vis* the majority.[40] Contesting the authenticity of an argument challenges the virtue of the speaker. The true voice reproduces oppression borne by the group. Only those who are recognized as members of the race are authorized to speak for that community. For race-conscious communitarians, one cannot mimic the voice; there can be no virtual representation no matter how empathic the speaker. However, members of the race may be deauthorized if their actions or words are perceived to be in enmity to the group.[41]

By asserting solidarity and speaking in the heretofore silenced "voice," the group establishes itself *vis-à-vis* the majority on its own terms. The minority group asserts the power to create and police orthodoxy. Failure to assert group solidarity reinforces the "ideology of white, European, Western supremacy."[42] Not all voices are heard. Depending upon how one reads society and one's conception of justice, the voices that need to be heard change. One thing is certain with respect to VRA litigation: unless the voice employs recognized legal categories, such as race and language minority membership, it is not heard.

Critical race theorists argue that liberating the private individual subordinates already oppressed peoples.[43] This view reflects a particular understanding of difference that brooks little dissent within the community. Political socialization involves learning the orthodoxy of ascriptive characteristics. They forge our expectations. The rhetoric of difference exerts a strong presence in representation jurisprudence. Some race-conscious communitarians assert that majority elected officials cannot understand or voice the perspectives of their minority constituents.[44] This is a controversial view. Those who do not share the minority's social space and physical characteristics cannot hope to replicate the minority's voice in law school, on the bench, or in the legislature.[45]

The outsider's rhetoric lays bare existing patterns of politico-legal domination.[46] Dominant legal scholarship, by contrast, replicates existing hierarchies. The method of explicating the marginal experience is storytelling. Storytelling encourages other stories to be told. Likewise, the minority representative voices concerns that ordinarily go unheard. Telling the story of the minority community presumably results in more responsive government. It also imposes a particular political discernment of the minority community *vis-à-vis* the majority community.[47] Those who claim marginal status advance storytelling not as a way to modify dominant legal discourse or political hierarchy, but as a means to include their rhetoric in that discourse.[48] Storytelling, by defining and demarcating the minority community, is part of dominant political rhetoric.[49]

YOUNG AND THE RHETORIC OF JUSTICE

Iris Marion Young believes in the power of the rhetoric of difference to do justice. In terms of representation, justice is unattainable when minorities fail to hold office in proportion to their percentage of the population.[50] According to Young, dominant political rhetoric shuts out women and other groups. Likewise, she believes that the dominant discourse of rational argumentation excludes "ritual, myth, passion, emotional expression, and poetic discourse," which impart much political insight. Yet, it is also true that cultural standards, as articulated in our discursive communities, define what is or is not privileged political discourse.[51] As such, much in rational argumentation that is ritualistic, emotional, mythic, poetic, and passionate goes unrecognized. The language of the law is a prime example. Young wishes to transcend dominant discourse in order to get to justice.[52] She believes that a commitment to neutral principles or formal equality for all persons and all groups universalizes the standards of the privileged group. This is relevant to our discussion of representation because it may mean that we may need to segregate the dominant from the subordinate group in order to empower the latter. It may mean that a "color-blind" solution to the problem of fair representation reinforces majority domination. But a critique of formal legal equality fails to explain how the VRA successfully set aside parts of political discourse for marginalized groups in the form of majority-minority districts, and increased public deliberation over its necessity.

Young bemoans the color-blind jurisprudence of the liberal state because it embraces "the transcendence of group difference or assimilation" as an ideal.[53] Yet by according special treatment to some social groups, we may replicate the same problems a color-blind jurisprudence hopes to correct.[54] Ordinarily, race should be irrelevant to a legal classification. But by employing a benign use of race in order to benefit a particular group, the law may reinforce the salience of classifications based on race. The point that Young makes, ironically, is that there is no true or false rhetoric. Yet she believes in extra-rhetorical claims to justice. She believes that justice pertains to the group, and that groups can voice their grievances effectively. However, she cannot tell us what the rhetoric of justice sounds like because it changes for different ears. She cannot articulate the rhetoric of justice without reflecting her politics and institutional space. No one can. Young's rhetoric of difference echoes the rhetoric of the politically dominant discourse of rational argumentation.

This does not mean that the rhetoric of difference is not somehow different from rational argumentation. In fact, I recognize and employ the difference between the two in this chapter. But the rhetoric of difference cannot describe a more just world from anything but another political standpoint. Additionally, there is much rational argumentation in the rhetoric of difference; passion, myth, and poetry are a part of rational argumentation. No discourse forecloses debate on what comprises justice. This is important in the consideration of fair representation because there are some who believe there is an authentic discourse, a politics of difference that leads to fair representation. But this rhetoric, like Young's, cannot exclude politics or forestall reinterpretation.

GLENDON'S IMPROVED PUBLIC RHETORIC

A way out of Young's dilemma that would enable us to emancipate the rhetoric of justice without imposing new inequalities may lie in critiquing how courts hear rights claims. I consider Mary Ann Glendon's typology of legal rhetoric because it is conceptually unambiguous and because it has a direct bearing on the discourse of fair representation.[55] Glendon wishes to improve public rhetoric with talk of community and interdependence. Somehow, if we just promote community and interdependence, things will improve. But what do these communities look like? Interdependence may materialize as stifling dependence. The proper forms of community and interdependence are intensely political questions. For instance, do we create a majority-minority district, or is it better to spread minorities out so that they may influence a greater number of electoral races?

Glendon reduces the jurisprudence of civil rights to a vocabulary exercise she calls "rights talk." If we can just get the words right, we can correct those wrongs which hold back the political community. She avers that we are stuck with an 18th century vocabulary of rights. Presumably the connotations of this vocabulary have not changed much over two hundred years. Glendon's argument, at the same time she wishes to display her command of rights talk historiography, strains under the objections that there are competing interpretations of history, and that the language of rights talk evolves.[56] It evolves even if the words remain the same.

Nonetheless, Glendon tells us that because we harbor a radical version of individual autonomy, programs that stress interdependence are avoided.[57] Yet, she does not spell out in detail what type of society fosters interdependence and nourishes the individual. This does not mean Glendon's criticism of American jurisprudence is not powerful. It simply means that her critique occurs within the practices of the political community she critiques. She cannot step outside of this community to delimit a new type of social relations around which the political community conforms.[58] Likewise, there is no pure language that informs fair representation because the concept of "representation" is an evolving practice. It is part of rights talk, and it has evolved immensely from the early reapportionment cases like *Baker* v. *Carr* and *Wesberry* v. *Sanders* to recent VRA cases such as *Miller* v. *Johnson* and *Johnson* v. *DeGrandy*.[59] The vocabulary of fair representation is utterly political. And this is fortunate, for representation is a political concept to be debated. It is not a creed learned by rote.

Glendon asserts that the liberal notion of individual autonomy ignores community membership and fails to reflect the reality experienced by most Americans.[60] What is not clear is how liberal practice excludes the recognition of communal membership, unless she limits this recognition to a particular political type. For Glendon, liberal rhetoric is exclusive of communitarian rhetoric and excludes the communitarian solutions she advocates. It is unnecessary to view communitarian and liberal solutions in opposition. Justice Harlan wrote in *Reynolds* that individuals vote, but they vote as members of groups. Individuals have many group affiliations, and these may change.[61] But individuals may also voice political concerns that have little or nothing to do with collective attachments.

Courts employ liberal and communitarian rhetoric in the same cases.[62] The case law of the VRA indicates that Glendon does not give the courts enough credit. The law conserves the political community.[63] Courts decide cases that recognize different types of communities and group rights. Government recognition of group claims in the context of voting rights intensifies a constitutional debate over the nature of representation and the relationship between individuals and groups within a republican form of government.[64]

TAXONOMY, THE LAW, AND LEGAL RHETORIC

We assert, and the courts countenance, group claims. It is a part of legal practice that draws little reflection. Political competition ordinarily pits group against group. Communal claims thrive within liberal practice.[65] This reality appears to represent the natural order of things. Factions thrive, and inform our particular liberal political community. Oppositions within this order are maintained by the persuasive power of their classificatory systems. Consider the following:

In a certain Chinese encyclopedia in which it is written that animals are divided into (a) belonging to the Emperor, (b) embalmed, (c) tame, (d) suckling pigs, (e) sirens, (f) fabulous, (g) stray dogs, (h) included in the present classification, (i) frenzied, (j) innumerable, (k) drawn with a very fine camel hair brush, (l) *et cetera*, (m) having just broken the water pitcher, (n) that from a long way off look like flies.

Contrastingly:

No Tagalog, born in this Tagalog, shall exalt any person above the rest because of his race or the color of his skin; fair, dark, rich, poor, educated, and ignorant—all are completely equal, and should be in one *loob* (inward spirit). There may be differences in education, wealth, or appearance, but never in essential nature (*pagkatoo*) and ability to serve a cause.

Each of the passages above illustrates how a society might choose to group things. It attempts to order phenomena so that perception rises above the idiosyncratic. In our society, the law attempts to order. The law is a special taxonomy. In it, categories and the oppositions they employ are at their most powerful when their arbitrariness remains uncontested.[66]

The United States Constitution, as interpreted by the United States Supreme Court, imposes order on a complex society when it forbids the denial of the right to vote on account of race, color, or previous condition of servitude. Likewise, equal protection jurisprudence recognizes the existence of "suspect classifications" and demands that the Court examine laws employing such classifications with greater rigor. Suspect classes may involve groups of people who are in a position of political powerlessness and, because of historical discrimination, must be protected from majoritarian tyranny.[67]   Race and religion are suspect classes.[68]   However, sex, mental retardation, sexual orientation, and wealth are not.[69]

Determining what is a suspect classification presents a complication. A court cannot recognize all communities, lest the notion of community become absurd. Courts answer incrementally what communities they recognize and what standards they employ to justify their recognition of, for example, race rather than income level as a suspect class. Answers to questions involving community recognition are intensely political. In a country with a history of profound racial division, where we view race as immutable but poverty as a category to transcend, perhaps the distinction between race and poverty makes sense. But we also have a profound history of sexism, and it is common to view sex as an immutable characteristic. Yet, courts distinguish between race, a classification requiring strict scrutiny, and sex, a classification that merits intermediate or heightened scrutiny. The unenviable task of the jurist is to construct an ever-changing chart into which she must put legal things. Legal taxonomies are contextual. They reflect a particular conflict involving the recognition of particular group claims at the expense of others. After the courts decide to recognize the group claim, the question of authenticity remains. Is the claim true or does it merely appear to be so? Authenticity is a comparison of this or that person in this or that context so that we are able to say, for example, that person A is a member of the Red group rather than of the Blue group. However, the comparisons we learn in order to make this determination are, in part, political determinations. The correct political determination is a matter of marshaling rhetoric more persuasively than your opponent does. It is not enough to be recognized legally.[70] The group must police its membership in order to successfully claim resources from the larger community.   For

Madisonian liberals, the problem with drawing up a list of groups to receive societal resources is that it reinforces social divisions. If these lines traditionally rend the fabric of the political community, the liberal is suspicious of government sponsorship.[71] However, if the state does nothing, it may reinforce long-standing social inequalities.

Glendon and Young misread American jurisprudence. We do not have a color-blind constitution, though it may be a strong aspiration for some.[72] Race-conscious redistricting is at the very heart of the 1982 amendments to the VRA.[73] The Attorney General, the official charged with enforcing the VRA along with the federal courts, is put in the anomalous position of requiring nondiscriminatory treatment within the context of a race-conscious drawing of district lines. The trick is to take remedial action without attracting the opposition of those who pillory such efforts as "affirmative action." It is not government action in and of itself that strikes some as unfair, so much as government action that for some reason appears contrived.[74] A legal taxonomy is respected by virtue of the will and ability that inform it, and not by whether or not it is color-blind.[75]

As a practical matter, due process is a means to normalize the legal order of things. Things that demand our attention, unless we have accepted their place in the rule-of-law, seem out of joint.[76] "Unnatural" power appropriations are tolerated at the cost of political capital.[77] At its core, law remains a tool by which the state categorizes society. The viability of the law depends on the relevance of the categories employed. Those who wish to use the law for change must argue for the relevance of their categories.[78] Groups advance politically liberal agendas through the law, such as increasing the racial diversity of elected bodies, but they do so within legal categories.[79] They must speak the law in order to use it. They use categories in which the legal community believes, unthinkingly, in order to persuade. Lawyers speak a specialized language. Much of law school and law practice is learning the vocabulary and the logic of the law. This is what makes lawyers powerful, for it is what enables them to exclude. In practice, the law rewards the powerful and the familiar.[80] This is borne out in VRA litigation, where institutions with experience and expertise shape the briefs that come before state and federal courts.[81]

REAPPORTIONMENT RHETORIC

One of the fallacies of representation jurisprudence is the belief that there is a stopping point. We might call this point "fair representation." Certainly, this is a political good that the political community ought to strive for by promoting robust public deliberation and the inclusion of minorities. But the standard of fair representation is, and will continue to be, an evolving one. As such, we must distinguish between static ideals and dynamic practice in order to evaluate the rhetoric of representation jurisprudence. Just as Plato wished to distinguish the ideal republic from the best attainable republic, so one distinguishes the ideal VRA from one shaped by political pressures. However, even Plato's ideal does not represent social and political justice. It is static. It does not account for "the continual re-creation of order in a living, plural society wherever new claims arise."[82]

Race is a dynamic concept. Unless we attempt to understand the changing significance of race, we are less likely to make effective use of the law to arbitrate among claims for political justice in ambiguous and contentious situations. We live in an intensely political and dynamic society with profound racial divisions. The ideal VRA would presumably be color-blind; the realistic VRA cannot be.[83] Of course, in an ideal world, the VRA would not be needed. Similarly, there is no static definition of fair representation. Each determination is political, and each voting district is a gerrymander. We discriminate among those districts that strike us as odd and those that somehow seem to fit. The rhetoric of objectivity distinguishes between illegal and racial gerrymanders. There is simply no apolitical measure of an electoral district. Depending upon which interpretive community we belong to, we may view a district as a gerrymander. The distinction between legal and illegal gerrymandering is rhetorical, but this does not make it any less real.

The rhetoric of redistricting became the centerpiece of *Shaw* v. *Reno* during 1993. The case involved the drawing of majority-minority congressional districts in North Carolina, a state that had not elected a black representative to Congress since Reconstruction. The 12th Congressional District, the second of two majority-minority districts created in North Carolina after the 1990 census and following the Attorney General's preclearance, drew the attention of white plaintiffs, who argued that North Carolina unconstitutionally segregated white voters from black voters. They claimed this violated their right to participate in color-blind elections as protected by the Equal Protection Clause of the 14th Amendment to the United States Constitution.[84]

The Court did not decide that the plaintiffs had the right to participate in a color-blind election, but that the use of race to fashion the odd shape of the 12th District was subject to strict scrutiny. The Court came to this decision despite the fact that the district was drawn to benefit blacks. The bizarre appearance of the district offended the Court. It unwound like a long snake: 160 miles long and in some parts no wider than the highway. The district was drawn with two major purposes in mind.[85] The first was to preserve the seats of Democratic incumbents elsewhere in North Carolina. The second was to congregate enough blacks so that they could elect the candidate of their choice. Reconciling these two purposes resulted in a curious shape. This proved fortuitous for the plaintiffs challenging North Carolina's 1990 reapportionment plan.

The shape of the 12th Congressional District was fortunate for the plaintiffs because the Court was not blind to its oddities. Indeed, the plaintiffs' brief called it political pornography.[86] The Court's reasoning in *Shaw* was criticized as *ad hoc*. It was likened to Justice Stewart's approach to identifying pornography in *Jacobellis*.[87] This is the "I know it when I see it" technique.

The Court was rebuked because it failed to articulate a systematic formula to determine whether a district was constitutional. It left the impression that the Court concluded whether or not a particular district's shape was constitutionally offensive according to its peculiar aesthetics. In short, the Court was faulted for relying on mere appearances rather than on something more substantial.[88] But how was the Court to judge reality except through appearances? Its mode of interpretation allowed it to discern political pornography. This was the Court's reality. Reality was a special kind of appearance. In this case, appearance was not open to further interpretation because it had, for O'Connor and the majority, explained itself. However, for the minority in *Shaw*, and the majority's many critics, O'Connor simply did not see what really happened in North Carolina.

Shaw certainly does not offer a means of limiting the Court's role in the apportionment process. It develops no clear guide for future political players. It does not lend jurisprudential clarity to progeny cases.[89] There is an Equal Protection Clause and there is a VRA, but their relevance depends on the fact situation. On the other hand, *Shaw* is an open letter to the states that if they send something to the Court as odd as the North Carolina district, it faces censure.

Some feel that if the Court acts in an *ad hoc* manner, it acts inappropriately. It acts politically.[90] This is as revealing an analysis of the Court as it is of the commentators who feel that the Court ought to "develop and supervise an extensive scheme" in this area of the law.[91] Despite revealing a profound mistrust of the political branches, this view displays an unrealistic optimism that the federal courts have the ability to develop and supervise litigation faster than the litigants manipulate and "supervise" the courts. If we cannot trust core political rights to political actors, why leave them to the courts? Nonetheless, the courts are a part of the reapportionment process. This is true despite the prescient warnings by Justices Frankfurter, Harlan, and others that the reapportionment process presents a problem with which the bench is ill equipped to deal.[92] Robert McCloskey, at the dawn of the Court's entry into the area of reapportionment, warned that the Court would find it impossible to exit apportionment politics. He believed this to be so because he advanced a strong dichotomy between the law (judicial process) and politics (legislative process).[93]

It is hard to see how the process of balancing the complexities and subtleties of communal and individual rights claims in the area of representation could be reduced to anything resembling an exercise of reason, how it could reflect anything more than a subjective *ipse dixit*. It is equally hard to see how the judicial process thus conceived could differ from the legislative process unless it would be by virtue of an abstract moralism that attempts to transcend reality. If the courts are to invade the center of this thicket, they must be prepared to grapple with the problems that inhabit it; and if they do, they are acting as legislators.[94]

Frankfurter, Harlan, and McCloskey were dubious of the judiciary's ability to umpire conflicts over fair representation because judges had to make overtly political decisions. McCloskey's law and politics dichotomy remains as robust as ever. Law is certainty. Law can lead to justice. Politics is contingency. Politics can lead to the capture of the legal process, caprice, and injustice, but this need not be the result. Of course judges, especially Supreme Court justices, make political decisions, but they are most effective when their decisions are presented as legal determinations arrived at by ascertaining the correct conclusion from the pertinent law. The judge employs the rhetoric of judicial restraint. She finds the law rather than creating it.[95] On the other hand, if we disagree with the decision, we can characterize her rhetoric as judicial activism. In the area of reapportionment, there is nowhere to moor the rhetoric of the law but upon the shoals of politics.

The Supreme Court can be more or less political, but few things are more political than the law. What is more central to the power of the state than to declare this or that action legal or illegal? Certainly the subject matter of *Shaw*, redistricting, gives the Court reason to pause. Here the Supreme Court comes into conflict with co-equal branches of government and state governments.[96] The Court remains in a political thicket. Its refusal to render programmatic decisions, as some wish, can be criticized. But, there is simply no way to predict how reapportionment jurisprudence will evolve other than that the interpretation of the law will remain political.

EXITING RHETORIC AND ENTERING REALITY

Commentators on the law have tried to capture the discourse of representation jurisprudence through different rhetorical strategies, though they have not claimed to engage in rhetoric. One reading of *Shaw* asserts there was a collective or communal wrong. This interpretation sounds the rhetoric of communitarianism. That is, the harm in *Shaw* was directed at the political community rather than the individual.

Expressive harms are therefore, in general, social rather than individual. Their primary effect is not as much the tangible burdens they impose on particular individuals, but the way in which they undermine collective understandings to describe these collective understandings.[97]

Professors Pildes and Niemi support their communitarian critique with a textual/extratextual opposition. They believe there are authentic collective understandings that can guide constitutional interpretation.[98] Something outside the legal text, the *Shaw* opinion, guides their interpretation. Their interpretation of *Shaw* seeks to end deliberation over the shape of electoral districts. For the material to be interpreted is not a legal text, but the expressive significance or social meaning that a particular governmental action has in the specific historical, political, and social context in which it takes place.[99] This contention makes sense if one believes a legal text can ever have meaning or be interpreted absent a historical, political, and social context. But legal texts are historically situated. They make sense to us because they are part of the socio-historical context we use to get at their meanings. We see legal opinions rather than menus, novels, or mathematical proofs because we understand what these other things are in relation to legal opinions. Likewise, the idea of transforming an "expressive harm" into a cause of action depends on how the jurisprudential community reads the text of that expressive harm.[100] Lawyers do not step outside of the text, the opinion, or law review article to understand an expressive harm if they conceive of it as conveying a cause of action. To think in terms of a cause of action, a theory by which to sue, places the reader in the legal community that supplies meaning to an expressive harm. Pildes and Niemi advance an untenable text/outside text framework to guide their interpretation of *Shaw*. There may be a benchmark to measure the verity of the Court's decision. But they do not tell us how to discern rhetoric from reality or misleading appearances from those we may trust. They posit an ideal VRA analysis by which to critique the opinion.

Yet, there is no Archimedean point by which to guide legal interpretation. Interpretation collapses the distinction between that which is read and that which is outside reading. We impose rhetoric on reality in order to make sense of things. One informs the other so that the legal opinion cannot be separated from the political, historical, and social contexts that inform its recognition. As the Court commented in *Shaw*, appearances do matter. But standards like "compactness" prove to be highly subjective. For example, population distributes in a highly uneven manner within states.[101] Topographic phenomena such as deserts, mountains, lakes, and rivers must be taken into account when drawing district lines. State shapes vary widely: Iowa is nearly a parallelogram; Hawaii is a cluster of islands; and Michigan looks like a mitten with a finger pointed above it.   Different topographical characteristics and population densities, not to mention different historical, economic, and ethnic concerns, change the standard of compactness. This is the dynamism of compactness.

The Court's efforts to define compactness may be "inconsistent, ad hoc, and unpredictable." This is not necessarily an undesirable state of affairs, since at the very least it invigorates the debate over what is legal redistricting. It is unlikely that a quantitative standard, even with qualitative guidelines, would solve the districting puzzle.[102] It is difficult to imagine how to generalize the use of qualitative and quantitative standards because each districting context presents different political, historical, geographic, and demographic factors.[103] The quantitative determination of compactness is likely to be "inconsistent, ad hoc and unpredictable" because appearances do not dissolve into reality. Reality yields more appearances.[104] Qualitative determinations are also a matter for debate;[105] aesthetics are political.[106] Compactness "does not mean that a proposed district must meet, or attempt to achieve, some aesthetic absolute, such as symmetry or attractiveness."[107] But do we not, no matter what standard we apply, summon some determination of symmetry or attractiveness? After all, the quantitative standard posits an aesthetic ideal.[108]

Even if we accept Pildes and Niemi's assessment of compactness, we are left with a gauge in which "compactness falls along a continuum," and where establishing a cutoff point is a political determination.[109]   Their standard of compactness bodes ill for the majority-minority electoral districts created after the 1990 census. Six out of thirty-one majority black districts, or approximately 19 percent, and four out of twenty majority Hispanic districts, or 20 percent, are by their standard "extremely noncompact" and open to a *Shaw* challenge based their appearances. Contrastingly, only 15 out of 370 majority white districts, or 4 percent, are extremely noncompact.[110]   It is not clear how noncompact a district would have to be for the Court to view it as "bizarre," as was the case in *Shaw*.

Perhaps this discussion misperceives *Shaw*. Instead, it might be argued that *Shaw* was an ordinary equal protection case. The 12th District expressed the rhetoric of race-conscious communitarianism. It concerned a law that treated classes of people differently because of historical differences in political power between races. This rhetoric is not in accord with a philosophically liberal interpretation of the Equal Protection Clause. In such a case,

(1) all race-dependent decisions are subject to strict scrutiny; (2) rule (1) applies (a) to policies that include an explicit racial classification; (b) to policies that are neutral on their face but which are found to have been based on an intent to draw a racial classification; and (c) to policies that, although neutral on their face, may be assumed to be race based because they defy explanation on any other ground.[111]

However, this reading wrenches *Shaw* out of the very institution that produced it. Presumably the justices, hardly political neophytes, are aware that race and ethnicity are contemplated in the districting process.[112]   If these decisions involve the weighing of racial and ethnic factors, how is the Court to identify which districts are unconstitutional? It is a political determination and one that is increasingly controversial. Evidence that a majority-minority district is negotiated by the state, the Justice Department, and the voting rights bar is virtually a plea to the Court to apply strict scrutiny, as was the case in *Shaw*.[113] Subsequently, North Carolina established a compelling interest and "saved" for a time the oddly shaped 12th Congressional District.[114]   The shape of voting districts and the motive of race continue to occupy the Supreme Court's attention.

Another theory to explain the Court's decision in *Shaw* is that one should not take a good joke too far.[115]   States are going to use race as a factor in redistricting, but race should not be the only or predominant factor. At least it should not be presented that way, because if it is, the districting plan will not be sold easily to others.[116] Furthermore, for aesthetic and legal reasons, it should not be so obvious. Districting is rhetorical, but not all rhetoric is equally persuasive. In other words, when we discuss the appearance of a district, we are talking about the power of rhetoric, or at least acknowledging that there is positively no district not infected by it.   Without rhetoric, a district is indecipherable. All voting districts are dynamic and distinct. They reflect a population with particular needs and concerns. In this sense, all districting is local. On the other hand, a districting plan presents us with a broad topography of the political community. Our sense of its space, of the propriety of its boundaries, is informed by those political and legal practices that order other districts.[117] If it is drawn offensively, a district may be termed a gerrymander: political, racial, or otherwise. A districting plan presents a partial view, but not one so partial that it must draw attention to itself with concomitant legal challenges.

I argue that meaning comes to us *via* rhetoric. Rhetoric does not make a shambles of an "objective" or "legal" explanation of reapportionment. Rather, it makes the production and reception of such a theory possible. Ironically, rhetoric makes possible theories that argue that we must expunge rhetoric from our analysis. Each text moves; it is an unfinished argument. No legal theory forecloses further legal challenges. A problem arises for those who disparage something as merely "rhetorical." This is just the type of objection some have when they criticize the Court for stressing appearances.[118] The Court would be wise to reply, "What else are there except appearances?" Appearances, like rhetoric, are criticized for being insubstantial. There must be something substantive behind the appearance. Rhetoric is criticized for disguising the "real" reasons of the opinion, but this presupposes that there could be real reasons absent appearances. But then, how would we recognize them? The recognition of something that is not apparent reflects a longing to establish an objective jurisprudence and suggests the limits of the Court's institutional competency.

These same commentators criticize O'Connor's use of the term "political apartheid," a characterization originating in the appellants' "brief on the merits," to describe North Carolina's districting efforts as bizarre or odd.[119] Justice O'Connor "paints a false picture of the actual districts drawn by North Carolina."[120] Apparently, there must be a real picture of the actual districts. This is an arguable point, but not one provable outside of appearances. The 12th District was open to many interpretations, not unlike a challenging work of art. O'Connor's interpretation was the most persuasive for a group of nine who have the power to set an ultimate legal interpretive standard. Therefore, it is inconsistent to claim that her interpretation of a picture is false at the same time one is describing politically constituted phenomena. It is inconsistent unless one believes there is some way to step outside of politics, outside of appearances, to situate the interpretation of an event like districting.

This is a rhetorical move on the part of O'Connor's critics to criticize her rhetoric. In other words, they and O'Connor do not have an empirical disagreement over the taxonomy of the *Shaw* case, that is, this is an Equal Protection Clause and VRA case involving North Carolina's 12th Congressional District. They have a political disagreement about what is significant. Such a disagreement is unresolvable unless one party or the other changes its politics.

This is possible. It is also possible that the rhetoric we use to name the political event changes that same event.[121] This alters the debate. It may disjoin things so that the former disagreement over districting becomes invisible and forces the debate into new areas.

CONCLUSION

Conflicts in the law reflect a highly stylized debate. The use of rhetoric to present the conflict and persuade others—a judge, a lawyer, or a scholar—is inextricably bound with the legal *res* in dispute. In the context of districting, how one describes the conflict is central to resolving the matter. For example, by describing North Carolina's 12th Congressional District as a snake, political pornography, and apartheid, the plaintiffs employed tropes that indelibly marked the suit. In fact, the plaintiffs' rhetoric found its way into the majority's vocabulary. Critics of the Court's opinion criticized it for letting appearances and rhetoric get in the way of reality. But what is reality without language and a mind to describe and perceive it? Rhetoric and appearance can no more be expunged from districting than politics from the law. This does not mean that reality is only rhetoric or that law is merely politics. It means that rhetoric enables us to make sense of reality. It is an indivisible part of it. Likewise, politics cannot be distilled from the law so that we have a pure sample untainted by partisanship.

The districting process is an ongoing debate. It is impossible to stop the districting process in order to delimit what is an acceptable appearance. Rhetoric allows us to perceive and describe districting. But rhetoric cannot be captured indefinitely to exclude alternative appearances or districts. It allows for opposition and change. For that, we ought to be glad that districting is merely rhetoric and appearance. It naturally follows that the next two chapters illustrate the elasticity and pervasiveness of rhetoric as the Supreme Court transformed representation jurisprudence and the measure of fair representation.

Chapter 3

Case Analyses of Fair Representation Ante *Shaw* v. *Reno*

This chapter explains the development of fair representation in the Supreme Court from the 1960's until 1993. I examine cases based on the VRA, the Equal Protection Clause of the 14th Amendment, and the 15th Amendment. The underlying motive for almost all of these decisions, after the initial reapportionment cases of the 1960's, is the desire to accommodate concerns for racial equality. This motive drives a rhetoric that seeks to resolve racial tension by articulating a result that accords minorities fair representation.[1] Persistent racial inequality urges the reconsideration of fair representation. The desire to accommodate race, in some form, is resolved by courts within liberal and communitarian narratives. The narrative of a particular opinion situates a concept of fairness by which race is accounted and given priority over other understandings of fairness. As this chapter demonstrates, politically liberal justices articulate philosophically liberal and communitarian narratives, depending on the fact situation of the case. The same is true of politically conservative justices. Thus, philosophically liberal rhetoric inheres intrinsically to neither the political conservative nor the political liberal. The same may be claimed for communitarian rhetoric.

The use of particular philosophical justifications by the courts is important because the consideration of fair representation is elemental to the legitimacy of a republican democracy. No philosophical position or political belief has a monopoly in the construction of fair representation. This is particularly true when the political community is characterized by stark cleavages among racial groups. As the cases reveal, the courts have not settled the matter of what constitutes fair representation, and further litigation will result. This is a healthy course of events for the political community because it means that factions continue to justify their interpretations of fair representation.[2] There is no such thing as fair representation. Were it not the case—were partisans relieved of the obligation of putting forward an argument for fairness—this would wither an important exercise for legitimating the political community: the deliberation of fairness among citizens and public officials.

The chapter concludes with a discussion of the consequences of the 1982 amendments to the VRA, which, for a time, rooted interpretation of fair representation within a race-conscious communitarian narrative. Such a narrative is based in a notion of the good defined by a historical understanding of the political subordination of minority races. Within such an understanding, the political community's health is dependent, at the very least, on certain racial communities being represented in rough proportion to their percentage of the population. Evidence for this reading is found in VRA cases brought subsequent to the 1982 amendments. The extension of the VRA by Congress and its interpretation by the Supreme Court led to unsettling results. The VRA was no longer seen solely as a means to correct for prior acts of discrimination. Rather, it became the legal and political authority for the construction of race-proportionate results. Some justices, as well as some commentators, found equating race proportionality with fairness to be troubling. As a result, race-conscious communitarian interpretations of the VRA were laid open to a radical liberal criticism. This revived liberal criticism pointed toward a wholesale reconsideration of using the VRA as a tool for political change and as a measuring stick of fair representation.

REYNOLDS v. *SIMS*: THE LIBERAL STANDARD OF FAIRNESS

In 1964, the United States Supreme Court, in an opinion authored by Chief Justice Earl Warren, enunciated three principles concerning the "right" to vote and voter equality that remain with us to this day:[3] (1) voting is a fundamental right because it is preservative of all other rights;[4] (2) equal representation means that one person's vote is worth as much as another's, and therefore, the constitutional standard is one person, one vote;[5] and (3) the individual, rather than the group, is the fundamental political unit of representative government.[6] These principles reflect liberal assumptions that individuals are the building blocks of the polity and that rights pertain to individuals prior to an explicit notion of the good.[7] People are not necessarily equal in all respects, but equality under the law is necessary to protect liberty.[8] The liberal concept of equality under the law may be criticized as disguising and legitimizing racial, ethnic, and sexual inequalities. Simply, there is not a *status quo*, nor has there been a *status quo ante*, characterized by nonhierarchical social relationships for the law to encode.[9] The law is an artifact of unequal power distributions. The liberal view describes equality of opportunity within an unequal distribution. Distribution of political power discriminates among people and groups. Only a few will pronounce a particular distribution to be fair.

Society is ordered many ways; one of these ways is through the law. Order implies some form of hierarchy. There is no natural way for society to order, nor is there an artificial manner. Whether the ordering is viewed as natural or contrived depends in large part on one's concept of fairness. If the ordering is in accord with our sense of how things are, or should be, it is unlikely we will view it as unfair. *Reynolds* v. *Sims* articulated a view of fairness in accord with philosophically liberal principles. In fact, *Reynolds* marked the acme of liberal reapportionment jurisprudence. Moreover, *Reynolds* was considered a politically liberal decision. The Court in *Reynolds* contemplated the apportionment plan of the Alabama legislature that had been found unconstitutional by a federal district court because it was not apportioned on a population basis.[10] In Alabama, some voters' votes were "worth" more because they lived in a political district that was substantially less populous than other districts. For example, voter X might live in Lowndes County which had one senator for 15,417 registered voters. Voter Y might live in Jefferson County which had one senator for 600,000 voters.[11] Under this scheme, voter X's vote is worth more than thirty-five times that of voter Y. Voter Y is not denied the right to vote, but her vote is devalued in comparison with that of voter X.

Liberal rhetoric dominated the Court's discussion in *Reynolds*. "The Constitution of the United States protects the right of all qualified citizens to vote, in state as well as in federal elections."[12] Further, "racially based gerrymandering and the conducting of white primaries which result in denying to some citizens the right to vote, have been held to be constitutionally impermissible."[13] The Court recognized that some individuals were denied the right to vote because of race. Group identity, therefore, may hinder an individual's ability to express her preference at the ballot box.

Neither did group identity preordain the individual's political preference. "The right to vote freely for the candidate of one's choice is of the essence in a democratic society and any restrictions on that right strike at the heart of representative government."[14] Individual choice legitimated representative government. In *Reynolds*, individual choice was threatened because rural Alabamians were overrepresented in comparison with their urban counterparts. This inequality debased the democratic process.

Once the geographical unit for which a representative is to be chosen is designated, all who participate in the election are to have an equal vote—whatever their race, whatever their sex, whatever their occupation, whatever their income and whatever their home may be in that geographical unit.[15]

The Court acknowledged that the individual possessed group identities including sex, occupation, race, income, and geography. Group allegiances altered as, for example, the individual changed professions or religion, or the need for ethnic solidarity dissipated. The Court noted that group identity, though strong, was malleable because "the complexions of societies and civilizations change, often with amazing rapidity."[16] One can hardly imagine that this last insight, also articulated by Madison at the founding of the Republic, became less relevant as time passed and the layers of complexity in our society increased.[17]

There is danger in putting the state's imprimatur upon a particular group identity. Politicians will not fail to appeal to these interests because that is where the political capital lies. The Court recognized that the law valued parts of social reality. The result was bartered for political power.[18] In reapportionment cases, it was once "natural" for the fault lines to demarcate urban from rural. In some places, the most salient feature of politics was to favor rural interests at the expense of city dwellers. This was the case in *Reynolds*, where rural Alabamians were proportionately overrepresented. In Alabama and many other states, it was the numerically inferior rural interests that controlled the state legislature and congressional apportionment to the detriment of the urban areas. This is not to argue that racial cleavages are analogous to the urban/rural divide in *Reynolds*. Rather, it is meant to demonstrate that our attention shifts from one set of concerns to another.[19] Increasingly, it is "natural" to assert ethnic or racial singularity in order to gain political office or challenge electoral practices.[20]

From the liberal viewpoint, interpreting legal reality in ethno-racial terms, especially with regard to representation, is dangerous. Categories may denigrate the position of an entire class of people. The legal categories we use do not come to us value-free. Moreover, we recognize their utility as categories while we can take action that affects a category's value. Perhaps that was why the Court in *Reynolds* v. *Sims* was reluctant to announce the salience of any political unit except the individual. This is significant because liberal institutions ordinarily avoid assigning rights to communal groups within the larger political community. For instance, the *Reynolds* Court did not explicitly recognize the right of any particular group to vote or be represented in proportion to its numbers so long as the individual participated in an arithmetically undiluted manner.

The *Reynolds* Court specifically referred to its language in *Wesberry,* also decided during the 1964 term. *Wesberry* held that the "principle of representative government . . . is one of equal representation without regard to race, sex, economic status or place of residence."[21] The ideal of representative government in 1964 was race-, sex-, and class-blind. Consider:

Neither history alone, nor economic or other sorts of group interests, are permissible factors in attempting to justify disparities from population-based representation. Citizens, not history or economic interests, cast votes.[22]

Unfortunately, this liberal formula presented a conundrum. If equality has no intrinsic value, if we cannot peg equality to some standard of fairness that is not ahistorical, then it must be that we fill in our notions of equality with those prejudices that strike us, from our position in society, as fair. Citizens may cast votes, but they do not do so in a vacuum. The problem is that we cannot exit that vacuum in order to determine in what position we are to locate equality. If the right to vote pertains to the individual absent an appreciation for historical and socio-economic inequalities, then for many citizens the equal right to vote remains an empty right.

Rule-of-law and liberal jurisprudence have been linked to color-blindness.[23] Blindness allows us to operationalize a brand of fairness.[24] Blindness does not mean that there is no recognition of race or ethnicity.[25] Rather, it is the method by which we establish a particular standard of equality. We say we are blind to this or that difference in the name of maintaining a standard of equality, the prejudices of which we do not countenance, in order to establish a condition of equality. Blindness in this context is not empty of assumptions about what ought not to be seen. Indeed, the very notion of blindness in our constitutional jurisprudence assumes that one can be blind to, for example, race, sex, and class.[26] One can ignore race, sex, and class inequity. But ignoring inequity does not make it any less equitable. Blindness may be an argument for a hands-off approach to racial, sexual, and class inequalities once an arbitrary equality of opportunity is naturalized. Blindness does not mean that we cease to see race, sex, and class differences, but that we cease to consider certain strategies for alleviating these differences in the name of fairness.

In sum, the majority in *Reynolds* v. *Sims* articulated a liberal vision of representative democracy. The state should safeguard the individual's access to the ballot, but not devalue one person's vote in relation to another's. Additionally, the state must not privilege particular groups; this impairs the individual's autonomy by circumscribing the universe of salient groups and limiting group competition.

The lone dissenter in *Reynolds*, the politically conservative Justice Harlan, offered a communitarian riposte.[27] He included history, class, geography, and occupation as legitimate factors that Alabama might take into account when establishing legislative districts.[28]

But it is surely equally obvious, and, in the context of elections, more meaningful to note that people are not ciphers and that legislators can represent their electors only by speaking for their interests—economic, social, political—many of which do reflect the place where the electors live. The Court does not establish or even attempt to make a case for the proposition that conflicting interests within a State can only be adjusted by disregarding them when voters are grouped for purposes of representation.[29]

For Harlan, the Court disregarded the constitution of the political community at the local and state level in order to reach a standard of equality measured by the worth of individual voters wrested out of context. The majority did not account for the sense of togetherness that defined political units in Alabama because community was not a strand in its narrative of fair representation.

Justice Harlan felt that the constitutional standard of population-based apportionment was no less a construct, and no less arbitrary, than the process it replaced. There were no "natural" markers for the reapportioners to employ. In this sense, every electoral district was potentially a gerrymander. Whether or not one found the resulting gerrymander offensive depended upon how successfully the district corresponded with one's conception of what ought to be. The advantage of the new standard was its accord with the liberal vision of representative democracy. This was a vision that a majority of the Court embraced. However, in its hurry to safeguard the rights of the individual, the Court's one person, one vote formulation trampled on historical means of structuring politics in Alabama. These means were in place long enough for them to seem natural and for the Court's recipe to seem artificial. The Court's solution to Alabama's districting problems devalued long accepted forms of political representation while it claimed to remedy the effects of vote devaluation.

It should also be noted that Justice Harlan was less sanguine than the majority about entering the area of legislative apportionment. *Reynolds* invited legal challenges to most if not all of the state legislatures. Harlan suspected that this display of judicial hubris lacked appreciation for the contextual nature of apportionment and promoted a particular and by no means uncontroversial interpretation of the 14th Amendment's Equal Protection Clause. Until *Baker* v. *Carr,* reapportionment was considered too political for the Court to consider, and therefore nonjusticiable.[30] Justices Frankfurter and Harlan, and law professor Robert McCloskey, among others, warned against entering this political thicket.[31] The Court became further entangled with questions of what constitute legal electoral and representational practices with the passage of the VRA.

THE ADVENT OF THE VOTING RIGHTS ACT

One year after *Reynolds* v. *Sims*, Congress passed the Voting Rights Act of 1965 to protect the right to vote. Later, the VRA dramatically changed representation jurisprudence. As amended and applied, the VRA ushered out the liberal ideal of *Reynolds* v. *Sims* and gradually replaced it with communitarian alternatives. It is astonishing how quickly and relatively uncontestedly the communal interpretation of the VRA became the orthodox version. Communitarian rhetoric favored a distribution of political power to racial and ethnic groups in proportion to their numbers. This prescription of proportional entitlements profoundly altered the fabric of American democracy.[32] It refocused representation jurisprudence from the individual to the group. The focus of equality broadened to include not only equality of opportunity but also proportionality of result.

The VRA proposed originally to enforce the 15th Amendment to the United States Constitution in states that excluded blacks from the ballot. In other words, it was intended to protect the integrity of the franchise in those states where it had been violated by racist acts. William Gillette wrote shortly before the passage of the VRA that because of voting discrimination, "the very integrity of the democratic process and national authority are [sic] in jeopardy."[33] This was entirely consistent with the liberal standard of fair representation. As the Supreme Court riterated the text of the VRA, which it found consitutional in *South Carolina* v. *Katzenbach*:

Whenever a covered jurisdiction shall enact or seek to administer any voting qualification or prerequisite to voting, or standard, practice or procedure with respect to voting different from that in force or effect on 1 November 1964, such State or subdivision may institute an action for declaratory judgment that such qualification, prerequisite, standard, practice or procedure does not have the purpose and will not have the effect of denying or abridging the right to vote on account of race or color, and unless and until the court enters such judgment no person shall be denied the right to vote for failure to comply with such qualification, prerequisite, standard, practice or procedure.[34]

Initially, the most powerful provision of the VRA was Section 5. Under Section 5, the Attorney General precleared redistricting plans or other voting procedures and practices in covered jurisdictions after finding that the changes did not perpetuate voting discrimination, or the particular state asked for a declaratory judgment as to the lawfulness of its procedures in the District Court for the District of Columbia. In practice, states seldom sought declaratory judgments and, instead, obtained preclearance of their plans from the Attorney General. If a plan decreased the ability of minorities to elect minority candidates, it discriminated. A plan had to maintain, at a minimum, the current ability of blacks to elect blacks. Because no decrease in black political strength was precleared, this was known as the nonretrogression principle.[35]

The provisions of the VRA were transformed by voting rights litigants and activists, the Justice Department, and the federal courts into a policy of race sorting in political representation.[36] This design was not created out of whole cloth but progressed incrementally.[37] From at least 1969, the federal government required states and municipalities to alter electoral districts and systems of representation so as to facilitate the election of minority candidates from groups protected by the VRA.[38]

These groups are privileged in the sense that they are the groups Congress reads. Congress could recognize any number and number of types of groups, but limited itself to a relatively few minorities. One motivation for limiting the number of privileged groups is demographic. As the demography of electoral privilege becomes more intricate, the number of potential group claims under the VRA increases geometrically. A second motivation is the astoundingly powerful lobbying on behalf of the existing covered groups to maintain the *status quo*. For example, the National Association for the Advancement of Colored People (NAACP) lobbied to limit the number of groups protected under the VRA because increasing the number of recognized groups potentially devalued black claims. Only after intense pressure, did the Mexican American Legal Defense and Education Fund (MALDEF) succeed in making the case for including Hispanics under the aegis of the VRA in the 1975 amendments.[39]

The race-consciousness of the VRA, as it was interpreted and amended, came to mean that a state could take race into account as long as it fit the Court's idea of what constituted reasonable discrimination.[40] "Reasonable" inevitably meant allowing the Court to consider the desirability of the ends of race-conscious legislation.[41] Though the Court did not say so explicitly, it acknowledged the historical boundedness of discrimination. Discrimination created the standards by which discriminatory behavior was judged.[42] As standards of reasonable behavior changed, what was discrimination changed. This is not an argument that there are not forms of discrimination that as a society we ought to avoid, but an acknowledgment that we as a society recognize certain forms of discrimination as reprehensible, such as denying someone the vote on account of race, while we countenance others.

Some pictures of discrimination are so reprehensible that it is impossible to make a credible argument in their favor. An act of discrimination may not be essentially evil, but for society its odiousness is self-evident. Denying blacks the opportunity to use the same rest rooms or lunch counters as whites is this type of discrimination. Other forms of discrimination may not be so apparent. Because of this, we do not seek their end. The use of racial categories on the census form may be an example of this type of discrimination.[43] Finally, there are some modes of discrimination that we recognize and that many or most of us tolerate because we understand that we must employ discrimination for compensatory purposes. We might call this affirmative action.[44] In part, the VRA is an example of this form of discrimination.

UNDERSTANDING THE VRA IN TERMS OF THE MOTIVE OF RACE

Justice John Marshall Harlan, the first Justice Harlan, advanced a flat prohibition of racial classification in *Plessy* to remove the issue from the discretion of the Court.[45] "Our Constitution is color-blind, and neither knows nor tolerates classes among citizens."[46] Simply, Justice Harlan was unwilling to rely on judges (or the state *writ large*) to distinguish good racial classifications from bad.[47] Of course, one can argue that refusal to acknowledge race, to be color-blind, simply reinforces the state's current distribution of benefits according to race.[48] It is the rhetoric of neutrality. This may be criticized as empty rhetoric where political power is already maldistributed across racial communities. Indeed, the rhetoric of race neutrality could prove insidious to race-conscious communitarianism because it is so rhetorically persuasive. We can be fair by simply doing nothing, including taking race into account. However, this presumes a *status quo* where the distribution of political power among racial groups is equal: a situation that unhappily has not been present in our history.   Alternatively, perhaps it merely recalls a practice and the assumptions that underpin it. Unfortunately, we cannot be color-blind because that would entail our not knowing to what we are blind. This is not an argument for color-sightedness. We see colors, though it is true that we learn the colors that we see. However, there is no spectrum by which we can justly redistribute politico-racial capital. By "just," I am thinking of a nonhierarchical distribution that somehow takes into account the intricacy and continual development of society. This is utopia, and does not exist. So, given the necessity of some failure, what do we do? We are driven by our desire to see race, and having done so, must consider it.

For Harlan, the danger in *Plessy* is that the law encodes a particular discrimination that outlives its relevance. Once the law fails to describe adequately the distribution of racial power and loses its political value, the discriminatory law falls out of favor, inspires backlash, and creates a legitimation crisis. Initially, those who employed communitarian rhetoric, as Justice Brown did in *Plessy*, did so to segregate the races. Those in favor of ending state-sponsored segregation consistently advanced liberal rhetoric. For example, as an attorney, Thurgood Marshall stated:

Classifications and distinctions based on race or color have no moral or legal validity in our society. They are contrary to our constitution and laws, and this Court has struck down statutes, ordinances or official policies seeking to establish such classifications.[49]

However, some political liberals recognized the potential for a communitarian conception of fairness as the liberal standard failed to account for group inequalities. Daniel Patrick Moynihan wrote, as Assistant Secretary of Labor in the Johnson administration:

The ideal of equality does not ordain that all persons end up, as well as start out, equal. But the evolution of American politics, with the distinct persistence of ethnic and religious groups, has added a profoundly significant new dimension to that egalitarian idea. It is increasingly demanded that the distribution of success and failure within one group be roughly comparable to that within other groups. It is not enough that all individuals start out on even terms, if the members of one group almost invariably end up well to the fore, and those of another far to the rear.[50]

Moynihan's prognostication came true. Ethnic and racial identities became legal artifacts. Using the census, another politico-legal artifact, the political representation of racial or ethnic groups in a representative body was easily compared with the general population.

In other words, certain indicia of success were flagged. Under the VRA, it was black voter registration and the number of black officeholders. These measurements were compared with those of the majority. These were not the only comparisons that reflected inequalities among the populace, but they became legally important. From these comparisons, differing rates of success were extrapolated to demonstrate discrimination. Fairness dictated that each group succeeded at roughly the same rate. If that was not the case, the rules of the electoral game needed to be amended. It was a simple concept to understand and demonstrate.[51]

CONSEQUENCES OF THE EARLY VOTING RIGHTS ACT CASES

The Court shifted gradually from its use of liberal to communitarian rhetoric. The Court was not merely concerned with the right to vote, it was concerned with the value of the vote as measured in terms of group representation. Fairness had to account for race. A race-conscious communitarian narrative easily articulated such a result. For instance, the Court recognized that a multi-member voting scheme could reduce a racial minority's voting strength.[52]   An early example of the development of this jurisprudence was Chief Justice Warren's opinion in *Allen* v. *State Board of Elections*. He based the decision partially on the rationale of *Reynolds* v. *Sims*. A voting scheme was unconstitutional if some votes counted more than others did despite population-based apportionment. This was vote dilution.

This case involves a change from district to at-large voting for dilution of voting power as well as by an absolute prohibition on casting a ballot. Voters who are members of a racial minority in one district, but in a decided minority in the county as a whole. This type of change could therefore nullify their ability to elect the candidate of their choice just as would prohibiting some of them from voting.[53]

Allen applied the one person, one vote standard of *Reynolds* v. *Sims* to at-large as well as single-member districts. But here fairness implied more than an individual's right to participate. The concept of dilution was linked to the influence of the racial bloc. The *Allen* Court embraced a VRA "aimed at the subtle, as well as the obvious, state regulations which have the effect of denying citizens their right to vote because of their race."[54]   This interpretation of the VRA, in particular of the preclearance provision of Section 5, signaled the significance of the Attorney General and federal district courts in resolving potential VRA disputes.[55]   In dissent, Justice Black, as had Justice Harlan in *Reynolds*, deplored the degradation of state electoral practices.[56]

For the majority in *Allen*, political participation meant enabling a black majority to elect a black candidate. An important aspect of encouraging this type of descriptive representation is the reliance on self-description. The state allows or requires us to sort ourselves using our conception of identity. The state facilitates the process by furnishing us with the categories it wishes us to adopt. It also helps the process along by offering incentives for using its categories. The majority-minority district is just such an incentive. Self-selection is a misleading description if it cannot be separated from state sponsorship of identification.[57] The political community is the product of many factors; the most important of these, in the area of voting rights, may be state action.

It soon became the case that a voting scheme was seen as suspect where numerically significant black voters could not elect black candidates.[58] It is important to recall the concept of representation and the function of the representative. These terms were, and continue to be, contested. As such, the administration of the VRA can be a legal morass. Nonetheless, racial identity informs representation. The representative is authorized by virtue of his racial identity to hold office. His election by minority group members ratifies the overwhelming importance of race. Here, race may be said to authorize the representative, inform his behavior, and constitute the task of representation.

If minority voters are unable to elect a candidate of their own race, and the *Reynolds* v. *Sims* standard is not violated, the problem must lie elsewhere. A voting scheme that fails to yield the desired result, that is, a minority representative, is unfair. This is the message of *Allen*. The ability to vote freely for the candidate of one's choice may disguise structural hierarchies and reinforce racial inequity. The quest for fair representation is a longing to reconfigure racial hierarchies. The question then is what types of racial inequalities we accept. The Court rejected certain voting practices despite the fact that they did not deny anyone the right to vote because of race. One such practice was the use of multi-member districts. Multi-member or at-large districts were challenged for their winner-take-all aspects, their tendency to submerge minorities, and their overrepresentation of the winning party.[59] While not unconstitutional *per se*, they were suspect.[60] This required switching to single-district voting and the construction of majority-minority districts, and led to a gain in the number of legislative seats held by blacks and other minorities.[61]

In *Whitcomb* v. *Chavis*, an Equal Protection Clause case, the Court considered the multi-member state Senate and House districts in Marion County, Indiana, and stated a strong preference for single-member districts. The Court stressed the importance of minority electoral success as an adjunct to minority participation. The electoral schemes worked to the disadvantage of the black minority. But because the Court discovered no intent to purposively discriminate against blacks, it found that the voting scheme did not dilute the black vote.[62] The concept of vote dilution linked with the right of the individual as group member to elect the representative of his or her choice. An important legal aside is that at this date, it remained essential for purposes of Section 2 of the VRA and the Equal Protection Clause that the minority group establish that the majority acted intentionally to discriminate against them. In other words, to prove vote dilution under Section 2 of the VRA, and the Equal Protection Clause, one had to establish purposive discrimination.

White v. *Regester* was another early attempt to flesh out the bounds of vote dilution. The Court found discriminatory multi-member state legislative districts in Texas that diminished the political influence of blacks and Hispanics. The Court continued to stress the importance of identifying evidence of discrimination beyond looking at electoral results.[63]

To sustain such claims, it is not enough that the racial group allegedly discriminated against has not had legislative seats in proportion to its voting potential. The Plaintiff's burden is to produce evidence to support findings that the political processes leading to nomination and election were not equally open to participation by the group in question—that its members had less opportunity than did other residents in the district to participate in the political processes and to elect legislators of their choice.[64]

In a similar vein, *City of Richmond* v. *United States* held that an extension of municipal boundaries that reduced the overall percentage of the black population abridged the right to vote on account of race. Unless a post-annexation districting plan fairly reflected the strength of the black community and afforded it representation reasonably equivalent to its political strength prior to the annexation, it was invalid.[65] The motive of race drove the estimation of fair representation. Framing the narrative in terms of group and community resolved the desire to construct an architecture of fair representation.

Consistently, *Beer* v. *United States* found that Section 5 of the VRA prohibited implementation of a plan that reduced the success of racial minorities in electing minority representatives.[66] Thus, reapportionment and subsequent redistricting could not reduce the prior political success achieved by a minority group. In *White, Beer, City of Richmond*, and *Whitcomb*, white majorities attempted to diminish black political success or to maintain white political success founded on racially discriminatory practices. In none of these cases was the issue the right to vote. The issue became the right to participate fairly in an electoral contest with the prospect of being able to elect the candidate of one's choice. Necessarily the issues were framed in group terms, black interests and white interests, because political power had been founded, in part, on white domination of the political process at the expense of blacks.

THE POLYCHROMATIC VOTING RIGHTS ACT

In 1975, Congress amended the VRA in such a way as to add to its complexity and power. Originally, the VRA guaranteed the franchise to blacks who had been disenfranchised by means such as intimidation, poll taxes, and literacy tests. The need for the VRA to protect blacks' right to vote in the South was unassailable. But with the alteration of the VRA from a narrow means to protect the franchise to a tool to recognize group representation, other voices demanded to be heard. The result was that Congress amended the VRA to include the "language minorities" of "Asian Americans," "Alaskan Natives," "American Indians," and "persons of Spanish heritage."[67] Thus, not just blacks could bring suit under the VRA. Nor was it clear what would happen when the interests of the other language minorities conflicted with that of blacks.

As interpreted, the VRA prohibited decreasing the chances that minority voters would elect minority candidates. No voting scheme, as long as it adhered to the *Reynolds* standard, denied equality of opportunity to a citizen. At this level, each citizen had the right to vote and have that vote weighed evenly. But these facets defined the right to vote incompletely. What was added was a vision of representational justice wherein members of different minorities had the same chance to elect members of their community as did members of the majority. It became clear that packing minority voters into "safe" single-member districts was the most effective way of assuring minority electoral success.[68]

Gradually, Attorneys General came to require the maximum number of safe minority districts with proportional representation as the goal.[69] By the mid-1970's, the Attorney General required state and local governments to gerrymander their districts along racial lines. As alluded to in Chapter 2, gerrymandering always occurs. It is only when "our" group is not privileged by the line drawer that we utter the epithet "gerrymander." Identifying gerrymandering is a political task. There is no essential or natural way to configure electoral districts. A plan that increases the political power of one group at the expense of another does just that. There is no apportionment or districting that has a greater claim to fairness other than how fairness is articulated within the prevailing politico-legal discourse.[70] Fairness is not just there waiting to be discerned.[71] The litigation process initiated during redistricting in accordance with the VRA produced and reflected the practice of political fairness articulated by interest groups, the courts, and the Justice Department.

Fairness is a result we may all agree to be desirable, though we may quarrel with the outcome.[72] We create the possibility of seeing and affirming our own limits by recognizing the limits of what we create. We cannot exit the set of conditions that allow us to make sense of and communicate what we see.[73] We cannot litigate a vision of the polity in accordance with the VRA if we are not already familiar with it. Expanding the VRA to include new minorities correspondingly increased ways of articulating legal claims for fair representation. Hence, the communitarian narrative, often informed by race-conscious communitarianism, became richer and more complex. However, the narrative was enriched did not mean it dulled contention over which groups ought to be represented and in what proportion.

Not surprisingly, the next issue to reach the Court was that of contradictory minority claims.[74] After the 1970 census, New York City reapportioned pursuant to the VRA. In 1974, the Attorney General objected to portions of the plan for the borough of Brooklyn. The city's plan had, he said, a racially discriminatory purpose because it did not maximize the number of viable majority-minority districts. This precipitated a lawsuit. The *United Jewish Organizations of Williamsburg, Inc.* (*UJO*) case was at heart about the complexity of diversity in New York City.[75] A new plan was accepted that divided the Hasidic Jewish community in Brooklyn. The Hasidim claimed that the new apportionment plan diluted the value of their votes in order to achieve a racial quota. This was true, but they were not members of any community protected under the VRA. For purposes of the VRA, they were members of the majority. Despite the fact that there was no demonstration that the maintenance of a Hasidic district disenfranchised blacks, it was permissible for the state to take action at the expense of the Hasidim as long as "other" members of the majority were not prohibited from participating in the political process.[76] The Hasidic community was not recognized under the VRA as a group in need of protection from retrogression of political power. They were simply a part of the white majority. Under the VRA, the claims of one community were sometimes recognized at the expense of another.[77]

VIRTUAL REPRESENTATION REDUX

The Hasidim were not disenfranchised or unfairly burdened because they were "virtually represented" by other whites in Brooklyn. This type of logic depends upon utilizing race as an essential category, a surprisingly easy task notwithstanding the now ubiquitous phrase that "race is socially constructed."[78] For the Court, race went a long way toward determining one's political outlook. A member of a race presumably shared many of the same political opinions as others who were members of that race.[79] Even if you are unable to elect a representative of your race in your district, as long as someone of your race is in the legislature, you may be virtually represented. Edmund Burke used the same type of logic to argue that Birmingham, which had a mercantile interest but no representative, was represented in Parliament because he, Burke, represented Bristol, which shared the mercantile interest.[80]

One might also consider the case of Adam Clayton Powell, the former Congressman from Harlem.[81] At one point during his career, there were only two blacks in Congress. The other was not the national figure that Powell was. Powell was vocal about looking after "black" interests. Under Burke's theory of representation, blacks outside of Harlem may have been virtually represented by Powell. One could also argue that white representatives directly represented blacks in jurisdictions containing majority and minority voters. However, some race-conscious communitarians assert convincingly that white and black interests are inimical. In such circumstances, white representatives cannot actually or directly represent blacks.[82]

One deficiency with equating the direct or actual representation of minority interests with racial correspondence is, simply, the dynamism of minority diversity. There is no end point for a just diversity at which we may rest. In practice, recognizing diversity means making political choices and persuading others that your choice is fair. Diversity conveys an entire cultural, social, and legal program. Is the VRA a special piece of legislation because of its attention to diversity?[83] Does it deserve greater deference from the Court than other affirmative action statutes, like minority business set-asides, because the representative function is politically fundamental?[84] Perhaps a more racially diverse legislature, an aim of the VRA, legitimates government by better representing the various interests in society.[85] Consider a contrary evaluation of diversity in Justice O'Connor's dissent in *Metro Broadcasting*.

The asserted interest [of the FCC] is in advancing the Nation's different "social, political, esthetic, moral, and other ideas and experiences." . . . yet of all of the varied traditions and ideas shared among our citizens, the FCC has sought to amplify only those particular views it identifies through the classifications most suspect under equal protection doctrine. Even if distinct views could be associated with particular ethnic and racial groups, focusing on this particular aspect of the Nation's views calls into question the Government's genuine commitment to its asserted interest.[86]

The competition to demarcate diversity among favored minority groups is now occurring in places like New York City, Los Angeles, Texas, and Florida: areas where there is a high percentage of both Hispanics and blacks. It is a battle over scarce resources, and pits minority groups against one another.[87] For example, in Florida during the round of reapportionment following the 1990 census, either an additional black or an additional Hispanic district could have been created, but not both.[88] Quarrelsome and ethnic politics distinguished the resulting clash. Each group tried to outdo the other in its claims to suffering greater political marginalization.[89] In response to the Hispanic demands for another district, one black state legislator retorted, "[when] the basis of an extra minority seat is the VRA, then we ought to look and see who it was standing on the Edmund Pettis Bridge in Selma getting trampled."[90] The struggle for fair representation is about politics. There is nothing untoward about this. The importance of remembering that it is political through and through is that one is not surprised or dismayed when civil rights activists, particularly lawyers, act like political animals.

ESCHEWING THE LIBERAL IDEAL OF REPRESENTATION

The Court's shift in the area of representation from a liberal to a communitarian ideal did not go unnoticed. Throughout the 1970's, in the context of reapportionment, the Court adopted the policy of "benign" racial sorting. Alexander Bickel summed up the displaced liberal conviction of the mid-1960's. Though he was not speaking specifically about the VRA, his comments were no less insightful for a liberal critique of the Court's race-conscious communitarian interpretation of the VRA. "Discrimination on the basis of race was illegal, immoral, unconstitutional, inherently wrong, and destructive of democratic society."[91] Likewise, "a racial quota derogates the human dignity and individuality of all to whom it is applied."[92] Bickel was wary of the Court's growing role as social constructor. The Court's vision of race relations was informed by the vagaries of its politics. It had no compass by which to chart a course except its tradition, history, and method of reason.[93] In the area of voting rights, the Court was caught in a double bind. On the one hand, the mere recognition of racial difference inscribed a racial hierarchy into the law. On the other hand, by claiming to be color-blind, the Court simply instituted racial distinctions in the area of political representation.

Bickel was concerned with the legitimacy of an overtly political Court. At some level, law should be separated from politics. The law and politics opposition is a familiar one, and is hidden in such phrases as "judicial activist" (too much politics) and "judicial restraint" (more law than politics, and sometimes not enough politics). It is sometimes suggested that more legal process can accomplish the task of finding the balance between law and politics. As such, procedure is the primary way that the law justifies its own political position.

The practice of the law, stylized and exclusionary, enables its adjudicators to make substantive determinations without appearing to do so.[94] This is done through the mechanism of due process. The practice of law allows the process/substance opposition to be taken seriously. Thus, adding layers of legal process to sanitize the law from politics is exactly the wrong strategy to prevent its contamination. However, it may also be the right strategy for the wrong reasons if procedure is seen as a means to level the playing field so that the powerful cannot dominate the powerless. Refining legal procedure does not cleanse the law of politics; quite the opposite occurs. Nonetheless, adding procedural layers may be a successful rhetorical strategy to prevent the law from appearing political.[95]

Sharing Bickel's concern with an increasingly political judiciary, John Hart Ely argued that the Court had a "representation reinforcing role." Ely embraced a procedure-justifying approach. Unfortunately, legal procedures do not operate like the invisible hand of the market: imperceptibly, impartially, and apolitically. According to Ely, the procedures of the electoral system should allow minority groups to be heard.[96] Yet, implementing any procedure requires substantive presumptions about the constitution of a just society. Not surprisingly, disputes over the procedural mechanisms of the VRA set off a round of litigation over its substantive goals.

THE UNBEARABLE ANNOYANCE OF PROVING PURPOSIVE DISCRIMINATION

The Court indicated it that harbored some uneasiness with the idea of communal racial sorting in *Mobile* v. *Bolden*.[97] The plaintiffs based their cause of action on the 14th and 15th Amendments to the Constitution, and the VRA. They argued that the at-large procedure of electing city commissioners diluted their votes because a majority of 50 percent plus one could win 100 percent of the seats. No blacks had been elected since 1911, although they were 40 percent of the population. Yet, it was difficult to find direct evidence of discrimination where one was not denied the right to vote and there was no ostensible plan to dilute the groups' voting strength.

The Court, in a plurality opinion by Justice Stewart, required those challenging purportedly dilutive electoral practices to demonstrate racially discriminatory purpose.[98] Moreover, Stewart stressed that the Equal Protection Clause did not require proportional representation of minority groups.[99] Justice Stevens, concurring in the judgment, emphasized the difference between state action that inhibited an individual's right to vote and state action that affected the political strength of groups. Echoing Bickel, Stevens argued that the Court should not, in the absence of compelling law and fact, restructure state political systems where no one was denied the right to vote.[100] Nonetheless, there had to be an awareness of group interests for the reapportionment process to work. Race, like religion, should be taken into account, although the government should be wary of providing incentives to define politics by racial group membership.[101]

In *Rogers* v. *Lodge*, the Court considered whether at-large voting schemes and multi-member districts in Burke County, Georgia, minimized the voting strength of minority groups by permitting the white political majority to elect all the representatives of the district despite no clear showing of discriminatory intent.[102] Instead of looking for purposive discrimination, the Court relied on a "totality of the circumstances" analysis.[103] Certainly the fact that no blacks had ever been elected in Burke County was an indication that black interests were submerged and that there was purposeful discrimination.[104] *Rogers* expanded the limits of the fractured opinion in *Mobile* with respect to what type of discrimination must be proved in order for a minority group to make out a cause of action.

Following the confusion created by *Mobile* and *Rogers*, Congress settled the dispute over the evidentiary standard needed to establish vote dilution claims under the VRA by amending Section 2. The amended Section 2 partially overruled *Mobile*. Under the 1982 amendments, one no longer needed to prove discriminatory purpose. Instead:

(b) a violation of subsection (a) is established if, based on the totality of circumstances, it is shown that the political processes leading to nomination or election in the State or political subdivision are not equally open to participation by members of a class of citizens protected by subsection (a) in that its members have less opportunity than other members of the electorate to participate in the political process and to elect representatives of their choice. The extent to which members of a protected class have been elected to office in the State or political subdivision is one circumstance which may be considered: Provided, that nothing in this section establishes a right to have members of a protected class elected in numbers equal to their proportion in the population.[105]

Purposeful discrimination need not be proved if discrimination can be inferred from a totality of the circumstances such as housing and employment patterns or the failure to elect a black representative in seventy-five years.[106]

In practice, this language made it easier to bring claims pursuant to Section 2. Paradoxically, Section 2 promotes the proportional representation of racial groups protected under the VRA where possible while it disclaims that it mandates such a result. This inherent contradiction in Section 2 spawned much of the current VRA litigation. As amended in 1982, Section 2 of the VRA encouraged race-conscious remedial procedures. In practice, this extended Section 5–type protections to all jurisdictions with significant minority populations. Discriminatory intent was no longer needed to prove vote dilution. Instead, the courts could rely on electoral results.[107] For instance, if there was a sizable minority of blacks or Hispanics in a city, and none were being elected to office, there was probably actionable discrimination.[108] The practical effect of Section 2 was reflected in the Court's rhetoric throughout this time period that confidently asserted communal entitlements to representation. Race-conscious communitarian rhetoric not only gave shape to what was fair; it provided the nomenclature by which a communitarian vision of representation was understood by the Supreme Court.

GINGLES AND THE SHAPE OF THINGS TO COME

In *Karcher* v. *Daggett,* a 14th Amendment case, the Court struck down a New Jersey congressional apportionment plan that included small population deviations across districts, thus violating the constitutional standard of one person, one vote.[109] More important, the Court considered the justification for some of the population deviations: namely, the necessity of preserving the voting strength of black voters.[110] The state failed to demonstrate the specific population variations necessary to preserve black voting strength in New Jersey.[111] Justice Stevens's prescient concurring opinion in *Karcher* identified problems that would dominate the Court's consideration of fair representation. These dilemmas included creating districts with race as the predominant consideration without violating the Equal Protection Clause, and the curious shape of some majority-minority districts. The desire to promote the representation of minorities influenced the bizarre shape of some of New Jersey's congressional districts and resulted in population deviations among districts. Stevens's eloquently described the political thicket entered into by the Court.

As I have previously written: "In the line-drawing process, racial religious, ethnic, and economic gerrymanders are all species of political gerrymanders. . . . From the standpoint of the groups of voters that are affected by the line-drawing process, it is also important to recognize that it is the group's interest in gaining or maintaining political power that is at stake. . . . The mere fact that a number of citizens share a common ethnic, racial or religious background does not create the need for protection against gerrymandering. It is only when their common interests are strong enough to be manifested in political action that the need arises. For the political strength of a group is not a function of its ethnic, racial or religious composition; rather it is a function of numbers—specifically the number of persons who will vote in the same way." *Mobile* v. *Bolden*, 446 U.S. 55, 88 (1980) (concurring in judgment). . . . More important, a mere numerical equality is not a sufficient guarantee of equal representation. Although it directly protects individuals, it protects groups only directly at best. A voter may challenge an apportionment scheme on the theory that it gives his vote less weight than that of other voters; for that purpose it does not matter whether the voter is combined with or separated from others who might share his group affiliation. . . . Regarding the noncompact shape of the districts and a possible Equal Protection Clause violation. Although I need not decide whether the plan's shortcomings regarding shape and compactness, subdivision boundaries and neutral decision making would establish a prima facie case, these factors certainly strengthen my conclusion that the New Jersey plan violates the Equal Protection Clause.[112]

The Court clarified the 1982 amendments in *Thornburg* v. *Gingles* and explained the revised Section 2.[113] While invalidating a plan for multi-member districts, the Court concluded that the VRA eliminated any requirement for establishing that the contested electoral practice was adopted or maintained with the intent of discriminating against minority voters. The *Gingles* majority interpreted Section 2 to require the determination of the feasibility of a single-member district remedy; whether there was a politically cohesive minority community; and whether minority candidates could be expected to lose as a result of their submergence in a racially polarized electorate.[114] *Gingles* spelled out the remedy for racial bloc voting in multi-member districts: the creation of majority-minority districts.

Gingles also clarified what plaintiffs must establish in order to prove a Section 2 violation. Before the 1982 amendments to the VRA, minority voters had to prove purposeful discrimination of voting standards and practices. After the amendments, minority voters needed only to demonstrate a discriminatory effect. In interpreting Section 2, the Court adopted a results test based on the "totality of the circumstances."[115] As Justice Brennan articulated the results test, of concern was the success of the group, not of any particular candidate in an election. Elections were contests between racial factions. Individuals mattered to the extent that they identified with a particular faction.

Consequently, we conclude that under the "results test" of Section 2, only the correlation between race and voter and selection of certain candidates, not the causes of the correlation, matters. . . .Under Section 2, it is the status of the candidate as the chosen representative of a particular racial group, not the race of the candidate, that is important. . . . Where multimember districting generally works to dilute the minority vote, it cannot be defended on the ground that it sporadically and serendipitously benefits minority voters.[116]

Gingles stressed Congress's admonition to consider the totality of the circumstances surrounding electoral practices. This included racially polarized voting, education, housing, and health services, as well as race-based appeals during elections. Courts should determine whether these factors, given the lack of minority electoral success in multi-member districts, prevented blacks from electing their preferred candidates.[117]

Justice O'Connor attacked *Gingles*'s logic. According to O'Connor, the Court's results test depended on *a priori* determinations of minority success. If a minority group elected candidates in proportion to its numbers in the population, there was no Section 2 violation. The problem with this was that Section 2 disclaimed a right to proportional representation.

Surely Congress did not intend to say, on the one hand, that members of a protected class have no right to proportional representation and on the other that any consistent failure to achieve proportional representation without more violates Section 2. A requirement that minority representation usually be proportional to the minority group's proportion in the population is not quite the same as a right to strict proportional representation, but it comes so close to such a right as to be inconsistent with Section 2's disclaimer and with the results test that is codified in Section 2.[118]

Gingles embraced the idea that the federal courts could read the social fabric and discover legitimate communitarian claims. Combined with the 1982 amendments to the VRA, *Gingles* placed the creation of majority-minority districts paramount among political issues for the Court to decide. It was the distribution of power among racial groups that merited carving out majority-minority districts under the VRA. This issue enmeshed federal and state courts as they struggled to define fair representation under the VRA. The right not to have one's racial voice submerged, found in Section 2 of the VRA, became the right to be represented separately, distinctly, and proportionately by race.[119] For a time, *Gingles* stymied contention over what constituted race and fair representation. The category of race, far from being problematic, was taken for granted in *Gingles*. It did not matter for the *Gingles* majority whether race was something to which one should be color-blind, or whether it was something around which empowerment strategies coalesced.[120] Race was simply there.

A recent law review article offers the following critique of the *Gingles* opinion.

By this reasoning, a violation might exist when there is a racial divergence in voting patterns, whether this divergence is attributable to racial prejudice, to accident, or to noninvidious differences in political perspective that may sometimes sort along racial lines. The plurality recognized that such divergence may be attributable to the differing political agendas favored by a white majority and a black minority but argued that, under Section 2, this should make no difference to whether there was a violation.[121]

Gingles considered the issue of vote dilution or submergence in the context of multi-member districts. In 1993, *Growe* v. *Emison* extended this logic to single-member districts when there was evidence that black interests were submerged.[122] Single-member, majority-minority districts were the preferred remedy where at-large voting patterns swallowed minority preferences. The remedy was a district where minorities elected minorities.[123] Ironically, single-member, majority-minority districts may replicate the same racial divisions in the legislature that characterize the use of multi-member districts.[124] That is, white representatives from majority-white districts will have little incentive to discuss race issues with minority representatives from majority-minority districts if they do not need minority votes to remain in office. Majority-minority districting may resegregate the legislature.

Race is but one of many factors around which people coalesce for political power. Perhaps the most familiar form of political faction is the political party. The Supreme Court considered the issue of vote dilution from a vantage other than that of the racial group: that of the political party. The issue in *Davis* v. *Bandemeer* was the ability of Indiana Republicans to district in such a manner as to dilute the votes of Democrats. The Indiana Democrats brought a suit claiming that the reapportionment plan violated the Equal Protection Clause by analogizing political gerrymandering to racial gerrymandering. The Court decided that the justiciability of a vote dilution claim was independent of whether the group asserting vote dilution was a racial or a political group.[125] The important point for the Court was whether or not the group was cohered around a set of interests.[126]

The dissenters criticized the majority for failing to treat the claims of racial and political minorities as analytically distinct in the context of the 14th Amendment. They had an inescapable and powerful point. Political affiliation was simply not an immutable characteristic.

While membership in a racial group is an immutable characteristic, voters can and often do move from one party to the other or support candidates from both parties. . . . Racial gerrymandering should remain justiciable, for the harms it engenders run counter to the central thrust of the 14th Amendment. But no such justification can be given for judicial intervention on behalf of mainstream political parties and the risks such intervention poses to our political institutions are unacceptable. "Political affiliation is the keystone of the political trade."[127]

As mentioned above, *Gingles* defined vote dilution in the context in which it most often occurred: multi-member districts. In multi-member district cases, the solution, single-member districts, seemed simple. But single-member districts were not inherently any more immune to vote dilution than the multi-member districts they replaced.

In the multimember context, the existing district boundary lines define the limited geographic territory within which to locate replacement single-member districts. One must still define compactness, but within a relatively small, predefined physical territory. In contrast, in challenges to existing single-member districting plans for congressional or state legislative seats, the only fixed boundary lines are those of the state itself. Within those boundaries, a [potentially] unlimited number of districting plans and individual district shapes are possible.[128]

With single-member districts, line drawing gets harder and the result may appear more unseemly, more political. This nettlesome issue continues to perplex the Court.

JUDGES ARE REPRESENTATIVES, REPRESENTATIVES ARE JUDGES

It was beyond dispute after *Gingles* that the Section 2 results test applied in multi-member district elections of representatives. But did it apply in multi-member district elections of judges? Just what types of voting practices and procedures were covered under the VRA? Were judges considered representatives for the purposes of the VRA? This semantic question was the sort that lawyers and judges revel in, and that may make little sense to legal outsiders. After all, a judge sits in a court, and a representative sits in a legislature.

Justice Stevens, writing for the majority in *Houston Lawyers' Association* v. *Attorney General of Texas* and *Chisom* v. *Roemer*, found that the VRA covered the election of judges.[129]   In *Houston Lawyers' Association*, once the determination was made that elected judges were representatives for purposes of Section 2 of the VRA, the Court found vote dilution without much trouble. The evidence of black underrepresentation was overwhelming. In one county with a population that was 20 percent black, only three of fifty-nine district judges were black.[130] Using the results test, this was a clear Section 2 violation.

The rationale behind finding that judges were representatives was established in *Chisom*. The voting practices and procedures in dispute in *Chisom* involved the election of justices to the Louisiana Supreme Court. No black had ever been elected to the seven member Louisiana Supreme Court.[131] If justices on the Louisiana Supreme Court were representatives, then black plaintiffs could establish an unassailable vote dilution case. In this instance, the results test was hardly open for interpretive dispute.

In and around New Orleans, the use of a multi-member district, which included a compact black population large enough to form a single-member majority-minority district, was alleged to have diluted black voting strength in judicial elections. Justice Stevens invoked the spirit of the VRA and divined that a voting standard, practice, or procedure "encompasses the use of multimember districts to minimize a racial minority's ability to influence the outcome of an election covered by Section 2."[132]

He further reasoned that the term "representatives" as it applied in the VRA was to be read expansively.[133] If the term "representatives" included all types of legislators, and executive officers such as sheriffs, prosecutors, and state treasurers because they were popularly elected, there was no reason to exclude judges.[134] It would have been anomalous for Congress to exclude such "an important category of elections from that protection."[135]

Justice Stevens's generous reading of the VRA, whereby a judge was rendered a representative, was critiqued in a vigorous dissent authored by Justice Scalia. First, Scalia attacked the general tenor of the majority opinion. "The Voting Rights Act is not some all-purpose weapon for well intentioned judges to wield as they please in the battle against discrimination."[136] Scalia also cast doubt on the concept of vote dilution that led the Court into the judicial management of democratic elections. Moreover, the concept of vote dilution diminished the individual while elevating the faction. This was discordant with Scalia's philosophically liberal concept of representation.

Indeed, it is the principle of "one person, one vote" that gives meaning to the concept of "dilution." One's vote is diluted if it is not, as it should be, of the same practical effect as everyone else's. Of course, the mere fact that an election practice satisfies the constitutional standard of one person, one vote does not establish that there has been no vote dilution for Voting Rights Act purposes, since that looks not merely to equality of individual votes but also to equality of minority blocs of votes. . . . I frankly find it very difficult to conceive how it is to be determined whether dilution has occurred, once one has eliminated both the requirement of actual intent to disfavor minorities, and the principle that 10,000 minority votes throughout the State should have as much practical electability effect as 10,000 nonminority votes. How does one begin to decide, in such a system, how much elective strength a minority bloc ought to have?[137]

Scalia's view of representation was rooted in liberalism. The right to vote was an individual right. Constitution of the political community resulted from elections conducted among equally endowed electors. Consideration of how the election should have turned out was an improper one for judges so long as individuals participated on equal legal footing. Group claims, for him, were more problematic. Indeed, the concept of vote dilution under the VRA required that the Court determine, with a lack of specific guidance, which groups increase their political power and which groups cede political influence.

LIMITS OF THE COMMUNITARIAN NARRATIVE OF REPRESENTATION

Scalia was skeptical of the justification behind vote dilution claims as well as of the use of majority-minority districts to increase minority political power. Soon after *Chisom*, proponents of an expansive VRA were dealt a setback in *Presley* v. *Etowah County Commission*.[138] *Presley* implicated Section 5 of the VRA, under which a covered jurisdiction must submit changes in voting standards, practices, or procedures to the Attorney General for approval or preclearance.[139] In *Presley*, a black commissioner was elected to the Etowah County Commission for the first time in the 20th century. Following the election, the duties, powers, and responsibilities of the five Etowah County Commissioners were reduced in the important areas of road funds and operations.[140] Black appellants argued that this diminution of a Commissioner's power constituted a change covered by Section 5.

The Court, in an opinion by Justice Kennedy, declined to find that diminishing the power of the Etowah County Commissioners was covered under the nonretrogression principle of Section 5 of the VRA. A change in the power of legislative officials was too murky of an area for the Court to enter. Kennedy reckoned that almost any budgetary change could be grounds for a Section 5 challenge in covered jurisdictions if it altered the power of elected officials. In short,

No one would contend that when Congress enacted the Voting Rights Act it meant to subject all or even most decisions of government in covered jurisdictions to federal supervision. Rather, the Voting Rights Act covers any voting qualification or prerequisite to voting or standard, practice or procedure with respect to voting. . . . Covered changes must bear a direct relation to voting itself. That direct relation is absent in both cases now before us.[141]

Justice Stevens's dissent excoriated the majority for giving Section 5 such a mechanical reading. He implored the Court to consider his history of the VRA. The purpose of the VRA was to alleviate grave racial injustices. Section 5 was strong medicine, but the disease it treated—poll taxes, literacy tests, and physical intimidation—was virulent. For Stevens, "[T]his is a case in which a few pages of history are far more illuminating than volumes of logic and hours of speculation about hypothetical line-drawing problems."[142]

Not surprisingly, voting rights activists supported Stevens's reading. Professor Kathryn Abrams argued Stevens's dissent was sensitive to political participation as an extended process that did not end with the election of the representative but continued in the process of governing. Representation involved a relationship between the representative and the electors.

This approach to the VRA makes it easier to understand why changes in the responsibilities of elected officials implicate the voting rights of constituents: they alter the political relationship through which those constituents exercise their power.[143]

Likewise, Professor Pamela Karlan found that the majority's opinion reflected confusion over the purpose of "integrating historically excluded minorities into the political process as that process is broadly understood."[144] Under this view, voting was essentially a group practice. For Karlan, *Presley* involved the qualitative malapportionment of a group of people. The majority's sensitivity that judicial supervision of post-election practices was too political was misplaced. "The real question is not whether federal courts ought to enter the thicket but how they should treat the handiwork of the other denizens they discover there."[145] For Karlan, the Court had a clear role that Justice Kennedy did not share. The VRA placed the Court into the political thicket of representation. The aim of the VRA was to promote the representation of minorities. Practices adverse to this end ought to be struck down. However, simply because the Court decides to enter the mire of representation does not mean that the results will suit race-conscious communitarians.

Marching headlong into the political thicket, the Supreme Court in 1993 heard three important VRA cases that made it plain that the Court was changing direction. I consider two of the cases in this chapter and save the third for Chapter 4. The first, *Growe* v. *Emison*, involved a federal district court invalidation of a Minnesota state court apportionment plan for state legislative and congressional districts.[146] The district court found that the state plan diluted the voting strength of minority voters in violation of Section 2 of the VRA. It applied the *Gingles* criteria to a case involving single-member, not multi-member, districts, and found vote dilution.

Justice Scalia, writing for a unanimous Court, determined that the federal court "erred in not deferring to the state court's timely consideration of congressional reapportionment."[147] Scalia's opinion harkened to Frankfurter's dissent in *Baker* and Harlan's dissent in *Reynolds*. In other words, representation intertwined with federalism, and federal court intrusion poisoned the process. Reapportionment was foremost a state political function, and here federal judicial preemption of state plans meddled with that function. The VRA was not a means to circumvent local politicians and place the reapportionment process in the hands of the federal courts and national interest groups.

Scalia also faulted the federal district court for failing to apply the *Gingles* criteria before finding vote dilution. According to *Gingles*, minority political cohesion and majority bloc voting against minority candidates could not be assumed.[148] Again, the reapportionment process was a state and local concern, as were the communities it affected. It required deference by federal courts to those state officials who conceived of the plan. Federal courts were not to upset state proceedings because they disagreed with the outcome.

The second case, *Voinovich* v. *Quilter*, in which Justice O'Connor authored the majority opinion, considered whether Ohio's creation of majority-minority districts as part of its decennial reapportionment diluted black political strength.[149] Ohio's plan created eight majority-minority state legislative districts. Black appellants claimed that the Ohio plan packed voters into majority-minority districts of such a high minority percentage that black votes were wasted. As an alternative, the appellants advocated the use of influence districts where the black vote was strategically spread to have as much political impact as possible.[150]

O'Connor correctly pointed out that vote dilution and influence dilution were different concepts. Dilution impairs the ability of minority voters to elect their candidates on an equal basis with other voters. This can be determined with some accuracy through the results test in Section 2 as interpreted in *Gingles*. Influence dilution claims set forth no clear-cut test. Influence is a highly subjective concept, and reasonable people might differ as to whether creating two liberal white coalitions with strong black influence would be less influential than creating one majority-minority district. This put the Court into the nettlesome position of determining how and to what degree minority political communities ought to be created to maximize minority political influence. O'Connor declined to determine whether influence claims were actionable under Section 2.[151]

The Court found that the federal district court erred when it held that Section 2 prohibited the creation of majority-minority districts unless they were necessary to remedy discriminatory voting practices. Furthermore, the district court failed to determine, under a totality of the circumstances analysis, the consequences of the Ohio apportionment plan. There was no showing that majority bloc voting impaired the ability of minority voters to elect their chosen representatives. Furthermore, the Ohio apportionment board had relied on assistance from the Ohio NAACP and two associations comprised of black-elected officials. The totality of circumstances did not demonstrate that the appellants had a claim under Section 2 of the VRA.[152]

There are practical problems with increasing minority representation through the single-member district: it requires the minority to be relatively geographically compact, and the number of districts at the state and federal levels is finite. Minority voters are not yet aggregated so as to maximize their electoral potential or political influence. However, we may be getting close to the number of feasible majority-minority districts.[153] For legal and practical reasons, majority-minority districting requires that minority voters live close enough in large enough numbers to create compact districts. So, what is compact? Suppose that a state has a district's worth of minority voters and that they are scattered across the state. It will be difficult, if not impossible, in such a circumstance to draw a majority-minority district for that minority. Now suppose that the distribution of black voters is scattered but concentrated enough so that with a little imagination, some handy interstates, and the requisite political maneuvering, the minority district can be drawn. Should this be considered legally compact? Should compactness matter? Should Congress or the states try to promote compactness by elucidating some guidelines for the courts to follow?

Majority-minority districting resulted in some odd-looking electoral districts. It also produced some interesting political issues. The Democratic Party, which traditionally supports civil rights legislation and can rely upon majority support from black voters, is uncomfortable with the implementation of the VRA whereby Republicans join with black litigants to create safe majority-minority and Republican districts.[154] After the 1990 census, in states as varied as Minnesota, Ohio, Florida, and North Carolina, race became one of the preeminent factors in establishing electoral districts. Whether the VRA allowed or compelled racial gerrymandering of congressional districts was a case of first impression for the Supreme Court and one of immense political importance.[155]

The increasing complexity of litigation surrounding the VRA and the 14th and 15th Amendments should come as no surprise. The VRA expanded in scope and power. The possibilities of claiming vote dilution increased correspondingly. Yet, the concept of representation remains elusive. We elect individuals to represent our interests in legislative bodies, but a representative's behavior may not correspond to that of his constituency. Moreover, we may find that some electoral practices are illegal. We trust that the courts are capable of determining the means necessary to end discriminatory practices. Nevertheless, after three decades of VRA litigation, we are no closer to determining what practices constitute representation and how we can determine when representation is fair.

CONCLUSION

Political representation was an area the Supreme Court entered with trepidation. The early cases, such as *Baker* v. *Carr*, *Reynolds* v. *Sims*, and *Wesberry* v. *Sanders*, asked the Court to consider the constitutionality of state apportionment schemes. The focus was on the individual's right to vote and participate in the electoral process. Under the guise of Equal Protection Clause analysis, the Court announced equal weighting of votes as the constitutional standard. Soon thereafter, this logic extended to federal elections.

The passage of the VRA allowed plaintiffs challenging voting practices and procedures to rely on statutory rather than constitutional claims. This created a dual legal doctrine regarding race and representation: the first stressed constitutional protections; and the second relied on the VRA. Consequently, the rate and scope of litigation expanded, particularly in those areas of the South covered by Section 5 of the VRA. The VRA was "strong medicine" needed to combat the institutional denial of the vote to blacks. It also became a means by which to promote the election of black officials. It was believed that this step was necessary in order to secure representation for blacks. Using the concept of "vote dilution," plaintiffs attempted to prove that a particular electoral practice rendered blacks unable to elect their chosen candidate. The focus of VRA litigation, after the vote was secured to individual black voters, was on the electoral success of the group. "Vote dilution" was a concept that measured the success of the racial group. It presupposed the existence of a racial-political group, and that the political interests of the minority voter and the minority community were nearly coterminous.

The 1975 amendments to the VRA expanded protections to Hispanics, Asian Americans, Aleuts, and Native Americans. The scope and the meaning of "minority" changed. In time, this complicated the recognition of communal claims brought under the VRA, as was the case in *Johnson* v. *DeGrandy*. But the 1975 amendments also made clear that the VRA was limited to ethno-racial minorities. Other types of minorities, such as religious minorities, did not enjoy protection under the VRA. This was starkly demonstrated in *UJO* v. *Carey*, where Hasidic Jews, surely a discrete religious minority, were treated simply as another facet of the majority white community of New York City.

The 1982 amendments to the VRA relieved plaintiffs of the onus of proving purposive discrimination in order to prevail under Section 2. Prior to the 1982 amendments, plaintiffs who argued that a particular practice was dilutive of their votes had to prove purpose or intent. After 1982, the plaintiffs had to show that under a consideration of the totality of the circumstances, the results of the election diluted their vote. Under this test, vote dilution occurred when the plaintiffs failed to elect representatives in proportion to their percentage of the population. They could demonstrate an adverse totality of the circumstances by referring to housing, education, and employment patterns illustrating that the minority suffered with comparison to the majority. The 1982 amendments sharpened the focus on the group. The premise of the results test was that lack of group success was actionable under the VRA.

Under *Gingles,* which clarified the requirements of Section 2, minority communities were presumed to be politically homogeneous. Moreover, they were presumed to be better represented by their own members. Fair representation meant proportional group representation. The VRA became a means to enforce this sense of communal political entitlement.

Despite many Supreme Court decisions and various amendments to the VRA, expectations for fair representation went unfulfilled, particularly when the desire was articulated in race-conscious communitarian terms. The desire to remedy minority underrepresentation, without an explicit end point, drove the rhetoric of fair representation back to its constitutional origins. In doing so, the clear rhetoric of a liberal vision of fairness again surfaced; the right to representation pertained to the individual prior to a conception of group political success. The reemergence of the liberal vision of representation concludes this chapter and is the major theme of Chapter 4, as the Supreme Court gradually began to rethink the means by which it accommodated the motive of race in the area of representation.

Chapter 4

Shaw v. *Reno*: What It Means, Does Not Mean, and Why

Shaw v. *Reno* is the most influential political representation case since the passage of the Voting Rights Act (VRA) in 1965.[1] *Shaw I* is not simply a VRA case; it is also a 14th Amendment, Equal Protection Clause case. It refocuses the debate over fair representation on its elements: Who is represented? How should the government ensure fair representation? Do some groups have a special claim on representation? The affirmative grant by the state to a minority group in the form of a majority-minority district, as was the issue in *Shaw*, must be justified.[2] As such, an effective narrative for majority-minority districting characterizes the need for more representation as compelling, and presents a remedy through the least burdensome means.[3] This chapter reviews how *Shaw* and subsequent cases reappraise the elements of fair representation in a newly emergent liberal rhetoric and brings into question certain justifications for majority-minority districting. Indeed, the rhetoric of liberalism successfully challenged the political edifice of the VRA and fundamentally altered its interpretation.

Before the passage of the VRA in 1965, reapportionment and voting rights cases were decided on constitutional grounds.[4] This was true of such landmark decisions as *Wesberry* v. *Sanders*, *Gomillion* v. *Lightfoot*, and *Reynolds* v. *Sims*, as well as the "White Primary" cases.[5] The difficulty with basing a cause of action on the Constitution is the general reticence of federal judges and Supreme Court justices to decide a case on constitutional grounds. If given the chance, courts prefer to avoid constitutional issues, especially those that might put them into conflict with higher courts or other branches of government. Instead, courts decide cases as narrowly as possible, and avoid constitutional issues by making factual distinctions among cases, issues, and facts, and by reinterpreting the meaning of statutes. This may entail creatively reading the statute that governs the particular fact situation in dispute.

The VRA provided plaintiffs and the courts with the means to negotiate the parameters of fair representation and, most important, mete out political power without raising constitutional questions. With rare exceptions such as *United Jewish Organizations of Williamsburg, Inc.* v. *Carey,*[6] the constitutionality of the VRA as amended in 1975 and 1982 was not seriously questioned until *Shaw* in 1993. Of course, *South Carolina* v. *Katzenbach*[7] considered the constitutionality of the VRA of 1965 soon after its passage and answered in the affirmative, but the VRA that *Katzenbach* considered had changed radically by 1982. Prior to *Shaw*, the federal courts articulated an underlying communitarian purpose in the VRA, and acted only to clarify its limits when presented with novel fact situations as happened in *Presley* v. *Etowah County Commission.*[8]

Shaw did not have to be a constitutional case. The Court could have decided, as it had in *UJO*, that the constitutionality of the VRA was not in contention since blacks were its beneficiaries. Instead, the Court entertained questions on the wisdom and constitutionality of using the VRA to segregate voters according to race for the purpose of increasing the political power of racial minorities. Such phrases as "political apartheid" and "segregate according to race" were not used lightly by the *Shaw* Court. The Court signaled that it was willing to return to a constitutional analysis of fair representation whose basic unit was the individual and not the group. The Court repeated this liberal theme in *Miller* v. *Johnson*[9] which found that the Equal Protection Clause prohibited the predominant use of race in districting. The Court in *Miller* came even closer to the brink of determining whether current interpretations of the VRA, particularly Section 2, were unconstitutional.

The result of these developments is that the VRA, unquestionably necessary in 1965, has become vulnerable like other affirmative action programs.[10] Simply because the VRA is vulnerable does not mean it is moribund. Blacks and civil rights activists are not being brutalized on the Edmund Pettis Bridge, but this does not obviate the necessity for some type of VRA. But it is an act in flux, and one whose shape reflects the uncertainty of race relations and political developments yet to come.

PRELUDE TO *SHAW* OR SOWING THE SEEDS OF DISCONTENT

Before *Shaw,* the federal courts regularly upheld challenges to districting plans that failed to achieve racial proportionality. For instance, one case in Los Angeles County dealt with the failure to create a majority-Hispanic district when it was not shown that racial bloc voting denied Hispanics the ability to elect a candidate of their choice.[11] In another case, from Arkansas, reapportionment of the state legislature resulted in one Senate and four House districts where the majority of voters were black. However, it was possible to create three Senate and thirteen House majority-minority districts. After a suit on behalf of black voters, Arkansas was found in violation of Section 2 and forced to redraw the districts with black majorities of at least 60 percent. It was hoped that black majorities of this magnitude would return black representatives and end vote dilution.[12] In short, the federal courts administered a program of political proportionality based on race. It was thought that the VRA required the creation of black and Hispanic districts where possible. States vetted their districting plans through the Justice Department. Some plans were challenged as contrary to the VRA even though they increased minority voting strength.[13]

Shaw v. *Reno* came a generation after *Reynolds* v. *Sims*. During the intervening years, the VRA changed the landscape of reapportionment. Under the procedure required by the VRA, redistricting of a covered jurisdiction must be precleared by the Attorney General or, less frequently, the state must obtain a declaratory judgment from the federal district court of the District of Columbia. Under the nonretrogression principle of Section 5 of the VRA, redistricting by a covered jurisdiction will not be precleared "if it will lead to a retrogression in the position of racial minorities with respect to their effective exercise of the electoral franchise."[14] Under Section 2, as many majority-minority districts, even in jurisdictions not covered by Section 5, must be created as is practicable, though Section 2 disclaims a right to proportional results.[15] Discrimination can be inferred from the totality of the circumstances, including, but not limited to, electoral results.[16] Section 2 is plaintiff-friendly and applies where there is a politically viable minority recognized under the VRA.

As mentioned in Chapter 3, the 1982 amendments worked profound changes in the VRA. The reworded Section 2 removed the onus of proving purposive discrimination by parties challenging voting practices and procedures. Of course, there is a good argument that purpose is still proven in practice. Patterns of discrimination may illustrate a purpose that we are unable to articulate but not unable to recognize.[17] The acceptance of examples of institutional discrimination, such as housing and education discrimination, as proxies for purposive discrimination and as an explanation for racially disparate electoral results is itself a sort of *mea culpa* for the difficulty in articulating what is discrimination.

According to two commentators in a 1993 law review symposium considering *Shaw* v. *Reno,*

The 1982 amendments to the VRA were written to condemn voting structures that relegated African Americans and other protected groups to perennial loser status. Congress knew that the inability of such groups to elect representatives of their choice could not be explained in terms of party affiliation or socioeconomic status; rather, race has been and continues to be of singular importance in the casting of votes in American elections.[18]

Yet, simply reading the strengthened VRA as a categorical good greatly simplifies matters, and may impair the position of blacks and the health of the political community. Broadening the interpretation of "voting practice and procedure" may, ironically, diminish the political authority of VRA claims. In other words, expanding the definition of "voting practice and procedure" in the

VRA may encourage politically and legally tenuous causes of action. It is hard to oppose a VRA that enforces the right to vote or proscribes practices that keep members of particular groups out of political office. It is easier to oppose a VRA that mandates the racial gerrymandering of districts in order to maximize the political power of a minority when there is little contemporary evidence that minorities suffer from discriminatory practices in that jurisdiction.[19]

The Voting Rights Act of 1965 reflected a deep commitment to racial equality in voting. Yet, 1982 was not 1965. By 1993, it was not asserted that anyone was denied the right to vote in North Carolina because of race. Access to the ballot was no longer an issue. The central question involved group empowerment once the ballots were cast. The 1982 amendments attempted to remedy the inability of racial minorities to elect their members by explicitly drawing the division of political power across racial communities.[20] The VRA made it feasible for minority groups to sue when they failed to win seats in proportion to their percentage in the population. Yet, not all races had equal grievances, and sometimes class and political preference eclipsed racial considerations.

In 1993, the VRA was thought by some to be politically and legally unassailable. A long line of Attorneys General had interpreted the VRA this way, as had the Supreme Court. Because of this, there were fewer justifications offered for the VRA, and remedial measures taken on behalf of minority voters were assumed to be legal, necessary, and correct. Opposing the VRA meant opposing racial equality in representation. Yet, by attempting to take the meaning of the VRA out of political contention, as its supporters wished to do, the law lost some of its relevance and vigor. As a result, challenges to the affirmative action aspects of the VRA began to percolate through the federal courts. A law placed above politics is without foundation, and invites critique.

Abigail Thernstrom suggested that the 1982 amendments to the VRA and their general tone of racial sorting resulted from a combination of disorganization by opponents of expanding the VRA and a strong, well-orchestrated civil rights community that pressed for a goal of proportional representation by race regardless of previous or existing discrimination.[21] The VRA was strengthened because it was in the interest of already politically powerful minority groups that it be fortified. The 1982 amendments led to presumptions about what was legally required under the VRA. What is required under the VRA is a highly political question despite the fact that it might be framed as a legal dispute.[22] What is necessary under the VRA is influenced by the text of the VRA, the Justice Department, the federal courts, institutional litigants, and the interested parties. For instance, in Houston, reapportioners were required, pursuant to Section 2, to accommodate black and Hispanic concerns for increased representation.[23] This resulted in the creation of two majority-minority districts in and around Houston: one for blacks and one for Hispanics.[24] The creation of these districts did not necessarily result in better representation for blacks, Hispanics, or whites. Rather, it changed the racial composition of officeholders. Under the VRA, the physical description of the officeholder conflated with fair representation.[25]

The *Shaw* Court's application of Equal Protection analysis to districting that classed voters according to race led to a constitutional evaluation of Section 2 of the VRA.

Should any court decide that the broad remedial purposes of the VRA compel districting akin to North Carolina's, or should any state purport to justify its districting as an attempt to avoid Section 2 liability, the question will be directly put whether such a justification is sufficient, under strict scrutiny analysis, to justify the overt use of race as the dispositive factor in the districting decision.[26]

Though the *Shaw* Court declined to strike down the district in question, it opened the door for constitutional challenges to the VRA. *Shaw* v. *Reno* illustrates the current condition of the communitarian/liberal debate over fair representation. By viewing *Shaw* within the context of narratives describing alternative political communities, instead of as a decision that indicates political conservatives on the Court have successfully limited the breadth of the VRA, we can better understand how preceding and succeeding cases articulate a fundamental but developing dialectic among communitarian and liberal images of the political community. We may also see that decisions and the strategies of justification within the decisions are not inherently politically liberal or conservative. Thus, the narrative that led to a liberal outcome in one case may be co-opted at a later date by a conservative majority.

WHAT HAPPENED IN NORTH CAROLINA WAS NOT SIMPLY A MATTER OF RACE

What follows is a short account of the dispute that gave rise to *Shaw* v. *Reno*. North Carolina attempted to satisfy the letter of the VRA when it reapportioned after the 1990 census. The results of the census entitled North Carolina to another congressional district, raising its total from eleven to twelve. Because of its history of denying blacks the right to vote, North Carolina was required to submit its redistricting plan to the Attorney General for preclearance pursuant to Section 5.[27] It was the usual practice of states to check with the Justice Department and the voting rights bar to forestall litigation.[28] The state devised a plan with one majority-black congressional district. The Attorney General objected, and North Carolina submitted a second plan with two majority-black congressional districts. This was a difficult task because North Carolina's black population was relatively dispersed: blacks were a majority in only 5 of 100 counties. On the other hand, blacks accounted for approximately 20 percent of the population.

To complicate matters, there were interests other than race, such as that of the political parties, that needed to be accounted for. Packing black voters into single-member districts was, in general, beneficial to Republican candidates in the remaining nonminority districts. Redistricting sometimes meant that a white incumbent sacrificed his or her seat.[29]   Because of the different interests involved, racial gerrymandering was sometimes difficult to separate from political gerrymandering.

At this time, redistricting under the auspices of the VRA for the benefit of racial minorities was embraced as a way of undoing political hierarchies that doomed minorities to a subordinate position.   That blacks were politically subordinate and the victims of long-standing discrimination was a historical fact. After the Civil War Amendments, blacks successfully elected other blacks during Reconstruction.   However, with the 1877 compromise following the election of 1876, black political power and representation gradually disappeared.[30]   In the 20th century, no black had been elected to Congress from North Carolina.[31]

Since *Thornburg* v. *Gingles*, the VRA had contemplated the race-conscious drawing of single-member districts to remedy the persistence of racial bloc voting.   North Carolina was a prime candidate for the drawing of remedial, majority-minority disctricts.   Nonetheless, some maintained that segregation by way of racial gerrymandering was a special type of wrong for historical reasons.[32]   This was the case even if the gerrymander benefited the minority group.   The creation of the majority-minority 1st and 12th Congressional Districts resulted in the election of North Carolina's first black Representatives since Reconstruction: Eva Clayton in the 1st and Melvin Watt in the disputed 12th.[33]   In order to construct the second majority-black district, North Carolina relied on innovative line drawing.   The Democrat-controlled North Carolina legislature used ingenious means to create the 12th Congressional District.[34]   The second majority-minority district was by some estimation "very, very ugly."[35]   By one quantitative measurement, the 12th District was one of the least compact districts.[36]   The redistricters' double goal was to preserve the seats of Democratic incumbents and to create majority-minority districts.   This was done, but not without stretching the boundary of political aesthetics.[37]

The creation of districts does not occur in a vacuum.   Districts are not simply there.   Their shapes are not "natural."   The political units they circumscribe fit together like a jigsaw puzzle.   In some sense, all districts are the result of gerrymandering.   Districting is a highly legal and political process. The creation of the 12th Congressional District attracted litigation, in part, simply because of its bizarre appearance. The mere appearance of the district indicated to observers that something was amiss.   In North Carolina, litigation over redistricting began with the 1990 census.   Litigation of reapportionment plans and the decennial census is now almost continuous.   In the other two 1993 VRA cases, [38] *Voinovich* v. *Quilter* and *Growe* v. *Emison,* litigation started before the 1990 census was complete. The reapportionment process is made more difficult by the impossibility of creating many more majority-minority districts.[39] Consequently, as the political pie is sliced into more intricate pieces, some pieces become harder to see as anything other than racial gerrymanders.   This is especially true in jurisdictions where the threat of VRA litigation influences redistricting.

The 12th Congressional District was 160 miles long and at most points no wider than the I-85 corridor. It snaked through the countryside, gobbled up black enclaves, and ignored whites. One state legislator claimed, "If you drove down the interstate with both car doors open, you'd kill most of the people in the district."[40] After some negotiation and reworking, the Attorney General precleared the plan, and litigation commenced.[41]

THE APPEARANCE OF REALITY IN *SHAW* WAS SUBJECT TO COMMON SENSE

The white plaintiffs did not claim that the plan violated the constitutional standard of one person, one vote, but that North Carolina created an unconstitutional racial gerrymander.[42] Neither did they claim vote dilution. Rather, they alleged "that the deliberate segregation of voters into separate districts on the basis of race violated their constitutional right to participate in a 'color-blind' electoral process."[43] In turn, the Court recharacterized the appellants' grievance. "What appellants object to is redistricting legislation that is so extremely irregular on its face that it rationally can be viewed only as an effort to segregate races for the purpose of voting."[44] The *Shaw* majority assumed there was a natural or original distribution of districting by race. Else, the Court could not use the words "irregular" and "segregate" to describe the North Carolina districting plan.

At this juncture, let us revisit the notion of district shape. Something enables us to define a shape as "natural" as opposed to "contrived." The naturally shaped district enjoys a presumption of constitutionality. Depending on how contrived the district shape seems, it may lose this presumption; this was the case in *Shaw*. What opposes natural to contrived is defined by experience.[45] We learn how to read this or that as odd and this or that as natural so that we hardly ever reflect on its contours.[46] Put another way:

[W]hile there may be no "natural district shapes," baseline expectations emerge from developed customs and practices. Social understandings, including those concerning the legitimacy of political institutions, are formed with reference to these developed practices.[47]

The notion of "playing" with our sense of community was picked up in the general media. A North Carolina paper said that it "plays hell with common sense and community." Even political scientist and VRA expert witness Bernard Grofman complained that its construction lacked "rational state purpose."[48]

The claim made in *Shaw* was distinguished from the standard claim made under the VRA in the mid-1960's and from vote dilution cases in the 1970's and 1980's. The first cases brought under the VRA considered the denial of the right to vote through various means. Since the enactment and execution of the VRA in 1965, the denial of the right to vote because of race was all but eliminated. Yet, blacks and other minorities remained underrepresented as officeholders. The claim of vote dilution because of racially polarized elections or electoral devices such as discriminatory multi-member districting emerged. Groups claiming vote dilution focus on discriminatory results. If election practices adversely affected a particular racial minority's political power (the ability to elect as many of their own candidates as was possible), vote dilution occurred.[49]

The new *Shaw* claim, a district appearance claim or an expressive wrong, centered "on the perceived legitimacy of structures of political representation, rather than on the distribution of actual political power between racial or political groups."[50] In other words, it was a rhetorical claim. Vote dilution was not claimed because it did not occur legally; no racial minority group was affected adversely by the redistricting plan. While some commentators argue that a vote dilution claim and a district appearance claim are birds of a different feather, it is doubtful that the appearance of the legitimacy of a regime can be separated from the distribution of political power among its politically salient groups.[51] It is just when some groups feel unduly bereft of political power that they question the legitimacy of the process. Likewise, separating the idea of legitimacy from power presupposes a concept of legitimacy that is not forged in a cauldron of power. Indeed, it was only under the most hegemonic of regimes that complete legitimacy might be contemplated because political power was so concentrated.[52] Ironically, it is only under circumstances where political power is relatively dispersed among different social groups that one can argue that power is unduly concentrated and that political structures are illegitimate.[53]

In reapportionment litigation, there is room to argue, and the rhetorics of liberalism and communitarianism drive the narrative. The result of reapportionment, and reapportionment litigation, is the distribution of political power. As such, it may be impossible to distinguish the perception of political power from the distribution of political power. The rhetoric of political legitimacy incorporates the perception and the distribution of political power. That is, the distribution of political power allows for a particular perception of political power and *vice versa*. Any dichotomization between rhetorical and real causes of action under the VRA or the Equal Protection Clause is simply a rhetorical move. Those causes of action which we perceive to be real are those which persuade. They are real because they recall our history in a highly persuasive (rhetorical) fashion. This was why the use of "segregation" and "apartheid" worked so well in *Shaw*.

It was asserted that the appellants in *Shaw* could not claim vote dilution, for none had occurred. Whites cannot bring a vote dilution claim under Section 2. However, assuming the possibility of making a white vote dilution claim, the potential plaintiffs still had a problem. To claim vote dilution under Section 2, a group identified a material deprivation of its relative voting strength. Even assuming that whites could claim vote dilution under the VRA, they would not be able to prove it.[54] After all, whites constituted approximately 76 percent of the population, and with ten of twelve districts controlled by white majorities, whites still controlled 83 percent of the districts.[55] Contrariwise, one could argue that no matter what the final distribution of officeholders as measured by race, any lessening of a group's voting strength by increasing another group's was a material deprivation of the latter's voting strength. This reasoning is disputable, but it is difficult to contest without replicating some of the same weaknesses of a formula that measures political strength by race among officeholders. In this context, it is a question of asserting what a particular group's strength ought to be. In order to articulate what a particular group's political strength ought to be, we develop coordinates by which to gauge political strength. The caprice of these coordinates is hardly ever called to account. We should not expect it to be, for the result, a particular power distribution, is prior to our determination of how we measure it. As such, districting reflects, and cannot help but reflect, the political results of a law, the VRA, informed by race-conscious considerations.

In *Shaw*, the standard of fair representation demanded by the Justice Department was one of proportionality. Any increase in black voting strength that did not cause white strength to dip below whites' percentage of the population could not result in vote dilution as measured under the VRA.[56] Whites in North Carolina did not have a VRA vote dilution claim.[57] However, the result of remedying black vote dilution pursuant to the VRA resulted in a white challenge to the redistricting plan on constitutional grounds.

A CONSERVATIVE REKINDLING OF LIBERAL RHETORIC

Justice O'Connor's opinion related the extensive history of racial gerrymandering in the United States and noted that the right of the individual to vote had been denied to many because of race.[58] She identified her uneasiness not only with what she perceived as racial sorting, but also with the notion that political equality was a group rather than an individual claim.[59] O'Connor believed state sponsorship of group identity in the context of voting rights was noxious because race-conscious redistricting resulted in elected officials who were "more likely to believe that their primary obligation was to represent only members of that group rather than their constituency as a whole. . . .'Here the individual is important, not his race, his creed, or his color.'"[60] O'Connor did not deny that individuals suffered racial discrimination. But she was wary of endorsing a remedy that based its necessity on its aims: creating more minority districts. O'Connor was loath to follow this logic absent a showing that individuals were denied voting rights. It exacerbated an illness in the United States known variously as discrimination, affirmative action, and racial preference.

Justice O'Connor employed philosophically liberal rhetoric: the right to vote was an individual right; and group identification that preordained for whom the individual voted, threatened freedom of ehoice. For her, the issue was equality of opportunity, not of results. O'Connor criticized the assumption that members of particular racial groups shared political preferences. She also disparaged the doctrine that only a fellow group member could represent minority group members. Group solidarity delimited the liberal concept of individual agency by presupposing a range of authentic activity based on the collectivity. For O'Connor, the notion of a districting plan that grouped or excluded people because of race was pejorative. "Classifications of citizens solely on the basis of race are by their very nature odious to a free people whose institutions are founded upon the doctrine of equality."61 Racial group identity, which informs the individual as to the possible conceptions of equality, nonetheless restrains the individual from achieving equality with respect to individuals from other groups. Strong racial group attachment may also confound the possibility of other equalities because it masks the prospect of the individual enjoying multifaceted and fluid group identities. The philosophically liberal O'Connor desired districting that:

seeks to realize a plurality of values: to ensure effective representation for communities of interest; to reflect the political boundaries of existing jurisdictions; and to provide a district whose geography facilitates efficient campaigning and tolerably close connections between officeholders and citizens.62

Shaw is not an argument against majority-minority districting but a liberal critique of the way group politics is played. "*Shaw* requires respect for value pluralism as a means, it seems, of ensuring that constitutional concerns for political legitimacy are not ignored or undermined in the process of enhancing minority representation."63

An interesting juridical trend is the shift by the politically conservative members of the Court to adopt the liberal, color-blind credo advocated by the politically liberal Justice Arthur Goldberg in the early 1960's when presented with Equal Protection Questions.64 Liberal positions become linked to politically conservative justices over time, and the same movement occurs with communitarian positions assumed by politically liberal justices, although there are recent exceptions.65

Racial classifications that suggested "the utility and propriety of basing decisions on a factor that ideally bears no relationship to the individual's worth or means" troubled the majority in *Shaw*.66 This left Justice O'Connor with a problem: the VRA as amended in 1982 prohibited legislation that resulted in the dilution of a minority group's voting strength. In other words, the VRA mandates that some states engage in racial classification when redistricting. The Equal Protection Clause tension inherent in Section 2 complicates matters, as does its extension to single-member districts. The simple fact may be that "proportional representation [according to race] and representation by single-member districts are incompatible."[67]   If the Court struck down the plan for a second majority-black district, minority voting strength would be diluted. The 14th Amendment and the VRA are potentially conflict when accounting for the persistence of racial inequality.

Justice O'Connor resolved this dilemma temporarily by distinguishing legitimate efforts to remedy the effects of past discrimination from establishing political apartheid. For O'Connor, racial sorting was a matter of style. She felt that North Carolina's plan perpetuated patterns of racial identification, reinforced racial divisions, and exacerbated race-based voting behavior. Yet, perpetuating a pattern did not foreclose a change in social or political capital, for perpetuation eventually drives change. A primary lesson of *Shaw* is that a coherent strategy of justification is central to affirmative representation. The representation of the perception of the need is essential to the reception of the need.

In Shaw, the story told by the Court stood in stark contrast to the rhetoric used to validate single-member, majority-minority districts. The promotion of majority-minority districts was a natural course of events rarely questioned before *Shaw.* O'Connor voiced an uncomfortable truth when she noted:

A reapportionment plan that includes in one district individuals who belong to the same race, but who are otherwise widely separated by geographical and political boundaries, and who may have little in common with one another but the color of their skin, bears an uncomfortable resemblance to political apartheid.[68]

One could read in this passage a preference for color-blindness as opposed to color-sightedness. But O'Connor attacked color preference in districting only when it overshadows all other interests. One problem with this interpretation of O'Connor's opinion is the unavailability of a color-blind position. Since we learn how to recognize color by our experiences, it is impossible to say whether something is in reality or objectively (something outside of our subjective determination) color-blind. Given our experience in a culture where color is learned and utilized ubiquitously, it would be astonishing to find that any law that affects the broad distribution of political power would not give preference to some group. But, there was a difference for O'Connor between noting that a law affects color and making color the basis of the law.

Last, O'Connor questioned the underlying assumption of the VRA: only members of a minority group speak for members of a minority group. Can representation authorized by description be reconciled with a philosophically liberal version of representative democracy? The permanence of the ascriptive or descriptive affiliation of the individual *qua* representative distinguishes this conception of the representative. For instance, a white Congresswoman could only represent whites and could never be an authentic representative of black individuals in her district. "This message that such districting sends to elected representatives . . . is pernicious."[69] It was baneful because it sent the message that the elected official represented groups rather than individuals, and because the basis of group political identification was race.   If the racial group superseded the individual, the result pointed toward a racially balkanized society and away from the liberal ideal of a color-blind society.

Consider how the concept of racially descriptive representation, which informs VRA analysis, conflicts with the liberal concern for discouraging permanent factions within the larger political community. It may mean that the racial faction retains special interests apart from the political community. Yet, opposed to racial and other political factions is the interest of the larger political community: this is the national interest, by which all factions are defined. The difference, in Madisonian terms, is that the political community's interest, stability and security, is different from the parochial interests vying for political power. Indeed, even a majority faction does not articulate the national interest, for the national interest may be contrary to political goals of the majority.[70]

RACE TO THE PAST: HISTORICIZING THE GROUP IN *SHAW*

For the dissenters, *Shaw* v. *Reno* remained a VRA rather than an Equal Protection Clause dispute. The VRA did not prohibit the type of communal segregation practiced in North Carolina redistricting. Instead, it encouraged it under Sections 2 and 5. However, treating groups differently on account of race potentially conflicts with the 14th Amendment. The dissenters in *Shaw* v. *Reno* emphasized that recognizing communal interests was not necessarily a violation of the one person, one vote standard.[71]   For the dissenters, an intention to separate blacks from whites was legally irrelevant to the dispute. Consistent with Section 2, the intention of state actors need not be determined in order to find vote dilution. The motivation of those who wished to create the maximum number of majority-minority districts also went unquestioned. Again, it was legally insignificant.[72]   What was significant was the distribution of political power with respect to race. The history of representation in North Carolina demonstrated that blacks were underrepresented in comparison with whites. Efforts to remedy this course of events were consistent with the VRA, and the 14th and 15th Amendments to the Constitution. It was not unconstitutional to remedy such an inequity and was required statutorily.

Does compactness have a special political value in the creation of majority-minority districts? Some commentators who favor the use of single member electoral districts argue that particularly compact districts promote community.

A particular aim of territorial districting is to facilitate the representation and interests of political communities. . . . because compact districting is thought, at least traditionally, to enhance political ties between representatives and constituents, abandoning compactness might be thought to undermine the value of representation.[73]

However, concerns for geographic compactness may diminish where a history of racial oppression describes an individual's social situatedness more powerfully than where he or she lives. For Justice White, racial bloc voting was a fact of life and trumped considerations of geographic compactness. Race is one of many factors taken into account when redistricting, along with class, religion, geography, and political persuasion. Because one cannot make a districting decision in many parts of this country, and certainly not in North Carolina, without taking race into account, he saw no need to treat race differently than any other consideration the state may legitimately take into account.[74] If we do not consider race in many jurisdictions, especially the South, there is little left to consider. One could argue plausibly that in some manner race permeates every issue in the North Carolina districting process.[75]

The question for White, after acknowledging that interest group politics defined our political system, was whether or not members of the majority group, whites, were denied access to the political system. As he noted, no one was denied the right to vote because of the North Carolina plan. The districts were arithmetically proportional. No *Reynolds* v. *Sims*– or *Wesberry* v. *Sanders*–type violation occurred.[76] The focus shifted to treatment of the majority rather than the minority, and no whites were denied the right to vote.[77] White acknowledged the benefit that redistricting accorded a historically disadvantaged minority. In a society defined by intense racism, striking down attempts to repair a polity wherein some minority groups were excluded from power perpetuated the *status quo*. The liberal view retarded social progress. Legitimating communal interests through redistricting carried the promise of advancement.

White rationalized group preference by resorting to an ahistorical notion of politico-racial equality. Unfortunately, such a resort is unavailable.[78] To repair an unequal or hierarchical *status quo*, we must either admit that our remedy will be inequitable or hierarchical, or believe that we can extract ourselves from our situation, from the process of law and politics, and institute the proper procedure. Those who use this type of rhetoric are either disingenuous or naive. Justice White was certainly not the latter. By shifting attention away from what is found discriminatory, White redirected the discourse of equality. For White, it was "an attempt to provide minority voters with an effective voice in the political process."[79]

Justice Blackmun's brief dissent explicitly recognized the historical and communal context of the dispute. It was a black-and-white dispute informed by North Carolina's history of race relations. He was unwilling to strike down a districting plan "under which North Carolina has sent black representatives to Congress for the first time since Reconstruction." The consideration of race required taking into account the political position of the white community *vis à vis* the black community. In Blackmun's opinion, conscious use of race in this context did not deny a particular group, whites, access to the ballot or minimize its voting strength.[80]

Justice Stevens's dissent also recognized the primacy of group politics. Stevens felt that the Court should not obstruct the majority when it facilitated the election of a member of a minority group lacking political power.

Interestingly, Stevens did not conflate the idea of group with race. A "minority" group included those defined by religion, ethnicity, class, political affiliation, and race.[81]

For Stevens, the difference between constitutional and unconstitutional gerrymanders had to do with the distribution of political power. Stevens acknowledged that all districting was gerrymandering. Whether or not a gerrymander was legal presented a political question. It was, however, not nonjusticiable. Constitutionality became a political determination framed by the coordinates of the law. It was political because the coordinates reflected competing understandings of the Constitution. Nonetheless, gerrymandering could be presented as an empirical fact. This rendered the assertion of constitutionality a powerful rhetorical device. What is constitutional is a historical fact produced and received through rhetoric. Justices interpret a case such as *Shaw* as they think it ought to look within the vernacular of the language games that describe their institutional space.[82] For Stevens, if the politically powerful group enhanced its political control by gerrymandering, this was unconstitutional. However, where the members of the weaker group voted as a bloc, and a gerrymander increased their political power, no constitutional violation occurred.[83]

Stevens found it incongruous that the Court singled out race for special treatment. It was ironic that Stevens felt it was necessary to make this point, since he singled out race for special treatment, too.

If it is permissible to draw boundaries to provide adequate representation for rural voters, for union members, for Hasidic Jews, for Polish Americans, or for Republicans, it necessarily follows that it is permissible to do the same thing for members of the very minority group whose history in the United States gave birth to the Equal Protection Clause.[84]

Moreover, Justice Stevens's dissents in *Fullilove* v. *Klutznick* and *University of California Board of Regents* v. *Bakke* noted the impropriety and arbitrariness of distributing public resources simply according to racial group membership.[85]

As did Justices Stevens and White, Justice Souter acknowledged that interest group politics defined the political spectrum. Classifications that took race into account, such as minority business set-asides or college admissions, often were viewed in zero-sum terms. A reward for a member of one race meant a deprivation for an individual of another race. But in redistricting, the result was different. Creating majority-minority districts did not deprive anyone in the majority of participation in the electoral process. Recognizing communal voting patterns and drawing voting districts to maximize the political effectiveness of minority groups did not deny any individual who was not a member of a minority group the right to vote or otherwise participate in the political process.[86] It did not restrict participation unless one adhered to the descriptive view of representation as the only means whereby a representative was authorized to speak for and directly represent his constituents.[87] This is why

Souter's reasoning, while politically acceptable because it gets to the same end point, is dangerous for race-conscious communitarians. It undoes the moral position it seeks to support because he criticizes descriptive representation in order to defend the use of race-conscious policy in the context of majority-minority districting.

For Souter and the other dissenters, communitarian and liberal narratives were not necessarily incompatible.[88] The definition of political community articulated by Souter encompassing both commonality and robust dissent, made O'Connor's critique of majority-minority districts less powerful. The problem for Souter and O'Connor is that it is hard to point out in the context of a lawsuit how a particular majority-minority district will function in practice.

As I understand his dissent, Souter asserted six factors that constitute electoral practices cleaved by race. First, individuals are members of groups. An individual's political identity is defined in terms of group membership. Of course this is not a new notion, it is the same liberal insight developed in *The Federalist.* Second, politics is largely interest group politics. Third, members of minority groups are politically underrepresented. This assumes a fairly specific definition of "minority" that allows fair representation to be measured proportionally: those groups covered by the VRA. Even this narrow definition is made problematic by our changing perception of what race is and what is important about race.[89]

Fourth, members of minority groups often vote as a bloc. This is an example of how ethnicity and race color our perception of society. The only things we can see are what we see. We do not articulate what we are blind to, though we may learn to see new things from a different vantage point.[90] Fifth, in racially mixed societies, it is impossible not to take race into account race when redistricting.[91] Therefore, it was not *per se* wrong to take race into account when districting, but reasonable and necessary to do so under many circumstances. Of course, "reasonable" is a highly political concept. The problem with current Equal Protection Clause jurisprudence is that the use of race as a category carries the presumption of irrationality. Hence, we apply strict scrutiny and require the state to demonstrate a compelling interest when race informs the use of legal categories. Doing away with the multi-tiered Equal Protection Clause analysis would be in accord with Justice Marshall's dissent in *Cleburne*.[92] That, it seems to me, is the logic of Souter's dissent in *Shaw*: Is it not reasonable for North Carolina, given the history of black political powerlessness, to create two majority-minority districts? This is powerful logic that may, in the end, carry the day politically and legally. But this logic benefits from using the rhetoric of liberalism rather than communitarianism to justify remedial measures. Rhetoric that speaks to the denial of political rights to an individual may be more impressive to the Court, and the public, than a blanket assertion that this or that particular group, because of past wrongs, deserves its recompense in the form of safe districts.

Sixth, and finally, redistricting that accounted for racial bloc voting among minority group members was not unconstitutional because it did not deprive a member of the majority group of participation in the political process.[93]   Of course, this is in many ways a liberal concern that traces its roots to *Reynolds* v. *Sims* and *Wesberry* v. *Saunders*. Still, this contention depends upon one's view of participation. The notions of participation and the right to vote had changed markedly since *Reynolds*.   Does participation entitle a voter to enjoy representation?   And if so, what do we mean by "representation"?   Under Souter's view, recognition of communal interests was not at odds with *Reynolds*, but in accord because the right of the individual was also   counted for.

Souter attempted to reconcile the liberal and communitarian narratives in *Shaw* v. *Reno*. Traditional liberal concerns such as equality of opportunity for the individual were not contrary to concerns for real and persistent group inequalities. This was especially the case in North Carolina, where race was such an important factor in political participation. Indeed, Justice O'Connor may be faulted for adhering to a liberal ideal of representative democracy that no longer described a political system in which politics was "a series of conflicts and deals among more or less transitory and fragmentary groups."[94]   By refusing to acknowledge the extraordinary nature of racial minority claims, Justice O'Connor and the majority reinforced a political structure in which the majority race wielded a disproportionate amount of the political power.[95]

SHAW CAUSED GREAT CONSTERNATION AMONG SUPPORTERS OF THE VRA

For the communitarian, Justice O'Connor's liberal rhetoric cast group claims as antidemocratic,[96] enabled the Court to define "the constitutional self by seemingly neutral but potentially biased forms of exclusion," and deconstituted the individual's race.[97] Her rhetoric mattered because the medium of law was language. Language remained subject to revision, and as language mutated, so did the law.   How Justice O'Connor framed the battle over redistricting forced subsequent writers to reply on her terms.[98]   In other words, she did not put a stop to interpretation but imposed a set of questions one needed to answer in order to develop a plausible counter-argument.   O'Connor challenged advocates of the VRA to justify its political aims, and advocates of the VRA were not used to doing so on her terms.

The Supreme Court remanded the dispute to the federal district court with instructions to consider the 12th Congressional District using strict scrutiny.[99] As a consequence, after *Shaw* v. *Reno*, the great worry was that the Court would roll back VRA protections and reverse decisions that interpreted the VRA as containing minority group preferences.[100]   The whole program of creating majority-minority districts was unsettled. The next two cases were decided in 1994, and reinforced part of the logic of *Shaw* that was to be skeptical of associating more minority officeholders with better minority representation. The fact that state reapportioners were compelled to create more majority-minority districts did not translate directly into more effective representation for blacks or whites.

AFTER *SHAW* THE VRA WENT INTO PLAY

In *Holder* v. *Hall,* the Court considered whether the size of a governing body, in this case a single-commissioner county government in Georgia, was subject to a vote dilution challenge pursuant to Section 2 of the VRA. It held that the size of a governing body was not subject to a vote dilution challenge.[101]

Bleckley County, Georgia had had a single-commissioner county government since its creation in 1912. Though the county was 20 percent black, it had never had a black commissioner. Furthermore, until the passage of the VRA, whites prevented most blacks from voting and participating in politics. Blacks suffered worse socio-economic conditions than did whites. The political atmosphere was so inhospitable to blacks that even the white federal district court judge noted that having run for public office, he would not do so in Bleckley County were he a black man.[102]

Nonetheless, no evidence indicated that the single-commissioner system discriminated against blacks' ability to participate in the electoral process. Given the method of government in Bleckley County, the VRA claim was legally unique. Respondents, a group of affected blacks supported by various civil rights organizations, claimed vote dilution and asserted that a multi-member commissioner system with single-member districts could be created with blacks as a majority in one district. This would replace the single-commissioner system that they viewed as structurally discriminatory. Applying the three-pronged *Gingles* criteria, the district court found that blacks could form a compact district, but that whites did not vote as a bloc to defeat black candidates and blacks were not politically cohesive. As a result, the district court declined to create a multi-member commissioner system including a majority-minority district.

The Court of Appeals reversed the district court, and the Supreme Court took the case on a *writ of certiorari.* In an opinion by Justice Kennedy, the Court reversed the Court of Appeals and held that a plaintiff could not challenge the size of a governing body under Section 2 of the VRA even if the size of that body was one person.[103] The justices split 5 to 4 in the judgment. This was due, in part, to the conceptual difficulties that vote dilution claims present. Read expansively, vote dilution can be found in any practice that fails to yield a result in accord with one's expectations. Justice O'Connor, concurring in part, wrote that vote dilution presented a potentially never-ending source of claims for the Court with no firm standards by which to demonstrate that something was not dilutive. Voting practices were always dilutive of some interests. Not everybody gets to win in democratic elections, which is why we have them.

Respondents argued that the single-member commission structure was dilutive in comparison to a five-member structure in which African-Americans would probably have been able to elect one representative of their choice. Some groups, however, will not be able to constitute a majority in one or five districts. Once a court accepts respondents' reasoning, it will have to allow a plaintiff group insufficiently large or geographically compact to form a majority in one or five districts to argue that the jurisdiction's failure to establish a 10, 15 or 25 commissioner structure is dilutive.[104]

Prior to Justice Thomas's appointment to the Supreme Court, Justice Scalia was the most acerbic critic of broad readings of the VRA, particularly those regarding Section 2.[105] Justice Thomas replaced Justice Scalia as the foremost critic of using the VRA as an omnibus vehicle for group preferences. He argued that it patronized blacks and divided the political community. In *Holder*, Justice Thomas, joined by Justice Scalia, concurred in the judgment. His reasoning was markedly different from that of Justice Kennedy and Justice O'Connor. It was not enough for Justice Thomas to criticize the difficulty of applying the concept of vote dilution to single-commissioner governance. Thomas wished to do away with vote dilution as a cause of action unless it involved the weight of one individual's vote in proportion to another's.

Thomas desired to recast the current state of representation jurisprudence. He argued that VRA vote dilution claims invited judges to engage in political theory, a role for which they were ill equipped.[106] Thomas's critique was reminiscent of Justice Frankfurter's dissent in *Baker* v. *Carr*.[107] The Supreme Court lacks the institutional capacity and the personnel to fashion legal remedies for questions of political theory.[108]

A review of the current state of our cases shows that by construing the VRA to cover potentially dilutive electoral mechanisms, we immersed the federal courts in a hopeless project of weighing questions of political theory—questions judges must confront to establish bench mark concepts of an undiluted vote. We devised a remedial mechanism that encourages federal courts to segregate voters into racially designated districts to ensure minority electoral success. In doing so, we have collaborated in what may aptly be termed the racial balkanization of the Nation. . . . In construing the VRA to cover claims of vote dilution, we have converted the VRA into a device for regulating, rationing, and apportioning political power among racial and ethnic groups. In the process, we have read the VRA essentially as a grant of authority to the federal judiciary to develop theories on basic principles of representative government, for it is only a resort to political theory that can enable a court to determine which electoral systems provide the "fairest" levels of representation or the most effective or undiluted votes to a minority.[109]

According to Thomas, the Court undertook to answer a question of political theory rather than of law. For Thomas, "political questions," unlike legal questions, do not have judicially manageable standards. Political questions lack objectivity, while legal questions are open to investigation and clear analysis.

Vote dilution, for example, came to stand for deviation from a standard of rough proportionality among racial groups. This was a standard dictated by our political sense of fairness, not by the law. For Thomas, law opposes politics, and reality is easily discerned from appearance. While Thomas wishes to get away from political theory, he seems all too well versed in the subject.[110] What troubled Thomas was the type of political theory, race-conscious communitarianism, until recently embraced by a majority of the Court in VRA and reapportionment cases.

Specifically, Thomas attacked the underlying communitarian assumptions that linked group claims for a proportional number of seats to vote dilution. Separate districts for different races did not so much raise up the subordinated race as reinforce its distinctiveness. This was a recipe for continued racial separation.[111] Of course, Thomas's castigation of the political motive behind making race a group entitlement for more representation offered insight into his own political theory. It was, in part, belief in the possibility of a color-blind Constitution. Blindness to the particularities of the individual was a central tenet of Thomas's libertarian liberal theory. Accounting for race militated against the rule-of-law, legal neutrality advocated by Thomas.

From the point of view of Thomas's liberal, color-blind jurisprudence, parts of the VRA were antithetical to a color-blind interpretation of the Constitution. In the VRA, political value was racial identity. This reinforced racial tensions and political divisions.[112] The VRA, according to Thomas, pitted race against race to secure political power. It was a device manipulated for the advantage of racial groups, not individuals. As interpreted, this law accommodated a vision of the good, one picture of racial equity, but in practice did nothing of the sort. It harmed rather than cured group divisions in the body politic.

We would be mighty Platonic guardians indeed if Congress had granted us the authority to determine the best form of local government for every county, city, village and town in America. But this Court is not a politburo. Properly understood, the terms "standard, practice or procedure" in Section 2 refer only to practices that affect minority citizens' access to the ballot. Districting systems and electoral mechanisms that may affect the "weight" given to a ballot duly cast and counted are simply beyond the purview of the VRA. . . . As four Members of the Court observed in *Gingles*, 478 U.S. at 84, there is "an inherent tension" between this disclaimer of proportional representation and an interpretation of Section 2 that encompasses vote dilution cases. . . . Few words would be too strong to describe the dissembling that pervades the application of the "totality of circumstances" test under our interpretation of Section 2. It is an empty incantation—a mere conjurer's trick that serves to hide the drive for proportionality that animates our decisions.[113]

For Thomas, the VRA had been interpreted within a race-conscious communitarian narrative that excluded liberal dissent. By limiting debate as to what comprised fair or effective representation, the race-conscious communitarian narrative aggravated racial tensions.

Not surprisingly, the race-conscious communitarian narrative was voiced by the dissent. Justice Blackmun, joined by Justices Stevens, Souter, and Ginsburg, argued that Thomas's and Kennedy's concern for judicial caprice was unwarranted.   Jurisprudence in the area of representation was grounded in history, custom, and practice. Indeed, it was the history and practice of racism in this country that militated for an expansive reading of the VRA.

The VRA was a bold and ambitious legislation, designed to eradicate the vestiges of past discrimination and to make members of racial and language minorities full participants in American political life. Nearly 30 years after the passage of this landmark civil rights legislation, its goals remain unfulfilled. The most blatant forms of discrimination, poll taxes, literacy tests and white primaries, have been eliminated. More complex means of infringing minority voting strength—including submergence or dispersion of minority voters—are still prevalent. We have recognized over the years that seemingly innocuous and even well intentioned election practices may impede minority voters' ability not only to vote but also to have their votes count.[114]

In short, the dissenters felt that Thomas's libertarian liberal rhetoric expressed in conservative politics was ahistorical. Thomas's argument made sense if one decontextualized the dispute, which meant ignoring decades of near political disenfranchisement of blacks in Bleckley County. The VRA did not have a meaning simply waiting to be heard. Instead, case law, a history of disenfranchisement, and the struggle for civil rights informed the text of the VRA. Denying this historical aspect drained the VRA of the vitality that made it arguably the nation's most effective civil rights law. The fact that blacks had equal access to the ballot did not mean that their votes resulted in commensurate political power.

Blackmun dissented in a fashion reminiscent of Justice Harlan in *Reynolds*. Harlan implored the Court not to consider the rights of the individual outside of the context and history of the community of which he was a part. If rural votes were arithmetically equal to urban votes, they counted for less. Rural interests would go underrepresented. Blackmun's objections to Thomas's concurrence reflected a concern with the solidarities that illustrate political life. The text of the VRA must be situated within a color-conscious, hierarchical political community; otherwise, criticisms of its practices touch only straw men.

In *Johnson* v. *DeGrandy*, the Court considered the nettlesome issue of competing minority claims.[115] After the 1990 census, Florida reapportioned its house and senate districts. In and around Dade County, the Florida legislature created Hispanic majorities in nine out of twenty House districts and three out of seven Senate districts. The legislature also created one majority-black Senate district and another with a near majority. Plaintiffs, joined by the Attorney General and civil rights groups including the NAACP, argued that this diluted the minority vote. The federal district court recognized a Section 2 violation and imposed a plan of eleven Hispanic House districts. The federal district court found that one more minority Senate district could be created, either

Hispanic or black, but not both.   It also found that racial bloc voting characterized the jurisdiction.[116]

Justice Souter, writing for a 7–2 majority, found no Section 2 violation:

In spite of continuing discrimination and racial bloc voting, minority voters form effective voting minorities in a number of districts roughly proportional to the minority voters' respective shares in the voting-age population. While such a challenge is not dispositive to single-member districting, it is a relevant fact in the totality of circumstances to be analyzed when determining whether members of a minority group have less opportunity than other members of the electorate to participate in the political process and to elect representatives of their choice.[117]

In other words, if the prevailing political practices work to a minority's advantage, despite racial bloc voting, the courts should not intervene in the districting process because there is no Section 2 violation.   There may be *de facto* racism, but there is no legal remedy because there is no legal wrong.

Justice Souter developed his argument by describing the nature of the claim.   Blacks and Hispanics claimed vote dilution not because they were unequal participants with whites in the political process, but because the largest number possible of majority-minority districts was not created.   Assuming, *arguendo*, that this was a Section 2 violation, fashioning a remedy was problematic because of the nature of group composition.   Racial bloc voting assumes the clear demarcation of a racial bloc, a problematic assumption in Dade County.

The Court recognizes that the terms black, Hispanic and white are neither mutually exclusive nor collectively exhaustive. We follow the practice of the District Court in using them as rough indicators of South Florida's three largest racial and linguistic minority groups.[118]

The claim for representation in *DeGrandy* was framed in communitarian terms: fair representation required blacks and Hispanics to be represented proportionately.   The problem was that whites, blacks, and Hispanics were neither exclusive of each other in membership and interest nor accounted for all diversity in Dade County. We may be able to view individuals and groups clearly, but in South Florida it was difficult to do simultaneously. The nature of group composition in South Florida did not comport with the clear definitions of group in the VRA.

The district court imposed the *DeGrandy* plan that called for eleven instead of nine Hispanic majority districts with at least a 64 percent voting-age population. Souter criticized the district court's findings despite the fact that the district court purported to employ the *Gingles* criteria. The three *Gingles* factors had been employed in a *pro forma* fashion. As such, they were not dispositive of a finding of vote dilution. Under *Gingles*, the district court acts as a fact finder and considers evidence of vote dilution and the viability of majority-minority districts within a "totality of the circumstances" analysis. The totality of the circumstances demonstrated that Florida's plan encouraged rather than thwarted minority participation. Yet, the district court focused on the maximum number of majority-minority districts possible, not on whether vote dilution occurred.[119]

But some dividing by district lines and combining within them is virtually inevitable and befalls any population group of substantial size. Attaching the labels packing and fragmenting to these phenomena without more does not make the result vote dilution when the minority group enjoys substantial proportionality. . . . Reading *Gingles* to define dilution as a failure to maximize in the face of bloc voting (plus some other incidents of societal bias to be expected where bloc voting occurs) causes its own dangers, and they are not to be courted. . . . However prejudiced a society might be, it would be absurd to suggest that the failure of a districting scheme to provide a minority group with effective political power 75% above its numerical strength indicates a denial of equal participation in the political process. Failure to maximize cannot be the measure.[120]

According to Souter, maximizing the number of majority-minority districts may do a disservice to minority voters. In reality, the voice of the minority community may be a multiplicity of voices. By squeezing minorities into separate boxes, the plaints of citizens may have as much to do with who they are not as with their concerns. Maximizing majority-minority districts reaches one measure of minority political potential. By this view, minorities have few incentives or opportunities to form coalitions with other voters in their districts, nor do white voters outside majority-minority districts have an impetus to seek the support of minority voters within those districts. Incumbents in such districts have less incentive to promote the interests of their districts when their seats are guaranteed through a racial supermajority.[121]

But minority voters are not immune from the obligation to pull, haul, and trade to find common political ground, the virtue of which is not to be slighted in applying a statute meant to hasten the waning of racism in American politics.[122]

In a powerful concurring opinion, Justice Kennedy lashed out at the underlying assumptions of race-based entitlements advanced in the district court plan. The problem for Kennedy was that the right pertained to the group within a conception of the legal good characterized by racial group proportionality. The district court turned the logic of our constitutional system on its head. Rights pertained to individuals so that they could participate and form effective groups. This is a liberal theme. Individuals participate in politics as parts of groups, but they have the autonomy to change groups. As such, groups or factions in the political community are, for the most part, malleable and short-lived. The notable exceptions in the context of VRA cases are, of course, ethnic and racial groups.

The Constitution protected the participation of groups in politics but did not give any particular group the right to political victory. Kennedy peppered his concurrence with references to previous Supreme Court opinions that extolled the virtues of race neutrality or color-blindness. Rights pertained to the individual despite, not because of, his particularities. Consider these examples.

The demeaning notion that minority members of the defined racial groups subscribe to certain "minority views" that must be different from those of other citizens.[123]

The moral imperative of racial neutrality is the driving force of the Equal Protection Clause.[124]

When racial or religious lines are drawn by the State, the multiracial, multireligious communities that our Constitution seeks to weld together as one become separatist; antagonisms that relate to race or to religion rather than to political issues are generated. . . . Since that system is at war with the democratic ideal, it should find no footing here.[125]

Kennedy's admonition against using race as the predominant factor in districting foreshadowed the Court's next move in its reconstruction of fair representation. And it was Kennedy who authored the closely divided Court's opinion in 1995 that interpreted *Shaw* to forbid the predominant use of race as the *modus operandi* of redistricting under the VRA.[126]

INTERPRETING THE SHAPE OF *SHAW* BUT NOT ITS BOUNDARIES

Miller v. *Johnson* considered Georgia's redistricting plan in light of *Shaw* v. *Reno*.[127] As had the plaintiffs in *Shaw*, the *Miller* plaintiffs stated an Equal Protection Clause claim challenging a state's congressional redistricting plan. In essence, the plaintiffs argued that the Georgia plan had no rational basis except to separate voters by race. The Court had to decide two questions: Did the Georgia plan give rise to a *Shaw*-type Equal Protection Clause claim? And if it did, was the plan narrowly tailored to meet a compelling state interest?[128]

Justice Kennedy, writing for the majority, started off by stressing his uneasiness with group distinctions and entitlements based on race. Employing a libertarian, liberal rhetoric, he extolled race-neutral government decision making. His was the narrative of the color-blind, autonomous legal individual. Because the law should not value one race over another, it did not matter legally which race was burdened in practice.[129] Yet, Georgia had to account for an unhappy history of government-sponsored discrimination, which was why Georgia was subject to Section 5 preclearance under the VRA.

Section 5 required Georgia to seek the approval of the Attorney General for any changes in voting practices or procedures, including reapportionment. From 1980 to 1990, one out of ten congressional districts in Georgia was majority-black. The 1990 census indicated that Georgia was entitled to an eleventh district. Because Georgia was 27 percent black, the General Assembly submitted a redistricting plan including two majority-minority districts. These districts took into account factors other than race, were relatively compact, and were of equal population in relation to the other ten districts.[130]

The Georgia plan failed to satisfy the Department of Justice, which wanted more than two majority-black districts. A new state plan attempted to maximize the voting strength of black communities in the 11th, 5th, and 2nd Districts. The new plan failed to appease the Justice Department, which advocated the so-called "max-black" plan designed by the ACLU and the Georgia General Assembly's black caucus.[131] Georgia acquiesced and adopted the max-black plan with three majority-minority districts.

The Justice Department imagined how the black community ought to appear. Using communitarian rhetoric, the politically conservative Kennedy derided the construction of the 11th District, which along with the 2nd and 3rd Districts, was majority-black. Ironically, it could be argued from a conservative, communitarian point of view that the Justice Department failed to protect the black community because it attempted to impose a blueprint for a community that did not exist historically. Georgia had historically distinct black communities, yet these singular groups were not addressed by the Justice Department.

The new plan also enacted the Macon/Savannah swap necessary to create a third majority-black district. The Eleventh District lost the black population of Macon, but picked up Savannah, thereby connecting the black neighborhoods of metropolitan Atlanta and the poor black populace of coastal Chatham County, though 260 miles apart in distance and worlds apart in culture. In short, the social, political and economic makeup of the Eleventh District tells a tale of disparity, not community.[132]

The white appellees characterized the 11th District as a monstrosity. It covered almost 7,000 square miles, and split eight counties and five municipalities. Nonetheless, the Justice Department precleared the plan because it promoted the political strength of black voters. In turn, this might make them a community.

The lawsuit was brought on behalf of five white voters residing in the 11th District who charged that the district was a racial gerrymander that violated the Equal Protection Clause as interpreted by *Shaw*.[133] The opposing parties stipulated that race was the predominant factor in drawing the district. Appellants argued that despite the legislature's motivation, this was not a valid *Shaw* claim unless the district could not be explained except by race. Kennedy claimed this misapprehended *Shaw*. *Shaw* was not about vote dilution: a VRA claim. It was about racial classification: a constitutional claim. The heart of *Shaw* was the admonition against assuming racial community and then segregating voters according to race for the purposes of assuring fair representation.

At the heart of the Constitution's guarantee of equal protection lies the simple command that the Government must treat citizens "as individuals, not as 'simply components of a racial, religious, sexual or national class.'"[134]

For Kennedy, placing the seal of the state on a particular racial classification retreated from the liberal, color-blind goal of a system where race no longer mattered.[135]

Kennedy also stressed that district shape alone may persuade us. Therefore, the bizarreness of the district's shape is a factor in determining an Equal Protection Clause claim. How a district appeared affected the legal reality. But a *Shaw* claim was not limited to mere appearances. Other factors, such as legislative intent[136] or an significant prior decision, may be influential.[137] Thus, if a districting plan expressed the motive of race, if it employed racial rhetoric, it could be found unconstitutional despite its ordinary appearance.[138] This was because liberals[139] on the Court such as Kennedy found it untenable for the state to assume that individuals of the same race necessarily constituted a single political interest.[140]

Justice Kennedy not only set liberal theory against communitarianism; he also used a law and politics opposition. Districting was political. Too much Court interference tarnished the legitimacy of the judicial branch. Districting was a legislative rather than a judicial function. The Court presumed that legislatures acted in good faith in the absence of evidence to the contrary.[141] Of course, the Jim Crow system was also based legislative action.

Kennedy linked a liberal, race-neutral ideal with his ideas of individual choice, traditional or natural communities, and good-faith legislating.[142] This rhetoric stressed not only that districting was more or less political and more or less race-conscious, but also that less was better than more in both cases. "Redistricting legislatures will, for example, almost always be aware of racial demographics; but it does not follow that race predominates in the redistricting process."[143] The General Assembly's motivation, the rhetoric of its motive, revealed its "prominent, overriding desire" to create three majority-black districts.[144] When the state assumes that members of a particular racial community have similar political interests, it stereotypes. It denies the diversity of that community and the autonomy of the individual. It disavows that singular individuals comprise racial communities.[145]

Because the Georgia districting plan employed racial classifications, the Court reviewed the plan using strict scrutiny. When employing strict scrutiny, the Court asks: Is there a compelling state interest? Is the legislation narrowly tailored to achieve this compelling interest? The Court refused to find that the VRA mandated the max-black plan. Moreover, the Court refused to find that the state had a compelling interest in complying with Justice Department preclearance demands.

Where a State relies on the Department's determination that race-based districting is necessary to comply with the Voting Rights Act, the judiciary retains an independent obligation in adjudicating consequent equal protection challenges to insure that the State's actions are narrowly tailored to achieve a compelling interest.[146]

Kennedy and the majority distinguished between valid and invalid racial classifications. The difference was one of appearances. As Kennedy pointed out, the judiciary had an obligation to question the motives of the political branches because the distribution of political power was at stake. At this juncture, the Court need not defer to the state or the Justice Department. Districting might be political, but it was also a legal issue. The issue here was whether the law, the VRA and the Georgia reapportionment plan, was in danger of appearing too political.[147]

The communitarian solution articulated by the Justice Department was predicated upon using race as a proxy for the political preference of minority individuals. This was a clumsy story to tell, given the cobbling of black populations from different parts of the state that shared little in common but race, and a hazardous one to promulgate. Far from eradicating discrimination, the Justice Department discriminated, and justified its course of action by reference to racial proportionality. From Kennedy's point of view, discrimination polluted, and pollution must be scrubbed from the political community by the law. Creating racial blocs did not eradicate discrimination even if the short-term effect resulted in the election of minority candidates. "It takes a shortsighted . . . view of the VRA . . . to invoke that statute . . . to demand the very racial stereotyping the Fourteenth Amendment forbids."[148]

Kennedy's unhappiness with the preclearance powers of the Attorney General revealed his general opposition to using the VRA to maximize the number of minority officeholders. The Justice Department's involvement took some initiative away from the state. Justice Kennedy saw the Justice Department demand virtual surrender by the state during preclearance: a ludicrous state of affairs.[149] A state could not have a "compelling interest" in complying with whatever directives the Attorney General issued.[150] Justice Department demands to enact its view of race equity, in Kennedy's opinion, brought the VRA into tension with the Equal Protection Clause.[151]

In dissent, Justice Stevens reiterated much of the communitarian analysis he articulated in *Shaw*. He did not believe a minority group could benefit from a gerrymander. A gerrymander reflected a political hierarchy whereby the powerful reaped the benefits. A gerrymander benefited a politically dominant group. His use of "dominant" and "majority" to describe whites and "minority" to describe blacks allowed him to argue persuasively for judicial restraint where the legislature acted to aid a politically powerless group.[152] Stevens stressed that segregation barred blacks from joining whites. Majority-minority districting had much the same effect. But the motive of race had to be understood within a communitarian context. Stevens stressed that the purpose and effect of majority-minority districting increased diversity in the legislature.

Segregation might occur among voters, but diversity increased among elected representatives.[153]

Justice Ginsburg's dissent, joined by Stevens, Breyer, and Souter, was the clearest communitarian narrative articulated by a justice since the *Shaw* decision. She tried to persuade by using such oppositions as black v. white, law v. politics, and majority v. minority. In each opposition, she relied on tools such as hyperbole, "true history," and stereotyping to drive home her point. For example, districting was a "political business." Judicial intervention was imperative to prevent "rank discrimination" against blacks.[154] For her, history was an easily charted graph and amenable to legal analysis. "Federal courts have ventured into the political thicket of apportionment when necessary to secure members of racial minorities equal voting rights . . . rights denied until not long ago."[155]

Ginsburg recounted the sorry history of voting rights in Georgia and examined the body of the political community. It was there to be found in flesh, blood, and travail. History was intimidation and violence. There were white primaries. There was a "Disenfranchisement Act." It was a political situation not open to "self-correction."[156] After the passage of the VRA, Georgia stubbornly refused to create a majority-minority district until ordered to do so. As Joe Mack Wilson, Chairman of the Georgia House Reapportionment Committee put it in 1982, "I don't want to draw nigger districts."[157]

For Ginsburg, the fulcrum of Equal Protection Clause jurisprudence was *Shaw.* Before *Shaw,* the Equal Protection Clause protected the minority's right to vote and prevented dilution of minority voting strength. After *Shaw,* the Equal Protection Clause was used to strike down majority-minority districts that empowered minorities.[158] Ginsburg did not simply argue that the post-*Shaw* analysis of majority-minority districting was wrong or political. To the contrary, she conceded that representation jurisprudence was political. Rather, she acted like a lawyer. Given the law, could she distinguish the Georgia district from the district that gave rise to *Shaw* in North Carolina? Of course she was able to do so, because the two cases constituted different fact patterns. She was able to distinguish on the facts, as opposed to the rule, and took three members of the Court.[159]

Finally, Ginsburg played her community card, and race was trump. The invocation of community is in many ways politically conservative, since so much of what is community is the conserving and romanticizing of solidarities existing just beyond the horizons of our memories. The politically liberal Ginsburg was less persuasive in this area. For her, racial communities were self-defined, and ought to be conserved. The problem with the majority opinion was that it took racial communities into account differently. For Ginsburg, race was a predominant factor to be considered when districting simply because it was so important. To make her argument for majority-minority districts, Ginsburg relied on a sense of the formation of the racial community whereby race existed prior to state action. But in practice, state action affects racial group solidarity. The racial group is prior to and a consequence of state action.

Apportionment schemes invariably influenced ethnic and racial groups.[160] "States do not treat people as individuals," so the important question to answer, as always, was what communities do we recognize?[161] For Ginsburg, the question was easily answered. "Special circumstances justify vigilant judicial inspection to protect minority voters—circumstances that do not apply to majority voters."[162] Vigilant surveillance of a state's practice is justified by a history of oppression. The VRA is designed "to make once-subordinated people free and equal citizens."[163]

Ginsburg did not present the idea of "free and equal" problematically. Yet, law that does not treat citizens equally and circumscribes their self-identification by group membership may not yield free and equal citizens. In other words, she does not offer a prescription for the illness she diagnoses. She should not be faulted for this, because who can offer such a panacea? Yet, her interpretations of history and the imperative of the present were based on conceptions of freedom and equality that did not invite reinterpretation. Freedom and equality for racial communities were ends prior to those communities, and justified legal means such as the "vigilant surveillance" of the state by the judiciary. This is worrisome to those who believe in the necessity of dissent within the political community, and that political virtue is arrived at through deliberation and disagreement rather than *a priori* impositions of the political good.

RECONSTRUCTING FAIR REPRESENTATION

The coordinates of the debate over representation change with the articulation of new case law. As this occurs, the narrative strategies of politically conservative and liberal justices on the Court may invert. In a 1996 case, political liberals on the Court reversed strategy and embraced a philosophically liberal rhetoric by which to strike down a registration fee of $35 to $45 to take part in the Virginia Republican state convention as a poll tax barred by Sections 5 and 10 of the VRA.[164] Conservatives on the Court opposed this characterization of the dispute and advanced a communitarian argument that stressed the associational rights of members of the Republican Party.

Justice Stevens delivered the judgment of the Court and was joined by Justices Ginsburg, Breyer, O'Connor, and Souter, although only Justice Ginsburg joined in the opinion. At issue was whether the preclearance provisions of Section 5 covered the Republican Party of Virginia. Section 5 is triggered if the change in practice or procedure relates to "a public electoral function of the party" and the party acts "under authority explicitly or implicitly granted by a covered jurisdiction."[165] If it was, then the new practice of charging a convention registration fee could be analogized to a poll tax. In any case, such a practice would have to be precleared with the Attorney General, and neither the Republican Party nor Virginia did so.[166]

Justice Stevens recognized the reality of the two-party system, and the entanglement of the Republican and Democratic parties with the commonwealth of Virginia. Virginia, in effect, endorses the two-party system and each party's method of determining their officers, nominees, and candidates. "The State function . . . may make the Party's action the action of the State."[167] A registration fee might limit the spectrum of voters who determine the party's nominee. It was directly analogous to a poll tax. As such, "political parties are covered . . . only insofar as the Party exercises delegated power over the electoral process when it charges a fee for the right to vote for its candidates."[168] A poll tax affected the individual voter's access to voting practices and procedures. In *Morse* a poll tax affected the ability of individual members of a group (Republicans) to elect the candidate of their choice. This regard for individual autonomy parallels Justice O'Connor's and Justice Kennedy's concern in *Shaw* and *Miller* that majority-minority districting limit individual choice.

In dissent, Justice Scalia, joined by Justice Thomas, felt that what was at stake was not only the breadth of Section 5 of the VRA but 1st Amendment protection of political association.[169] The majority's interpretation of the VRA put the 1st Amendment in conflict with Section 5. As interpreted, Scalia argued that Section 5 preclearance worked a prior restraint upon associational freedoms.[170]

The Court makes citizens supplicants in the exercise of their First Amendment rights. . . . That is the most outrageous tyranny. A freedom of political association that must await the Government's favorable response to a "Mother, may I?" is no freedom of political association at all.[171]

Though Scalia framed the right to associate in opposition to the VRA, this need not be the case. Some preclearance of party nomination procedures does not unavoidably affect the internal practices of the party. Yet, Scalia conceived of the right to associate free of government interference as a group and an individual right. And what bothered him was the intrusion by the judiciary into the group's, the Republican Party's, internal decision-making process.

In a separate dissent, Justice Thomas agreed that in this case political association involved advancing the group's goals. It was not an area in which the state should be involved.[172] This was especially the case because here, as opposed to the "White Primary" cases, no one was excluded from participation because of race. An intriguing aspect of Thomas's dissent was his comfortable use of communitarian images. This was true despite the fact that he was politically conservative and often embraced a libertarian liberal political philosophy. Ironically, it was the politically dogmatic Thomas who demonstrated the compatibility of communitarian and liberal rhetoric.

A convention to nominate a party candidate is perhaps the classic forum for individual expression of political views and for association with like-minded persons for the purpose of advancing those views.[173]

But language is captured by no man and is used only at his risk. The same liberal rhetoric advanced by political liberals in *Reynolds* became their bane in *Shaw*. Communitarian narratives are just as politically contingent. Thus, there will always be room for dissent, that is, a means for dissent. Consequently, there remain further interpretations of fair representation, and these interpretations touch at some level the tension between the individual's right to join or stand apart from a group and the group's ability to assert its presence in the political community. Nowhere was this more true than in the North Carolina and Texas redistricting cases decided at the end of the 1995–96 term, *Shaw II* and *Bush* v. *Vera*, which again demonstrated the elusiveness of fair representation.[174]

In *Shaw II*, the Supreme Court considered whether the 1992 North Carolina reapportionment plan, in particular District 12, was narrowly tailored to meet a compelling state interest. District 12 was the district which gave rise to the dispute in *Shaw I*, where the Court held the districting plan was subject to strict scrutiny and remanded the case to the district court. The district court found that although the plan classed citizens according to race, it survived strict scrutiny.[175]

The Court's opinion, by Chief Justice Rehnquist, stressed the majority's uneasiness with redistricting plans where the predominant factor was race.[176] In the trial record, appellees acknowledged that the state drew District 12 to ensure black majorities.[177] For the majority, this smacked of discrimination because it treated individuals differently because of race. This was antithetical to the 14th Amendment. Individual political rights were circumscribed by government-sponsored racial factionalizing.[178] With the Court placing its analysis within such a straightforward philosophically liberal narrative, it is not hard to see why it found deliberate racial gerrymandering in North Carolina constitutionally offensive.

The Court asked whether there was a compelling state interest in majority-minority districting. In doing so, it characterized majority-minority districts as state discrimination and placed the onus on the state to justify its plan. It decided that there was not enough evidence to support a finding that District 12 was necessary to combat past and present discrimination.[179] The Court also found that District 12 was not required under the nonretrogression principle of Section 5, nor was it narrowly tailored to meet the state's interest in avoiding Section 2 liability.[180]

The Court chided the Justice Department for advancing a maximization program for black districts in North Carolina similar to the plan found offensive in *Miller*.[181] It was a program whose end, the proportional representation of racial groups, where possible, in jurisdictions covered by Section 5, did not comport with a liberal notion of the individual, whose political autonomy and identity were not limited by state promotion of group membership.

To accept that the district may be placed anywhere implies that the claim, and hence the coordinate right to an undiluted vote (to cast a ballot equal among voters), belongs to the minority as a group and not to its individual members. It does not.[182]

The dispute, as framed by the Chief Justice, involved a determination of to whom the right to vote pertained. It is not surprising that Justice Stevens's dissent came to a different conclusion. Reminiscent of his decision in *Shaw I*, Justice Stevens stressed the factional nature of politics. Under the 14th Amendment, historically disadvantaged groups enjoyed a special status, and efforts to ameliorate their political powerlessness should not be viewed with the same suspicion as "is appropriate for oppressive and exclusionary abuses of political power."[183] It was ironic, for Stevens, that the majority, in the name of combating the reduction of politics to race, reduced the controversy in *Shaw II* to race. The majority downplayed a crucial dimension in the redistricting plan. There was not only a racial dimension but also a partisan dimension. The white plaintiffs were Republicans who found themselves in a black and Democratic district. Stevens opined that the Republican plaintiffs would not have been nearly so exercised about the creation of District 12 had the districts not been so carefully drawn to preserve the seats of Democrat incumbents.[184]

Leaving partisanship aside, even if one were to reduce *Shaw II* to a dispute over the proper utilization of racial categories, blacks are affected differently than whites under the Equal Protection Clause because they are a disadvantaged minority. For Stevens, because no individual was denied the right to vote, it was hard to understand what the racial gerrymandering claim sought to remedy. No matter how the lines were drawn, race would have an impact. It was either a question of what ends you endorsed or of what group you were a part.

I know of no workable constitutional principle, however, that can discern whether the message conveyed is a distressing endorsement of racial separatism, or an inspiring call to integrate the political process. As a result, I know of no basis for recognizing the right to color-blind districting that has been asserted here.[185]

Stevens recognized the conflict in *Shaw II* for what it was, a philosophical difference about the constitution of representative democracy. "Fair and effective representation" was delivered to minority voters in the form of majority-minority districts facilitated by Sections 5 and 2 of the VRA. This remedy maximized racial solidarity. It conflated racial group membership and political partisanship. Whether or not one agreed with this remedy was not a question for the Court to settle. Indeed, Stevens was worried about the attempt by the majority to settle the question of the constitutionality of many majority-minority districts. It took initiative away from the federal and state actors in the political branches who were trying to hammer out the difficulties of intertwining politics and race.[186]

In a companion case, *Bush* v. *Vera*, the Court considered the 1990 Texas reapportionment scheme. As a result of the 1990 census, Texas gained three seats. In turn, Texas created three new majority-minority districts.[187] In order to comply with Section 5 of the VRA, Texas submitted its reapportionment plan to the Justice Department. The Justice Department precleared the plan. A federal district court found these three districts unconstitutional.

As in *Shaw I* and *II*, and *Miller*, this case involved an alleged racial gerrymander. Because the concept of a racial gerrymander is so contested, the Court's opinions in this area have left much to be settled and have been difficult to put into practice. In *Bush*, the Court was highly divided. Justice O'Connor announced the judgment of the Court and was joined by the Chief Justice and Justice Kennedy, who filed a concurring opinion. Justice Thomas concurred in the judgment and was joined by Justice Scalia.

Justice O'Connor, as she had in *Shaw I*, castigated the use of race as a proxy for political preferences. It constituted the individual with group traits that he or she might not share. It was state-sponsored racial stereotyping that struck at the individual's right to participate freely in the political process.[188] To establish her contention, O'Connor had to look no further than the words of the Texas Section 5 submission.

Throughout the course of the Congressional redistricting process, the lines of the proposed District 30 were constantly reconfigured in an attempt to maximize the voting strength for this black community in Dallas County. . . . The goal was to not only create a district that would maximize the opportunity for the black community to elect a Congressional candidate of its choice in 1992, but also one that included some of the majority black growth areas which will assure continued electoral and economic opportunities over the next decades.[189]

O'Connor made her case by discussing the racial motive of the district plans and their bizarre shape. They reduced the political relevance of the minority voter to race and ignored economic, city, and neighborhood boundaries.[190] Because the three Texas districts were the products of racial considerations that subordinated all other concerns, they were subject to strict scrutiny. As such, the state had to establish that the districts were narrowly tailored to meet a compelling interest. As had North Carolina in *Shaw II*, Texas relied on a three-pronged argument to meet the compelling interest test: the districts were necessary to avoid Section 2 liability; to remedy past and present discrimination; and to satisfy the nonretrogression principle of Section 5.[191]

The plurality assumed, without deciding, that avoiding Section 2 liability was a compelling state interest. But because the districts were, in O'Connor's opinion, bizarrely shaped and drawn with traditional districting principles subordinated to race, they were not narrowly tailored.[192] The shapes of the districts served to intensify racial identity and deemphasize other forms of political identity.[193]

As for the record of past and present racial discrimination against minorities, Texas had an inglorious history to remedy, which, it argued, served as a compelling interest for the creation of the three majority-minority districts. But merely asserting a record of discriminatory behavior was not enough. The harm must be specific, and the state must conclude from a strong basis in evidence that remedial action was necessary. The Court wanted present proof of discrimination against individual minority voters. Again, the Court assumed, without deciding, that Texas had a compelling interest but that the remedies, majority-minority districts, were not narrowly drawn.[194]

Finally, Texas argued that the nonretrogression principle of Section 5 compelled the creation of a majority-minority district. As O'Connor pointed out, the Texas plan went beyond nonretrogression in creating a new majority district. Therefore, the plan was not narrowly tailored to maintain the current ability of minorities to elect representatives of their choice.[195]

Justice Stevens's dissent echoed his prior dissents in *Shaw I* and *II*. He asked us to consider the historic treatment of Hispanic and black minorities in Texas and their present situation. History compelled the creation of majority-minority districts.

While any racial classification may risk some stereotyping, the risk of true "discrimination" in this case is extremely tenuous in light of the remedial purpose the classification is intended to achieve and the long history of resistance to giving minorities a full voice in the political process.[196]

Moreover, he castigated the majority's application of strict scrutiny analysis. The districts were not odd-shaped so much because of race as because of the caprice of partisan politics.[197] As such, race was not the predominant factor in setting the district lines. If this was the case, then the districts should have passed strict scrutiny. The districts were not gerrymandered solely to increase black representation. They were gerrymandered for a great number of reasons that included fairness, race, land use, transportation corridors, and communities of interest, but the most important factor was reelecting Democrats.[198]

Stevens expressed his concern that the standards set in *Shaw I* and *Miller* were unworkable. They presented the Court with social and political decisions best left to the "political branches of our Government."[199] By requiring states to be race-conscious under the VRA, but not too much according to the Equal Protection Clause, Stevens argued, the tension resulted in blacks being packed into compact districts that stood out as islands surrounded by oddly shaped white districts.[200] Ironically, the effect of *Shaw I* and *Miller* may be to resegregate minorities in the name of color-blindness.[201] Because only three out of thirty-nine black United States Representatives at the time were from majority-white districts, the Court's opinion would, in all probability, work adverse political effects on blacks.[202]

In his dissent, Justice Souter addressed the conceptual core of the *Bush* suit: the *Shaw I* claim. He asked what harm racial gerrymandering caused and what were the contours of the *Shaw I* claim. He argued that the failure to describe a practical standard for distinguishing between the lawful and unlawful use of race left confusion in the state legislatures.[203]

Turning back the jurisprudential clock to 1964 and borrowing heavily from Justice Harlan's dissent in *Reynolds* v. *Sims*, Souter argued that voters naturally act as parts of communities of interest that, in turn, give life and legitimacy to politics. Moreover, the Court, in its zeal to protect the individual, ignored the federal structure of the Republic and sacrificed state and regional diversity of interests.

Voting is more than an atomistic exercise. Although it is the law of the Constitution that representatives represent people, not places or things or particular interests, the notion of representative democracy within the federalist framework presumes that States may group individual voters together in a way that will let them choose a representative not only acceptable to individuals but ready to represent widely shared interests within a district. The Court has recognized the basically associational character of voting rights in a representative democracy.[204]

Part of associational character, along with geography, occupation, economic interests, partisanship, and history, is race. Likewise, the accommodation of racial communities of interest need not take the shape of "political apartheid."[205] In *Shaw I*, the Court characterized the segregation of white and black voters as an expressive harm, but it did not distinguish who was hurt from who was not. It provided no clear way to distinguish legitimate attempts to accommodate racial communities of interest from political apartheid other than the majority's political opinion of illegal race-conscious districting.[206] The majority pushed the Court into the arena of political theory by offering an abstract notion of what amount of race-conscious districting was allowed by the Constitution. Then it avoided articulating a concrete legal standard and invited the states, the Justice Department, and lower courts to guess as to what that standard might be.

As the dissenting opinions pointed out in *Shaw II* and *Bush*, the Court started to enter into an area of reapportionment where manageable judicial standards may remain inevitably elusive. A 1997 case, *Abrams* v. *Johnson*,[207] illustrates the intangible nature of the debate over fair representation and the shape of the political community when the Court employs the rhetoric and logic of *Shaw I*. There is no game for the Court to play because no end, no good, is articulated clearly enough to drive the Court toward a singular conclusion.

In *Abrams* v. *Johnson*, the progeny of *Miller* v. *Johnson*, the Court again considered the propriety of Georgia's congressional redistricting plan. All the concerns that characterized *Miller* remained.[208] In *Miller,* the Court identified the political and legal wrong as using race as the *predominant* factor in redistricting and found the 11th District unconstitutional for that reason.

Although it was not a VRA case, Johnson based her cause of action in the VRA because the Georgia redistricting plan reflected the concerns of the Justice Department, which possessed preclearance powers pursuant to Section 5 of the VRA. As discussed above, white plaintiffs cannot bring a vote dilution action under the VRA. Instead, as they had in *Shaw I* and *II*, *Bush*, *Miller*, and *Hays*, white plaintiffs articulated how a districting plan enforcing the VRA violated their Equal Protection Clause rights. The Court's recognition of a constitutional cause of action in *Shaw I* and *Miller* based on the 14th Amendment enabled Johnson to articulate a argument against using race as the predominant factor in redistricting. The logic of such redistricting treated individuals primarily as members of racial groups. Justice Department and state approval of race-based redistricting placed the government in the odd position, from the majority's perspective in *Abrams*, of supporting racial divisiveness by making currency out of racial identification. Again, this is an archetypal liberal argument against a race-conscious communitarian solution to the underrepresentation of minorities. Nonetheless, no one has successfully argued that the VRA is contrary to the Equal Protection Clause, and the Court has engaged in gymnastics to avoid answering such a query.

In *Abrams*, Justice Kennedy wrote the majority opinion joined by Justices O'Connor, Scalia, Thomas, and the Chief Justice, a solid bloc of political conservatives.[209] The case came to the Court in the following fashion. After *Miller*, Georgia's eleven-district plan was remanded to the federal district court. The district court deferred to the Georgia legislature to draw a new political map. The Georgia House adopted a plan with two majority-minority districts, and the Senate adopted a plan with only one. Unable to compromise, the Georgia legislature reluctantly left resolution to the district court. In the meantime, Johnson amended her complaint to challenge the 2nd District on the same grounds the Supreme Court used to strike down the 11th. The district court, working with the original plan remanded by the Supreme Court, found the 2nd District unconstitutional. This ruling was appealed, but implementation of the district court plan was not stayed. As a practical consequence, one majority-minority district remained for the 1996 congressional elections.[210]

Upon remand following *Miller,* the district court was placed in the unenviable position of trying to fashion a political remedy with legal tools, a situation anticipated by Justice Souter in *Bush* v. *Vera*. It found the task unwieldy and noted with disdain the already polluted political waters caused by the Justice Department's "'subversion of the redistricting process' since the 1990 census." It attempted to remedy this fall from grace by taking as its point of departure Georgia's 1972 and 1982 redistricting plans.[211] Although it considered creating a second majority-minority district, the district court declined to do so, claiming it would "subordinate Georgia's traditional districting policies and consider race predominantly, to the exclusion of both constitutional norms and common sense."[212] The district court cast aside objections to the plan based on Sections 2 and 5 of the VRA and the constitutional standard of one person, one vote.

The ruling was appealed, and for the second time in the 1990's Georgia's congressional redistricting plan reached the Supreme Court. The Supreme Court in *Abrams*, as it had in *Miller*, found that following the precleared Georgia redistricting plan of 1992 as a model did not show deference to the democratic process. Much was made of Justice Department involvement in the legislative process. The Justice Department had pressured Georgia to adopt its approach, which maximized the number of majority-black districts. Following the Justice Department's lead, as the district court refused to do, would perpetuate constitutional errors and reduce legislative authority in redistricting.[213]   The Supreme Court noted with disdain the *modus operandi* of the Justice Department at oral argument. The Justice Department suggested it was proper under the VRA to segregate voters to support a majority-minority population.[214] The majority noted, however, that in practice it was unnecessary to draw majority-minority districts in Georgia in order to elect black members of Congress. After the 1996 congressional elections, the three black incumbents were returned with significant white support. Only one of the black incumbents ran in a majority-minority district.[215]

Justice Kennedy's opinion concluded with a theme he stressed in *Miller*. The redistricting exercise is in the best of all worlds left to the legislature and the democratic process. However, acting under the aegis of the VRA, the Justice Department so perverted the process that it was difficult to determine the will of the people.   The Justice Department interposed itself into the redistricting process so thoroughly that the Court was unwilling to accept the representations of parties claiming to speak for Georgia.   Ironically, the Court relied on the district court to account for traditional districting factors and represent the will of the people.[216]

The newest member of the Court, Justice Breyer, stated the dissent for Justices Stevens, Souter, and Ginsburg. For Breyer, counting the number of whites and comparing that with the number of blacks was a large calculus in determining the propriety of the Georgia districting plan.   In that sense, he echoed the race-conscious communitarian analyses of Stevens, Souter, and Ginsburg in *Shaw II* and *Bush* v. *Vera*. However, Breyer took another tack, one reminiscent of Justice Harlan in *Reynolds* v. *Sims*, Justice Frankfurter in *Baker* v. *Carr*, and Justice Thomas in *Holder* v. *Hall.* He stressed the inherently political nature of redistricting and the superiority of the legislative bodies in devising redistricting plans. He found that the Georgia legislature, Department of Justice pressure notwithstanding, displayed a preference for two majority-minority districts.[217] The majority's reasoning was flawed because they refused to take Georgia at its word and consistently read between the lines to find the nefarious presence of the Justice Department. Justice Breyer went on to ask why it was legitimate for special interests, but not the Justice Department, to cajole a state legislature. Of course, Justice Breyer understood that local chambers of commerce and farmers associations do not possess preclearance power or unprecedented access to the Supreme Court, as does the Justice Department.218 Nonetheless, as Justice Breyer saw matters, the district court usurped the democratic process. As a result, Georgia went from having three, to two, to one majority-minority district. Furthermore, Justice Breyer could find nothing "in the record not to take at face value what all the legislature's plans thereby suggest, namely that two majority-minority districts represents the [preference of the legislature]."219

According to Breyer, the *Abrams* majority risked further entangling the federal courts in the redistricting process with its oracular warning about the predominant use of race. Indeed, Breyer is correct. If we are not to place race out of bounds when redistricting, where does it lie? Are state legislatures to be constantly second-guessed by the federal courts when it is apparent that race is a factor? And what of Justice Department pressure and pressure from groups such as the NAACP-LDF and MALDEF? All three of these organizations stress the protections afforded minorities under Sections 2 and 5 of the VRA. The VRA compels legislatures, at least those covered by Section 5, to account for race. A question remains poignant for Breyer and the state of Georgia: When is race too much of a factor? If the courts cannot define this concept, then perhaps they should, as Breyer suggests, show more deference for traditional redistricting practices.220 Of course, Breyer's politics allows him to see the VRA as a means to recompense racial groups for years of discrimination. This view of the political game allows him to make a democratic process/deference to the legislature argument. Were the Department of Justice and the Georgia legislature not submitting plans increasing the number of majority-minority districts, one wonders what his feelings toward the democratic process and judicial deference to the Georgia legislature might be.

CONCLUSION

The United States Supreme Court reinstated a "liberal" interpretation of representation in *Shaw* v. *Reno*. The motive of race was expressed in terms of a color-blind ideal whereby individuals were to be treated equally by the law despite their race and differences in their ability to elect a candidate of their choice. The practical effect of such an interpretation was to return to the Constitution when deciding districting cases. The Constitution provided a means by which to describe representation as an individual right while at the same time it made problematic such communal concepts as vote dilution and majority-minority districts.

In general, political liberals on the Court such as Ginsburg and Stevens, remained committed to a communal interpretation of representation. For Stevens, *Shaw I* was flawed because it should have been a VRA case instead of an Equal Protection Clause case. Given VRA jurisprudence, and the presumption of community among blacks in North Carolina, Stevens persuasively if not conclusively argued for the continued creation of majority-minority districts. Certainly, the dissenters in *Bush* and *Shaw II* put forth credible communitarian critiques of *Shaw I*, and it is not clear how far, given the existing case law, state legislatures can go to accommodate racial communities when districting. [221]

From *Reynolds* to *Shaw*, there evolved a narrative in districting and reapportionment cases. The majorities in *Reynolds* and *Shaw* relied on philosophically liberal rhetoric under which the right to vote and be represented was not conflated with communal membership. In *Rogers* and *Gingles*, the Court articulated a vision of the political community whereby the law was used to affirmatively increase the political power of racial minorities. Grouping individuals of a race together did this. The presumption was that these individuals were a ready-made political faction.

Importantly, a unanimous Court embraced neither the liberal nor the communitarian rationale. This is fortunate. If a particular narrative of representation establishes an orthodoxy to choke off debate as to what constitutes fair representation, the political community suffers. Moreover, liberal and communitarian narratives are not mutually exclusive. The concern for the representation of the minority community is also, at some level, a regard for equal political access for the minority individual. Appeals to protect the federal structure of the Republic, and state and regional communal diversity, have been sounded by conservatives and liberals using liberal and communitarian arguments. Both liberal and communitarian narratives have at various times been on the ascendancy. The Court continues to incorporate themes from each. The lesson of the case law is that the definition of representation is not self-evident. The practice of representation must be negotiated continuously. For instance, *Miller* forbade the predominant use of race when districting. But what constitutes "predominant," and how this affects future VRA cases, remains an open question. That there is no firm answer as to the remedial limits of the VRA or of the scope of *Shaw I* portends well for those who subscribe to the idea that in deliberation a democracy flourishes.

Likewise, in *Shaw I*, *Shaw II*, *Bush*, and *Abrams*, justices in the majority and in the dissent argued for a more fluid sense of racial community than that espoused by those who hold a rigid view of race proportionality in representation. This, too, is a fortunate state of affairs because it promises to increase debate over the rights of the group, the constitution of the group, and the political identity of the individual *vis-à-vis* the group. In the next chapter, I hope to put these legal and political debates into the philosophical narratives of liberalism and communitarianism. These narratives are not in opposition, but in a process of a continuing dialectic in which the concept of representation evolves.

Chapter 5

Liberalism, Communitarianism, and Fair Representation

As I argued extensively in previous chapters, the Supreme Court resolved disputes over political representation by recourse to communitarian and liberal rhetoric, often using variants of each concept in the same opinion. In this final chapter, I situate the concept of fair representation in competing but not exclusive political theories: liberal theory and communitarianism. For example, if we articulate a claim for fair representation as a right, the discussion might be framed as: Does the right pertain to the individual absent a conception of the good?[1] Answering this question leads to more objections. The discourse produces new problems as it replaces and renames old ones. The law surrounding representation is characterized by a constant modification of the terms of the debate.[2] For example, there is a vibrant and expanding common law of the Voting Rights Act (VRA) and Equal Protection Clause stirring political controversy over the means used to promote the minority representation.[3]

Predictably, the Supreme Court is not of one mind on the subject of fair representation, but the multiplicity of the justices' views raises several questions relevant for a culturally plural society. For instance, do voting rights pertain to the individual or to the group with whom the individual identifies? Must they pertain to the former at the expense of a claim by the latter? If the individual articulates rights claims through group membership, we may still ask which groups are recognized, and whose voice represents the group.[4] By one view of representation that stresses the group nature of politics and the special perspective of minorities, one cannot make a claim to speak on behalf of a minority group, to represent, absent group membership. One must possess traits and experiences that demarcate the group from the majority.[5] As a corollary, outsiders cannot criticize the story told by group members because they lack the very traits that make the story possible.[6]   In part, this is a justification for the creation of majority-minority districts represented by minorities. This is also an argument for taking race into account when redistricting, whether the goal is to right past wrongs or simply to increase the number of minority political officeholders.

The authorization of representation is complicated further by the fact that we live in a heterogeneous society. Cultural plurality, diversity of experience, and varied viewpoints are the norm. It is a society characterized not only by a large population, but also by a multiplicity of associations and communal groups with whom individuals share an affinity.[7] Groups are in a never-ending process of reconstitution.[8] Moreover, individuals possess more than one group connection and shift their allegiance among groups, depending on the context.[9]

Determining whether rights pertain to the individual or the group redirects political and legal discourse.[10] If the individual articulates rights claims through communal membership, we must still ask which communities are recognized, and whose voice represents them. Employing a liberal framework may lead us to   argue   for   fundamentally   different   resolutions   than   if   we   adopt communitarianism. However, a particular liberal or communitarian philosophy need not necessarily lead to politically conservative or liberal results.   The philosophical debate between liberal theory and communitarianism is central to this consideration of the rhetoric of fair representation. It allows us to step back from the legal and political arguments for increased minority representation and place the debate into a philosophical framework.

LIBERAL THEORY AND REPRESENTATION

I argue that the philosophical debate between liberal theory and communitarianism is relevant to this consideration of the rhetoric of fair representation because when one adopts the communitarian as opposed to the liberal position, one speaks of fair representation in a different manner.[11] One formulates different questions and comes to different conclusions if the lexicon of liberal theory is used instead of communitarianism. This is true whether one adopts a libertarian as opposed to an egalitarian liberal position or a conservative versus a race-conscious communitarian stance.

Broadly construed, in liberal theory the individual rather than the group is the fundamental political unit of representative government. Rights pertain to the individual prior to an explicit constitution of the good. Individuals have the right to vote. Individuals vote, not groups, though individuals express group preferences when they vote. The individual exercise of the right precedes consideration of the constitution of the political community.[12] Liberals do not assume that people are equally capable, but that equality under the law is necessary to protect liberty, though liberals may disagree over what constitutes equality under the law. The law is applied neutrally despite existing social inequalities. This is procedural neutrality and is elemental to the rule-of-law.

The neutral application of the law may accurately be criticized for failing to account for capability disparities among legal institutions and players. Nonetheless, procedural neutrality prescribes a base level of equal treatment, creates institutional expectations, and does not presume a particular outcome for parties coming before the law.

By "liberty," the liberal refers to personal autonomy. Rights in a libertarian, liberal sense preserve the private sphere. They delimit the power of the state.[13] In liberal theory, participation in the public sphere is largely lacking of considerations of those aspects of social life, such as gender, race, and class, which constitute our identities. These aspects of social life influence our ability to recognize and assert rights, and make the invocation of the law a meaningful event.

ELEMENTS OF THE COMMUNITARIAN CRITIQUE OF LIBERAL THEORY

Communitarians critique the liberal concept of the individual and the public sphere as excluding particularities and, thus, denude political theory of many communal aspects of experience. As Michael Sandel summarizes:

As a political matter, our deliberations about justice and rights cannot proceed without reference to the conceptions of the good that find expression in the many cultures and traditions within which those deliberations take place.[14]

However, making specific the range of particularities we consider in our deliberations of the good may unintentionally limit our conception of the good. This re-creates the same paradox that Sandel identifies. A liberal polity is understandably wary of a prescription that reduces the range of dissent or diversity.

Within the communitarian position, broadly speaking, rights pertain to the group within an explicit conception of the good. Consideration of the good is appropriately debated within a reference to the traditions and solidarities of the political community. For the communitarian, the group displaces the individual in importance. The self becomes encumbered with all the historical particularities of communal existence, such as religion, sex, race, occupation, family, and geography, that fill our life experiences.

The communitarian critique of liberal theory questions the assumptions upon which liberal theory relies. For instance, liberal theory assumes that "no man or group of men possesses the capacity to determine conclusively the potentialities of other human beings."[15] By contrast, the race-conscious communitarian version of voting rights recognizes the paramount role of the racial group in shaping the political behavior of the individual. It prioritizes particular group claims for remedial legal measures and articulates a goal of proportional representation of racial groups. This provides an important framework for fair representation in a society where racial minorities have historically been discriminated against and unable to elect the candidates of their choice. The political individual acts as part of a group. Practically speaking, elections in a representative democracy reflect competing group claims.[16]

In the context of fair representation, the individual right to vote starts rather than stops the consideration of fair representation. Each person should have an equal opportunity to cast an equally weighted vote. However, the individual's right to vote conveys a partial view of fairness because it ignores those circumstances and prejudices which affect his ability to vote "freely" and assure that his vote is worth as much as the next fellow's. Such an idea of fair representation may be worth little without an appreciation of prevailing political practices and institutions.[17] Our notion of fair representation is produced by political institutions and practices, and our expectation as to how these institutions and practices ought to work.

As shown above, Sandel critiques liberal theory's conception of the unencumbered self: a dissociated individual shorn of particularities, that is an individual apart from the group, stripped of the social characteristics, such as race and gender, that implicate how he is treated in the political community.[18] Sandel's conception of political identity reflects the culture of which the individual is a part and the collectivities with which the individual identifies, such as race, ethnicity, class, religion, and sex. An electoral system that encourages racial minority community success fosters a sense of inclusion in the political community. By contrast, a representative system that ignores the barriers to political participation of a racial group denies political representation to individuals who identify with that group because it disavows the importance of the race as a factor shaping their perspectives as political actors.[19]

We may employ liberal rhetoric when making arguments about the assertion of legal rights, as for instance, the right to vote. As an example, we assert that the right to vote is an individual right or that vote dilution measures individual access to the ballot. We might instead employ rhetoric that stresses the right to vote in solidarity with a particular minority. The right to vote interweaves with the community's ability to elect a member of that community. Of course, we might use one or both strategies to convince others, such as a federal judge, of the wisdom of our arguments. Political conservatism or liberalism does not inhere in either liberal or communitarian rhetoric. Using a particular philosophical rhetorical strategy may make more sense in the context of one legal dispute rather than in another. Thus, it is not surprising that Justices Thomas and Ginsburg use variants of a communitarian justification, but for opposed political purposes.[20] The practical effect is that the rhetoric any of us uses frames our debate and delimits the possible problems and resolutions we are apt to discuss.

Further muddling the apparent opposition between communitarianism and liberal theory is the fact that communitarian and liberal tenets are not mutually exclusive. An opposition exists to the extent that we invest it with properties that exclude mutual recognition. But the elements of the opposition need not oppose. Thus, one could easily accept the communitarian thesis of the social embeddedness of individual identity while maintaining the liberal insistence on guaranteeing individual liberty against the state.[21] Furthermore, the strong criticism of liberal theory as underestimating or banishing our communal nature is not as convincing when applied to liberal practice. The United States, the most individualistic liberal state, continues to flourish.[22] Despite its liberal practices and institutions, solidarities based on race, occupation, sexual preference, wealth, and gender thrive.[23] Additionally, procedurally neutral legal frameworks in the United States, at the state and federal levels, either do not inhibit or actually promote a diversity of communal political and legal claims.

While the communitarian critique of liberal practices and institutions may not be as powerful as the communitarian critique of liberal theory, communitarian rhetoric remains alluring.[24] Communitarians accentuate interconnectedness.[25] The individual participates in a political community with a well-defined notion of the good, such as increasing the diversity of elected officials. This has resonance in a society where we are told its members are suffering alienation due to extreme individualism.[26]

Identity politics such as that expressed in race-conscious communitarianism, a type of political communitarianism, presents challenges for the jurisprudence of representation. The identity of the speaker, whether denoted by race, gender, sexual persuasion, or some combination, invests the speaker with authority. Politics becomes intertwined with the expression of identity. Identity politics asserts the perspective of a particular group based on that identity and an individual's membership in that group. In the context of representation, a primary question is: Which groups ought to be represented?[27] This is only the beginning. It is also important to dissect our inquiry by asking what we mean by group, and who are its members. Even if we can answer those questions, the politics of identity remains problematic. It does not remove patterns of domination from the home, workplace, or state. Furthermore, the responsibility the individual owes to others in society is at the core of politics. This is especially true when we consider to what extent the state influences the social sphere, such as the family and the workplace. The size of what we might call the public sphere, as opposed to the size of the private sphere, fluctuates and is the subject of intense political and philosophical debate.[28]

The entrance of the individual into politics, singularly or as a member of a group, fills the public sphere with meaning and legitimates its institutions. The distribution of political power among groups and individuals may serve to underscore a particular claim to representation that goes unmet. The law plays a fundamental part in determining the rules by which politics is played and how the fruits of politics are distributed. Ultimately, the imprimatur of the state is placed on a particular distribution of political power among groups.

How important are questions of fair representation, and at what level do they affect the political community? Certainly, the Supreme Court has struggled with these questions and has failed to give determinative answers.

This body may never articulate to what degree a state may consider race when redistricting. Indeed, the Supreme Court may be the wrong institutional body to manifest a solution to such fundamental political questions within a representative democracy that has coped fitfully with institutional racism. Yet, we have, at least since *Baker* v. *Carr* and *Reynolds* v. *Sims,* and more recently in *Miller* v. *Johnson,* asked the Supreme Court to "fix" problems in the political framework where answers are not legally apparent. What are the political contours of society, and what should the governed expect from those who govern? It is suggested that voting rights and reapportionment jurisprudence are "at the core of American political life."[29] The challenge to reapportionment jurisprudence, including considerations of the VRA and the 14th and 15th Amendments to the United States Constitution, is to answer the question of what is fair and effective representation.

What is fair and effective representation, and how should the polity be structured to create institutions that approach this ideal? These questions concerned political theorists and lawyers long before the founding of the Republic. How to structure representation and governance in a political community was a question asked by Plato and Aristotle.[30] Though their differences were many, each recognized corporate divisions within society and the communal nature of politics. They were communitarians, though they espoused an ordering of society much different from that embraced by modern communitarians.

For both Plato and Aristotle, the integrity of the political community required curtailing individual liberty in order to achieve a good for the community as a whole. Being a part of the political community required limiting individual autonomy in favor of solidarity to the political whole.[31] We might characterize this as allegiance to a large and complex politico-legal regime, such as the United States, or fidelity to a smaller, less complex political community.

For Plato, different classes of people were endowed with different capabilities. Accordingly, the rights and responsibilities assigned to various classes in his *Republic* differed. Representative functions were reserved for the excellent in society, who were relatively few. They were responsible for divining the interests of the different classes and articulating a plan that benefited the polity as a whole. They were, in short, responsible for developing the political good.[32]

Citizens, those individuals with political rights, comprise the polity. Though citizens differ in capabilities and interests, they share equal political rights. This is true in our political community in form if not in substance. Among these citizens, the law is applied equally. There is procedural neutrality. From this, we deduce the rule-of-law. The law is neutral to existing social and political inequities except in special circumstances including representation.[33] Representatives of citizens divine the national interest. The polity has some interests, such as security and renewal that must be articulated. This does not mean that the political community's interests are unchanging—quite to the contrary. But it is what makes politics such a necessary and vital exercise. Other interests of the polity, such as certain occupational or regional interests, may be exclusive of the national interest, but they, too, are subject to politics.

For better or worse, we did not choose the Platonic alternative though we may have adopted Law Professor Duncan Kennedy's option.[34]   Plato's guardians, the men of reason, do not administer the contemporary American state. Our diverse culture is leery of accepting a single standard of wisdom. Plato's division of society into groups treated differently according to their capabilities is inconsistent with our constitutional regime that recognizes equality under the law.[35] Nonetheless, hierarchies order the distribution of economic, social, and political power. However, these hierarchies are, for the most part, not written into law based on innate differences among the capabilities of citizens. Rather, they are the result of applying the law equally to classes of citizens who differ in their capability to use the law for their benefit.

ARISTOTLE'S INSIGHTS INTO THE LIFE OF A POLITICAL COMMUNITY

In his *Politics*, Aristotle argued that there were goods for which a just society ought to strive. It was within the ambit of the state to structure society so as to achieve these goods. The good citizen did service for the political community. Debate among citizens defined the political good. The citizen had responsibilities to the political community. For Aristotle, citizenship required moral training and participation. Likewise, political justice was not necessarily the will of the majority.[36]

Concepts like community, responsibility, and justice drive much of the discussion over what is fair representation. Likewise, one of the reasons there remain unsolvable legal contentions in VRA and Equal Protection Clause doctrine is that Supreme Court justices have differing interpretations of "community," "responsibility," and "justice." Aristotle can clarify some of the confusion that transpires when political theorists invoke notions of community as a remedy for dissociating or individualistic liberal practices. In addition, Aristotle's notion of community allows us to concur in the social nature "of individual character and actions without suggesting the necessity of any specific form of communal life."[37] Aristotle's use of community is markedly different from that of modern communitarians. This is because "he treats community as a generic rather than a specific social category." If we use Aristotle's conception of community, "his account of politics loses much of its romantic and moralistic glow and some of his most interesting insights into everyday political life emerge more clearly."[38]

Aristotle referred to social groups when he used the term "community." The community consisted of diverse individuals who shared some commonality and engaged in some activity related to what they shared. They were tied "by some sense of friendship and some sense of justice."[39]   There were several different types of communities, and they were composed differently.   Aristotle eschewed the civic republican desire for collective identity in his understanding of community, and he did not romanticize communal membership.[40]

Aristotle's notion of shared identity contrasts with the strong sense of collective identity asserted in contemporary identity politics, including that of race-conscious communitarians, where group membership is something more than sharing common elements.   It is membership forged by a mixture of history, experience, and their relationship with the majority.[41]   This emphatic sense of collective identity advances the claim of a special voice.[42]   This assertion has ramifications for our consideration of fair representation since representatives stand in or speak for their constituency.   If the voice of the representative does not express the identity of the group, we may ask whether or not the group is represented.   Aristotle, however, did not conflate this specific sense of collective identity with political community.   For Aristotle, "there is little sense of collective identity among community members precisely because their individual identities are shaped by the communities in which they live."[43]

COMMUNITARIAN CRITIQUES OF LAW AND THEIR RELEVANCE TO THE VOTING RIGHTS ACT

Communitarian concerns with the social embeddedness of individuals and groups remain politically and legally relevant.   The political identity of an individual is not separate from the groups with whom the individual identifies. Since 1975, the VRA has recognized and protected the following groups: blacks, Hispanics, Asian Americans, Aleuts, and Native Americans. Contemporary political competition pits group against group and individual against individual.   One voting rights litigator argues that a representative system which ignores the representational "right" of a particular group denies true political representation to individuals who identify with that group.[44]

Just as liberal theory can be distinguished from liberal politics, so political communitarianism, such as identity politics or race-conscious communitarianism, is different from communitarian theory.[45]   Opposed to communitarian theory that critiques liberal theory because it posits the political individual as shorn of those characteristics and group solidarities which define social existence, identity politics reduces the number of salient particularities to a comparative few.   Political existence is diminished to, in some instances, race, sex, sexual preference, or a combination thereof.[46]   Of course, these characteristics are important politically, but the tendency to reduce the interests of political communities to the few categories listed above may diminish consideration of the individual.   Identity politics does not so much promote diversity as redefine it.   Identity politics withers under the same communitarian criticism leveled at liberal theory: it posits an unnecessarily eviscerating conception of the individual and fails to account for the varieties of experience that inform our conceptions of the good. Identity politics is inward—rather than outward—thinking, and as a result those particularities outside our immediate political perspective remain unseen and unheard.

Political communitarian concerns are not exclusive of liberal practice. Pamela Karlan, a law professor and voting rights litigator, articulates a race-conscious communitarian program that reduces the good to a particular nonhierarchical relationship of racial groups in the context of political representation, and embraces liberal practice to advance her program.[47] Race circumscribes the individual's political autonomy; there is no color-blind original position.[48] Nonetheless, personal autonomy remains an important element in liberal institutions such as the courts, where individuals vindicate individual and group rights claims.[49]

Let us consider the politics espoused by communitarians who desire a standard of fair representation that enhances the representation of a particular community. Is there an inherent direction to their politics? The use of the term "community" or "identity" does not presuppose that individual responsibility to the good necessarily entails left-leaning politics or a right-wing mythology of the past.[50] The advancement of political freedom defined by responsibilities undertaken for the good of the political community—for the national interest, in Burke's terminology—does not presuppose any type of politics, left or right.[51] Political communitarians like Hitler, Mussolini, Mao, Robespierre, and Stalin advanced strong notions of the good, went to great lengths to define who was a competent political individual, and linked political membership to the realization of the good.[52] The desire to construct a specific "community" transcends ordinary political classifications such as left and right or liberal and conservative.

What interests should be included for representation to be fair? The relevance of any particular interest is not a fact of nature but rather a political and historical phenomenon. The state, in all its manifestations, continually recharts the map of politically significant terrain.[53] Given the rights claim of a particular group for representation, admitting the rhetorical persuasiveness of its map of the political community, we may ask, "Does it represent the world as many of us see it?" Are we asked to understand something that strikes us as commonsensical?[54] Once recognized in the law, a group claim to representation is politically (rhetorically) and legally powerful. However, the claim is by no means incontestable. Indeed, the 1975 amendments to the VRA added to the number of groups protected by the VRA, and this addition was highly contested. Gradually, the artifice apparent in the addition of a group disappears. We recognize the claims of those particular groups as natural, as having always been with us. Do any of us reflect upon artificiality of the Hispanic claim to protection under the VRA? We reflect not on the legitimacy of the claim, but on how the claim ought to be interpreted within our practices. When a particular group's claim to representation becomes law, the contrivance of that claim is gradually lost. It begins to seem natural that this group has a legal claim for representation.[55]

Likewise, those who successfully weld group membership to fair representation and enact that vision into law are unlikely to have to fight a rearguard action to protect a legal category that acknowledges the right of a particular group to representation by its members. For example, those groups privileged by the VRA, blacks and certain language minorities, are unlikely to find their claims erased from the VRA though different causes of action under the VRA may arise or foreclose.[56]

The trend had been to enlarge the VRA to cover more jurisdictions,[57] more groups, and more causes of action, although a retrenchment seems to be occurring in recent Supreme Court cases.[58] Once a rights claim is inscribed, once a group is recognized, once the prevailing practices employ a specific group claim or remedy, its practice is a part of the logic of the law. Whether we agree with a specific suit under the VRA is another matter. The ability to assert a claim by any of these groups is unquestioned, though the scope of that claim may no longer be.[59] The legal community that formulates, argues, and adjudicates VRA and reapportionment cases uses without reflection categories like vote dilution, majority-minority district, and protected minorities. These terms shape how a conflict over interpreting fair representation is articulated and resolved.[60]

What is it that contemporary race-conscious communitarians advocate in the context of representation? Some advocate the "civic inclusion" model whereby legislatures "reflect as nearly as possible the demographics" rather than "the geographics of the state."[61] Democracy should promote the inclusion and representation of groups such as ethnic and racial communities.[62] Elected officials should empathize with, and if possible share, the racial and ethnic identities of their constituencies.[63] This empowers minority communities by creating a sense of political efficacy and encouraging greater participation in the political process.[64] A question remains: To what extent ought minorities depend upon the Supreme Court to protect or extend this relatively recent sense of political empowerment? Certainly the Supreme Court and the courts in general are an important facet of the strategy to relieve the underrepresentation of groups protected under the VRA. However, the Supreme Court will not necessarily, over time, promote counter-majoritarian or minority interests. Recent opinions such as *Shaw* v. *Reno, Shaw* v. *Hunt, Miller* v. *Johnson,* and *Abrams* v. *Johnson* evidence this. These decisions are perceived to be inimical to increasing the number of minority officeholders. Commentators such as Professors Girardeau Spann and Gerald Rosenberg suggest advancing long-term political strategies for minority groups outside the courtroom.[65]

THE ASCENDANCY OF THE RACE-CONSCIOUS COMMUNITARIAN PERSPECTIVE

In the context of fair representation, race-conscious communitarians conceive of the political community differently than does liberal theory. Where one prioritizes decontextualized individual rights, the other insists we can speak of rights only within a specific conception of the proportional representation of groups. Race-conscious communitarians insist that fairness dictates certain groups within the larger polity be represented at specific levels. Fairness is discernible; it is out there. Fairness can be reduced, in some contexts, to counting heads among elected officials.[66] Race-conscious communitarians urge us to measure fairness from the viewpoints of minorities. For the political community to move toward fairness, the structures of governance must be integrated. The viewpoints of minorities are heard when they hold political office.[67] This standard of fairness is measured by the identity of the speaker. Even empathic majority officeholders may not be able to articulate minority concerns. Consequently, the perspective of the majority, no matter what its political sympathies, does not yield fairness but reproduces the inequities that give rise to minority political powerlessness.

An unfair political system, for race-conscious communitarians, submerges the interests of racial minorities to the majority. This occurs, by definition, when the institutions of representation are controlled by and reflect the majority's concerns. Because the majority does not hear their complaints, minorities do not feel connected to the political process. Muting these voices stifles democracy and decreases the intensity of deliberation. In order for a political system to correspond to such a vision of justice, political power among the pertinent social groups should be proportionate.

Roughly opposed to the classical liberal ideal of equality of opportunity is the race-conscious communitarian aim of equality of result. Race-conscious communitarians deny the possibility of individual equality of opportunity absent a rough equality of result among the various groups comprising the community. In the arena of representation the measure of equality is reduced to counting the number of minority officeholders. If the result corresponds roughly to the racial makeup of society, it is more or less fair. We might call this a descriptive theory of representation. Hannah Pitkin tells us that descriptive theories of representation do not read themselves.[68] Descriptive theories leave us the problem of "reading" the demographics of the political community in order to decide which groups merit equality of result. In the reading, there will be interpretive dispute. This results in legal conflict over what the state should look like and what is fair.

Thus far I have argued that liberal theory is different from liberal practice and that communitarian theory is distinguished from race-conscious communitarianism. I also have asserted that liberal practice accommodates communitarian arguments for the representation of specific social groups. Yet, identity politics may delimit the range of interests represented. Ironically, identity politics does not allow for diversity that is not self-referential, and polices politics to that end. The focus and narrative of identity politics is inward rather than outward. This criticism of difference-eviscerating identity politics replicates the communitarian critique of liberal theory.

The task of the theorist, liberal or communitarian, is somehow to rise above the idiomatic, apply a framework, and order phenomena. Yet, there is some difficulty with describing the individual and the group with clarity. The closer we bring the individual into focus, with all his oddities and attributes, the fuzzier becomes the group. Accurately defining a group leaves us with a blurred picture of its individuals. There is no natural way to order things. Order is not out there waiting to be revealed. The order of things reflects both the plan of the organizer and the politico-historical position she occupies.

Those traditions or histories used to circumscribe community membership may reflect values we no longer countenance. Some communitarian programs may sound fanatically religious or may emphasize a familial structure that strikes us as outmoded or oppressive. The theorist has the task of appropriating those traditions which define and rally the community while constructing new virtues to account for different social contingencies. Communitarians hope to build on widely shared moral precepts emphasizing responsibility to the whole. Of course, a terribly difficult process is determining which moral precepts are widely shared and galvanizing enough to form a political program.[69]

From a political standpoint, the communitarian approach raises some concerns. Manufacturers of community do not simply find and delimit rights and responsibilities in a neutral fashion. They reflect a particular conception of the good.[70] This violates the liberal belief that "the government should be neutral among competing conceptions of the good life."[71] Race-conscious communitarians interpret these conceptions according to their aspirations, and the end result is bound to be contentious. This is politics, and it characterizes the debate over the political good that is the subject of this book: fair representation.

We should be wary of representatives whose perspective renders them immune to critique from others in the political community. Certainly the political community is in part a reflection of political power of the majority faction. But, it also must reflect the demands and political power of minority factions.[72] If race or ethnicity identifies a faction, it is considered legally to be a group whose membership is based on immutable characteristics.[73] This type of faction is distinguished in legal discourse from a group whose membership is more or less fluid. One of the most important differences between these two types of factions involves the concept of choice. One cannot join a faction based on immutable traits. One is born into it.[74] The exclusivity of group membership is important in Equal Protection Clause jurisprudence and the VRA because it delimits the universe of claims based on unequal treatment due to race or ethnicity.

A claim involving representational authority made by some race-conscious communitarians implicates perspective. Members of a particular group whose membership is based on immutable characteristics share a perspective, a manner of viewing the political. This may reflect historical oppression and/or current political marginality. By virtue of their unique perspective, political officeholders who are part of this group articulate interests unarticulated by the majority. One may criticize this view of race-based political groups because it ignores the important role of the majority faction in constructing the political rhetoric of the minority. After all, oppression and marginality do not occur in a vacuum. In addition, not all members of the minority group are marginalized or oppressed. While its very marginalization informs its distinctive claims, it is hard to conceive of such total or complete group political powerlessness in a dynamic society.[75] This view underestimates the political power minority groups exercise in the political community even if their members are not elected in numbers proportional to their percent of the population.[76] Moreover, it countenances too cropped a view of political power. Racial correspondence between the electors and the representative is hardly the only measure of political influence, and even if it is the most important, this leaves the daunting task of delimiting the boundaries of race.[77]

The exclusive interests of racial minorities may be an argument for the maintenance of the minority's social and political segregation in the form of majority-minority districts.[78] Indeed, one might ask whether minority factionalism is exclusive of political community with the majority.[79] This conception of minority community diminishes individual agency by race or ethnicity. Factional membership delimits individual political autonomy. Politics becomes the competitive rending of the fabric of the political community along racial and ethnic lines. Yet, the interests of minority factions ought not to be exclusive of those of the national interest. Madison warned against permanent factions adversely affecting a political community's health.[80] He conceived of the individual as having shifting, multiple attachments that pass into and out of political discourse as the larger community develops its priorities. Encouraging the full play of factional politics decreased rather than increased the destabilizing potential of factions. Certainly, political factions are a fixture of political life. Interest group politics constitutes liberal practice. The individual has the ability to join and quit most types of interest groups as preferences change.[81] Still, the question remains of how best to accommodate the interests expressed by racial minorities who do not fit neatly into a Madisonian framework.

It is not enough simply to talk about political communities, their interests and their needs. Communities are made, not discovered. There will always be communities, even those characterized by a high degree of individualism. The question is: Who defines those communities? What attributes will people fix upon in order to group themselves? Communitarianism in practice is not new, nor is it necessarily a good thing.[82] To say the least, Orwell's vision of a total

community was not benevolent. Perhaps the antebellum South was characterized by a higher sense of community than is the contemporary, post-VRA
South. We need not be nostalgic for forms of community that heighten
oppression and diminish humanity. Liberal practice may be beneficial to the
extent that it limits the possibility of total communitarian programs becoming
political reality while allowing for the formation and interplay of communal
interests.

CAN LIBERAL PRACTICE ACCOMMODATE CLAIMS FOR COMMUNAL REPRESENTATION?

Does our culturally specific form of liberalism have something to offer
racial minority claims for representation even if it cannot accommodate all
cultural claims?[83] Iris Marion Young is pessimistic, and emphasizes the poverty
of the abstracted liberal ideal of the neutral self. She argues that the possibility
of impartial reason depends on deploying a position outside of perspectives that
constitute social action.[84] This position denies that the particularities of the
reasoner inform her reasoning process.[85] Law professor Mary Ann Glendon
also despairs. The liberal state lacks the vocabulary and traditions necessary to
recognize and nurture group claims. She conceives of alienated, self-dealing
individuals who struggle for advantage within a radically liberal state bereft of
community.[86] She addresses how it is that liberal theory is wrong about the
individual occupying a departicularized original position. This view of the
individual ignores the primacy of group life to the construction of the
individual. However, Glendon offers little evidence that liberal practice in the
United States, which she reduces largely to legal practices and institutions, does
not foster a shared sense of political belonging. She criticizes American
jurisprudence as exceptional because it reflects and promotes a radically
individualistic picture of the legal self. She is able to make this argument, in
part, because liberal practice in the United States fosters a robust debate over
liberal standards of justice. Her thesis of an exceptional American jurisprudence
characterized by a radically autonomous sense of the individual incorrectly
describes the context of representation. Strong group solidarities and the
communal nature of representation describe VRA and Supreme Court decisions
from *Allen* v. *State Board of Elections* in 1969 through contemporary cases.[87]
The debate in the courts is not over whether to recognize communal claims for
representation but how to prioritize these claims. For example, do we impart the
same legal recognition to group claims based on religion and race as we do to
those claims based on party affiliation?[88]

COMMUNITARIAN CRITIQUES OF LIBERAL THEORY DO NOT EXTEND TO LIBERAL PRACTICE

Communitarians such as Young and Glendon use terms like "identity,"
"community," and "rights." Much of their theoretical language and many of

their analytical categories find their roots in classical political thought. Aristotle's conception of politics remains relevant to the current liberal and communitarian debate for several reasons. Aristotle is an author one must read in order to discuss political theory. Aristotle's works are ubiquitous in the discourse of political theorists. Moreover, current liberals and communitarians invoke Aristotle to demonstrate the veracity of their arguments or the falsehoods of their opponents.[89] Aristotle is central to the discussion of fair representation, but the debate must be appreciated, as must Aristotle, in historical context.[90]

Race-conscious communitarians often fail to distinguish between communion, the sublimation of individual identity characterized by an emotional sense of belonging to a group, and community. They urge diversity-erasing communion that undermines community. The community theorized by Aristotle "does not necessarily provide us with the source of increased trust and cooperation that we will find in communion." Trust and cooperation may emerge, but they arise from "conflict and competition" among different kinds of individuals.[91]

The communitarian critique of liberal theory extends to liberal practice. Yet, the communitarian critique of liberal practice is much more tenuous than the communitarian critique of liberal theory. The assumption of the primacy of communal life for individuals is relatively uncontroversial. Individuals cannot transcend their social conditions. But the assertion that liberal practices are inadequate is contestable. As Bernard Yack explains:

For it is the central premise of the communitarian critique of these theories that self-constituting or dissociated individuals exist only in the fevered imaginations of liberal theorists. It follows from this premise that even if modern individuals feel less associated with each other, they still must, like all other individuals, draw a large part of their character and identity from their shared life. Modern individuals may experience a relatively large degree of alienation from each other, but such alienation is no less a social phenomenon, a shared culture, than patriotism or the celebration of tradition.[92]

In sum, the communitarian position is controversial because it critiques liberal practices and institutions on the same grounds as it finds fault with liberal theory. In turn, it asserts a specific form of community as a cure for our dissociating practices.[93]

In discussions of fair representation, opposing sides often characterize their positions as just. They treat justice as if it were tangible. Certainly the concept of political justice is coherent enough to discuss. On the other hand, it cannot be reduced to a formula. Searching for political justice is a rhetorical exercise.[94] For Aristotle, different forms of justice correspond to different forms of community. Justice results from social practice. Laws attempt to codify and enforce patterns of obligation among members of the political community. Debating, constructing, and enforcing these standards is the practice of justice. Political justice implicates public institutions and the law. For a representative democracy, political justice involves evolving political and legal standards of fair representation. Political justice is the product of a historical tradition of reasoned debate among the members of a political community.[95]

Citizens bring with them different skills and capabilities. They bring to the community different opinions and interests, and convey different concerns. They are strangers who do not necessarily share virtues or affection. They will hardly be predisposed to treat one another like family. Diverse citizens form a community to strive toward the good life, not because of *a priori* conceptions of the good.[96] They are likely to have radically different political views and ideals of fair representation. Citizens debate the standards of political justice to persuade others of the justness of their position. This debate is ongoing and not subject to final resolution. Resolution is displaced by further deliberation. The practice of politics does not stop, nor will, in all probability, litigation under the VRA.[97] Standards of fair representation remain usable but inchoate.

The law is an essential part of the debate over political justice. Interpretation of law in the area of representation frames what is fair, equitable, and just for the individual and the group. Members of political communities are subject to law, which is why deliberating the wisdom of a particular law is essential. Political justice, as articulated in the practice of law, "expresses standards of mutual obligation."[98] Aristotle's notion of political community is consistent with liberal practice and is more inclusive than an understanding of political community wherein moral consensus among community members is a necessary predicate.[99] The political practice of a citizen, his part in the debate, improves the citizen and makes possible the good life.[100] This is relevant for our consideration of political representation. We employ reason to demonstrate the correctness of our position. Yet, what is reasonable is a contested category and one that drives politics. We are continuously testing the limits of what makes sense or what is persuasive within our interpretive communities. Standards change as to what is just, fair and equitable. Speech used to delimit claims for representation expresses different conceptions of what it means to be represented. This movement in standards is rhetorical. It is expressive. The rhetorical aspect of reasoned speech informs and reveals the practice of representation. Our notion of representation changes, in part, because the boundaries of what is reasonable alter.

Arguing about the wisdom of correct courses of action is political practice. It is indispensable to the health of the political community. In part, it is found in the "rhetoric" of Supreme Court opinions. Questioning the fairness of political representation implicates the constitution of the political community. Certainly we argue to secure narrow political advantage. We also argue because the soundness of the political community, a broader political good, is of concern to all of us though we may disagree as to what the configuration for which we should strive.

COMMUNITARIAN CRITIQUES OF LIBERAL PRACTICE IN
THE DEBATE OVER FAIR REPRESENTATION

Some communitarians desire to remove important areas of politics, large spheres like representation, from contention. Iris Marion Young does not countenance debates over justice inconsistent with her politics of difference. This is true despite the fact that she fails to offer a specific program for protecting difference and overcoming group oppression, except to note that it is permissible for oppressed groups to segregate on their own terms, and it is impermissible for dominant groups to do so.[101] Similarly, Cass Sunstein and other civic republicans who advocate differential treatment of groups because the neutral application of the law reinforces existing social inequalities do not seem to anticipate debate over their conceptions of the good.[102]

Part of the controversy over the lack of fair representation is over to what degree groups protected by the VRA are underrepresented and how this ought to be remedied. As a result, a program that redistributes political power along lines benefiting those groups characterized by marginality or oppression advances an alternative conception of political justice. The trick is to promote a relatively uncontroversial plan. As we have seen, plans using majority-minority districts of novel shape based primarily upon race have proved to be legally and politically contentious.

Debate over the political good presupposes that individuals possess divergent conceptions of the good. Even uncontroversial conceptions of the good are likely to become controversial over time. Race-conscious communitarians propose a relatively specific notion of the good in the area of representation. It is the desire to remove certain aspects of the good from controversy that distinguishes race-conscious communitarians from liberals. It is an aspiration to curtail debate over certain standards of justness and fairness that remains unfulfilled because disagreement is inevitable in a political community where diverse individuals debate standards of political justice.[103]

Still, communitarians accuse liberal society of failing to promote a strong sense of community.[104] It is one thing to call for an intense feeling of community, and it is quite another to consider how a strong community may conflict with values that a liberal community promotes, such as individual autonomy, tolerance of dissent, and freedom to contest the core tenets of the political community. In fact, liberal practice does promote a particular type of community. The problem for many communitarians is that they have different and more specific expectations of community.

Communities formulated in the abstract do not have to answer hard questions put to liberal communities in concrete form. The most troublesome of these questions may be how to accommodate powerless individuals and minority groups who seek protection from the political community. In the context of representation, the political community may invoke the law, such as the VRA or the Equal Protection Clause, to protect minority interests.[105] A legal regime, which disdains treating divers people differently on account of status, may still be hospitable to claims for protection by marginalized groups. This is especially true when we consider how effectively the VRA guarantees the right to vote and promotes minority representation. However, negotiating a political settlement in reapportionment or redistricting entails legal challenges to the practices of the political community. No group will be successful all of the time. The resolution of the challenge to the prevailing practices of political representation is ongoing. Given the stakes involved, the legitimacy of our form of representative government for large segments of the population, it is essential that political and legal conflict over what constitutes fair representation continue.

In this vein, H. N. Hirsch considers the modern communitarian challenge to liberal practices and warns against those who sanguinely invoke the recognition of "community" as a panacea for our constitutional ills.[106]   The problem of marginal or oppressed groups for a political community is not obviated by the communitarian prescription.   Assuming a radically different worldview for marginal people, a common assertion in identity politics, may mean that standards of reasoned speech cannot be universalized. If reason cannot be universalized to all citizens because of inequalities among groups, then group members can debate the good life only among themselves. There will be little discourse between the marginalized and the majority because they reason and experience in different ways.[107]   The identity politics assertion of group singularity may serve to segregate racial minorities in liberal political practice. Courts may in practice reinforce inequitable differences among the majority and various minorities because, despite their counter-majoritarian role, they remain majority institutions.

The same identity politics that asserts community based on group identity also militates against members of that group participating as full and equal members of the political community.   For instance, the fact that a county commission is integrated through voting rights litigation does not mean that it will not resegregate internally.[108] The communitarian critique of liberal theory does not answer how a political community can be cobbled together out of diverse and exclusive groups possessing different views of the good.[109] The spirit of identity politics is bent on establishing a political community more specific than one established by liberal practice.   Political communitarians envision a more dynamic public sphere; state action blurs the distinction between public and private. For political communitarians, the private informs the public.[110] As Young and others note, the personal is the political.[111] In the context of representation, race-conscious communitarians demand no less than proportional correspondence between the race of the representative and the constituency.   Personal description becomes political authorization where fair representation is measured by how the racial makeup of the legislature.

CHALLENGES FOR LIBERAL THEORY IN THE AREA OF REPRESENTATION: MARGINALIZED GROUPS

In the area of representation, the challenge for liberal practice is to integrate individuals and groups whose relationship to the political community is partial. Their partial position may be a consequence of historical oppression. Discriminatory laws and practices may hinder their political participation. Marginalized groups may advocate the formation of communities within the larger political community with special rights and privileges.[112]   Liberal constitutionalism can accommodate marginal voices but may not provide this type of strong community.[113]

Identity politics does not rise above the abstract in its call to engage the political community and transform society. Change, if it does occur, transpires from the same group practices and beliefs that give rise to critiques of group practices.   Change cannot arise external to the community's beliefs and transform them because this would entail exiting one way of knowing, adopting an emancipatory epistemology, and integrating that vantage into a heretofore oppressive practice without becoming part of that practice. In short, it is part of practice to critique practice but this does not entail transformation. Furthermore, the models that communitarians offer often are drawn from a nostalgic past and small communities where a high level of consensus was assured, and do not adequately reflect contemporary political reality.[114]

Some communitarians criticize the rule of law because it perpetuates liberal, dissociating practices and social inequalities.[115] Ironically, they employ the law to find solutions. A case in point is the VRA. Although *Bush* and *Shaw II* hint at the limits of using the VRA to accomplish race-conscious communitarian objectives such as increasing the number of minority officeholders through redistricting, the VRA remains a vital instrument to prevent discrimination against minorities in a wide range of voting practices and procedures. It offers a baseline of fair play. Indeed, Hirsch defends the rule of law on these grounds. It offers a modicum of fairness or impartiality without which the marginalized or oppressed may suffer further.[116] This understanding of the limits of liberal practice is not contrary to a program seeking to create a greater sense of belonging and consensus while integrating marginal groups into institutions of governance.[117] Furthermore, identity politics does not offer an alternative to the rule-of-law.[118] It is not the impartiality of the rule-of-law that race-conscious communitarians criticize. They criticize the politics of liberal impartiality.[119]

Erasing the rule-of-law, a formal commitment to procedural and substantive neutrality, denies to marginal groups the very means, the fulcrum, by which they pressure the larger community. This paradigmatic liberal practice fostered solidarity and gained them political and legal recognition.[120] Banishing the rule-of-law from our practice might result in embracing a legal regime based on status.[121] Under such a legal regime, the application of the laws corresponds to the differential treatment of individuals based on their status.   The personal defines the legal. Group membership determines the legitimacy of political representation. Such a system was implemented in India to remedy the underrepresentation of the lower castes. Whether it has been a success or a failure is a matter of dispute.[122] The historical and economic context of group conflict is different in the United States than in India, but the latter's experience with group preferences in representation is an important lesson.

Race-conscious communitarians, in their zeal to promote community, may embrace a form of political organization that extinguishes social diversity in favor of relatively permanent legal classes that reproduce their rigidity in the private sphere.[123] This is inconsistent with liberalism but not inconsistent with a specific form of community that promotes a strong sense of belonging and inclusion. In this limited sense, the race-conscious communitarian program may not promote social diversity but diminish it. The desire to impose a good and establish a specific community requires enormous political mobilization. Even if the goal is the representation of underrepresented minorities, it may entail the exclusion of types of people and opinions that typify the heterogeneity of the community.[124] It reduces the breadth of political dialogue around a set of collective representations that allow the community to restrict the telling of its story.[125] For the purposes of enforcing legal standards of fair representation, this may be particularly dangerous for racial and other easily distinguishable minorities.[126]

In practice, the law may not be neutral with respect to different individuals and groups in society. Members of some racial and ethnic minorities may enjoy the formal privileges of membership in a political community, yet still feel as though they are outsiders because of prejudice. This exclusion may discourage these individuals from seeking political office or leadership. The choice to engage in politics is absent because the person in question was never inclined to seek political office. Simply guaranteeing the right to vote, a formal legal privilege, does not make blacks or other minorities meaningful participants in the political community. More is needed, and we have a complex bureaucracy promoting a minimum level of minority representation through federal and state legislatures, courts, and the Justice Department. Without involvement by the state, social losers will be political losers.[127]

Absent the creation of a specific community, race-conscious communitarians promote the institutionalization of the social community's political interests. Federalists such Madison and Hamilton wished to mitigate the effect of factions whose interests were adverse to the interests of the political community.[128] They designed a system meant to thwart the rise and influence of factions. Conversely, the Anti-Federalist's critique was based on a commitment to community they saw lacking in the Federalist constitution.[129] The race-conscious communitarian's critique is an examination of the political community they wish to create and one that is lacking. They wish to retain the status to critique the political community while they remold it into one where their distinctiveness is maintained. The race-conscious communitarian critique of institutions of representation forces a reexamination of the practices undergirding the legitimacy of the political community.

Again, let us consider the relevance of our discussion to the problem of fair representation for underrepresented groups.   Can we enlist notions of community to empower marginal groups in the United States?   Should the government take the lead?   Can the Supreme Court foster the inclusion of marginal groups?   Certainly the Supreme Court and the federal judiciary wield great authority in the area of representation.   For example, whether or not the Court determines an electoral practice to be dilutive of a group's voting strength, or whether a district is an unconstitutional racial gerrymander, may create large numbers of lawsuits and eventually affect the makeup of Congress and state legislatures.   Still, there are institutional constraints to consider.   Most important, the fact that the Supreme Court makes a ruling does not mean that it will be followed or that people will change the way they think about one another.[130]   Additionally, the Supreme Court will not refrain from reinterpreting its decisions.[131]   A judicially imposed conception of the good cannot be successful without social change whereby long-standing attitudes and patterns of exclusion alter.

We ought not to be too pessimistic in our estimation of the limits of procedural justice in a liberal state.   The rule-of-law does improve on previous legal systems that rest explicitly on social status.   We should be circumspect in attempts to collapse the rule-of-law into a preconceived social structure as part of a strategy of minority empowerment.   This may worsen matters for marginal or oppressed groups.   The law may not make an immediate difference, but this does not mean that it is an ineffective instrument.   Legal change is a slow, evolutionary process.[132]

Multitudes of social communities characterize a healthy political · community.   Individual membership changes constantly.   Race-conscious communitarians miss this insight, even when they advance notions of intersectionality.   They tend to reduce identity to race or sex or an uneasy combination of both.[133]   Claims to fair political representation by social groups are contingent and highly political.   We can argue and draw conclusions, but there is not a road map, absent the practice of deliberation, guiding us to our destination.[134]

CONCLUSION

Let us end this last chapter, and our general discussion of fair representation, by summing up the major issues and explaining why they are relevant for our discussion of fair representation. In this discussion of liberal theory and communitarianism, the shape and pervasiveness of the political community were disputed.   Aristotle felt that the political community should contribute toward the development of the individual.[135]   Yet, Aristotle recognized the maintenance of a strong and diverse private sphere.   It is the

maintenance of the boundaries between public and private that communitarianism so forcefully brings into dispute.   The public deliberation over fair
representation benefits from the race-conscious communitarian critique.[136]

In the context of fair representation, communitarians asserted that "to affirm
rights in society was to visualize rights, less as products of the discrete choices
of individuals, than as interdependent acts of social groups."[137] In a society of
over 250 million, it states the obvious that to be heard, most of us speak as parts
of group interests as well as individuals.   However, something more is being
asserted. Membership in some groups means the individual is a recipient of
special rights or is unfairly denied rights basic to citizenship. An individual's
assertion of group membership need not diminish her distinctiveness. But an
individual's assertion of group A membership rather than group B membership
may affect how the state treats her claim. As courts arbitrate among group
claims, a conundrum develops. A court cannot recognize all communities lest
the notion of community become absurd. Recognition simultaneously includes
and excludes. For example, a space must exist between A and B for there to be
A and B. It is at the interstices that hard political and legal choices are made.
The difficult task of the jurist is to construct an ever-changing blueprint onto
which she places legal things. It is an unenviable task because it is a political
task open to dispute.   Legal classification situates an event within a legal
category. Legal taxonomies are contextual and reflect particular conflicts the
state resolves by recognizing some group claims at the expense of others.[138]
Legal taxonomies are political artifacts subject to revision. Yet, the contingency
of legal categories does not mean they are any less powerful. As a result, how
the state maps group claims is neither correct nor false in an absolute sense,
although "correct" and "false" may be used to describe how they appear. In the
context of fair representation, this means that we may take strong positions
regarding the justness of a particular Court decision. We may even say that the
result is unjust.   In essence, we are saying that given the circumstances, the
interests at stake, and our political goals, we disagree strongly.   That
disagreement may change how we ascertain what is just. It may even have
some effect on future decisions by the Supreme Court. But it does not establish
that a particular opinion is unjust, because an opinion is part of a taxonomy that
is neither just nor unjust, but argued and employed.

In the area of representation, it is liberal practice to recognize the political
centrality of the individual. The individual votes. The individual is represented.
Contrastingly, race-conscious communitarians stress the necessity of ensuring
the political presence of particular social groups in their estimation of fair
representation.   Race-conscious communitarians stress the essential group
nature of political competition and largely reduce that framework to racial
competition. Liberals who fear the institutionalization of a racial spoils system
meet this reduction with opposition.   They argue that the state should not
compromise individual autonomy in order to reach a vision of the good in
accord with a partial notion of racial equity. Moreover, the very use of the

group as a means to distribute political recourse stigmatizes the individual with all the traits, virtues, and vices that have been ascribed to that group.

I spoke about the concept of representation in the context of the liberal and communitarian opposition. It is representation, a voice, that we all wish more of, and bemoan its lack. To understand the current conflict over fair representation in purely political terms, by which we see conservatives advancing an agenda and liberals putting forth a counter-argument, is certainly a large part of the story, but it excludes much analysis of the legal reasoning used to resolve conflict. Understanding fair representation in terms of the language of a statute or the Constitution requires that we examine the pertinent Supreme Court decisions. Understanding how the Court determines and characterizes what is or is not vote dilution, or what is or is not an unconstitutional racial gerrymander, is an important portion of the consideration of fair representation. Stepping back and placing the legal and political analyses of fair representation into a philosophical framework enables us to bring the dispute over fair representation into focus without falling into the political battle or the legal contest. A philosophical framework that places the political and legal debate about fair representation into the broader narratives of communitarianism and liberalism allows us a vantage from which to analyze the practice of hammering out what is fair. It is a means to supply a narrative to an unavoidably contentious enterprise while acknowledging that contention is necessary.

The health of the political community depends on there being no permanent winners or losers in political representation. As such, it is a good thing that the notion of fair continues to evolve. For many in the political community, it may seem that there have been no permanent legal or political losers or winners. However, some racial minorities have lost more than their share for far too long, and their claims for greater representation must be heard. By analyzing the liberal and communitarian debate within a liberal and communitarian narrative, a narrative that promises to continue, we gain the perspective to sanguinely accept the contentious nature of the political and legal struggles without losing the immediacy of the claim for fair representation.

Notes

INTRODUCTION

1. *Bush* v. *Vera,* 1996 U.S. LEXIS 3882; *Shaw* v. *Reno,* 125 L.Ed.2d 511, 113 S.Ct. 2831 (1993) *(Shaw I)*; *Shaw* v. *Hunt,* 1996 U.S. LEXIS 3880 *(Shaw II)*; *Abrams* v. *Johnson,* 1997 WL 331802; *Miller* v. *Johnson,* 132 L.Ed.2d 762, 1995 U.S. LEXIS 4462.

2. *Baker* v. *Carr,* 369 U.S. 186 (1962); *Wesberry* v. *Sanders,* 376 U.S. 1 (1963); *Reynolds* v. *Sims,* 84 S.Ct. 1362 (1964).

3. Most notably, *Shaw* v. *Reno.*

4. Hannah Pitkin, *The Concept of Representation* (Berkeley: University of California Press, 1967).

5. As I explain in more detail later, I use the term "race-conscious communitarian" to refer to those theorists who adopt a communitarian framework informed by sociopolitical inequalities among races.

6. There is no metalanguage by which to ground theories of representation, much less constitute fair representation. A metalanguage, if there were one, would provide the lexicon to interpret a subordinate language perfectly. It would remove contingency from meaning. Such a language would be unrecognizeable.

7. Of course, I consider and discuss cases prior to *Reynolds* v. *Sims* (1964), such as *Baker* v. *Carr* (1962) and *Gomillion* v. *Lightfoot,* 364 U.S. 339 (1960), but close analysis of the actual language of the cases starts with *Reynolds.*

8. Communitarians, civic republicans, and other critics of liberalism like Cass Sunstein, William Galston, Lani Guinier, and Frank Michelman tend to assume or articulate a left-leaning and progressive good. I argue that communitarian programs misjudge the extent to which the notion of the good, usually cast as a multicultural, inclusive, and tolerant political community, is possible or even universal. See Sunstein, *The Partial Constitution* (Cambridge, Mass.: Harvard University Press, 1993); Galston, *Goods, Virtues and Diversity in the Liberal State* (Cambridge, Mass.: Cambridge University Press, 1992); Guinier, *The Tyranny of the Majority* (New York: Free Press, 1994); and Michelman, "Law's Republic," 97 *Yale Law Journal* 1493 (1988).

9. *Voinovich* v. *Quilter,* 113 S.Ct. 1149 (1993).

10. For instance, many parts of the South are covered by the nonretrogression

principle of Section 5. Northern states are often subject to Section 2 liability under the VRA. See *Voionovich* v. *Quilter* (1993) and *Growe* v. *Emison*, 113 S.Ct. 1075 (1993).

11. *Miller* v. *Johnson*, 1995 U.S. LEXIS 4462, *8 (1995).

12. As the court noted in the *Miller* progeny case of *Abrams* v. *Johnson*, white majority constituencies reelected black incumbents after the original majority-minority districts were redrawn.

CHAPTER 1: ASSESSING REPRESENTATION

1. The Voting Rights Act of 1965 (VRA) was not passed to address this problem initially, but to protect the right to vote. However, the vote without other measures did not put minorities into political office.

2. Descriptive correspondence is reduced to an amalgam of physical and cultural characteristics we call "race."

3. I borrow these terms, in part, from Wendy Brown-Scott's exhaustive discussion of racial inequalities that inhere in our legal order in particular and our society in general. See Wendy Brown-Scott, "The Communitarian State: Lawlessness or Law Reform for African Americans?" 107 *Harvard Law Review* 1209 (1994). For a discussion of race-conscious informed scholarship and a strategy for practice, see Anthony D. Taibi, "Symposium on Race Consciousness and Legal Scholarship: Race Consciousness, Communitarianism, and Banking Regulation," 1992 *University of Illinois Law Review* 1103.

4. James Madison, "Federalist No. 10," in Alexander Hamilton, John Jay, and James Madison, *The Federalist*, introduction by Edward Mead Earle (New York: Modern Library, 1960).

5. Groups that are not historically disadvantaged are secondary and "should receive consideration only if a district lacks a significant number of historically disadvantaged minorities." Grant Hayden, "Note: Some Implications of Arrow's Theorem for Voting Rights," 47 *Stanford Law Review* 295, 311 (1995).

6. *Colegrove* v. *Green*, 328 U.S. 549 (1946) (plurality opinion), apportionment was a political thicket the Court should not enter; *Gomillion* v. *Lightfoot*, 364 U.S. 339 (1960), relying on the 15th Amendment, found unconstitutional the drawing of municipal boundaries of Tuskegee, Alabama to deny blacks the right to vote and political power; *Baker* v. *Carr*, 369 U.S. 186 (1962), Tennessee apportionment was justiciable; *Wesberry* v. *Sanders*, 376 U.S. 1 (1963), Georgia apportionment of congressional seats found unconstitutional; *Gray* v. *Sanders*, 372 U.S. 368 (1963), found unconstitutional Georgia apportionment of county political strength; and *Reynolds* v. *Sims*, 84 S.Ct. 1362 (1964), Alabama and other state apportionment schemes found unconstitutional as not meeting the one person, one vote standard.

7. Section 2 of the VRA changed the focus from protecting the right to vote to promoting the ability of minority members to elect members of their own choice. Subsection (b) of Section 2 of the VRA looks to whether minority group members "have less opportunity than other members of the electorate to participate in the political process and to elect representatives of their choice." 42 U.S.C. sec. 1973 (1988).

8. It is now applicable in voting districts where there is a concentration of 5 percent or more of a protected group. See 42 U.S.C. sec. 1973 (1988). Language minorities include Hispanics, Native Americans, Aleuts, and Asian Americans.

9. As will be explained in Chapter 4, the ideal of representation promoted by the VRA formed gradually, and now promotes group and individual interests measured by the Section 2 results test.

10. Kathryn Abrams discusses the special relationship between minority represen-

tatives and their constituency in the context of *Chisom* v. *Roemer*, 111 S.Ct. 2354 (1991) and *Presley* v. *Etowah County Commission*, 112 S.Ct. 820 (1992). Abrams, "Relationships of Representation in Voting Rights Act Jurisprudence," 71 *Texas Law Review* 1409 (1995).

11. Samuel Issacharoff, "Polarized Voting and the Political Process: The Transformation of Voting Rights Jurisprudence," 90 *Michigan Law Review* 1833, 1845–50 (1992).

12. Madison and Hamilton were concerned with the debilitating effect of factions, majority and minority, on the health of the political community. Madison, "Federalist No. 10" and "Federalist No. 15," and Hamilton, "Federalist No. 9," in *The Federalist*.

13. This is the case with Supreme Court justices. The President may wish to appoint a justice who is confirmable, competent, and somewhat in conformity with the President's agenda. The President selects his candidate from a list compiled by a search committee. Does a Supreme Court justice govern? Not in the usual sense. But his or her position in our system of self-governance is vitally important. Moreover, the Chief Justice of the Supreme Court does have important administrative duties, including the promulgation of federal rules of procedure and administering the federal court system and Supreme Court. These duties are subject to legislative veto by Congress.

14. The apportionment process is complex and occurs in every state at least every ten years. In many cases, it is the state legislature that plays the major role in determining the reapportionment and redistricting.

15. T. Alexander Aleinikoff and Samuel Issacharoff, "Race and Redistricting: Drawing Constitutional Lines After *Shaw* v. *Reno*," 92 *Michigan Law Review* 588 (1993).

16. A judge may be a representative of a race or a language minority. For the purposes of the VRA, a judge may be a representative because her election ratifies group preference.

17. This is less directly the case with nonelected judges. For instance, the President appoints federal judges with the advice and consent of the Senate. He does so with an eye to his political relationship with the Senate and with an eye to his electorate. For instance, he may appoint judges who, he assures us, are tough on crime or strict constructionists. He does this to gain or retain political popularity. In the case of the President and federal judges, the electors give the President the initial authority to appoint judges by electing him. They retain some authority over the President by constructing the limits of what is an acceptable appointee through public opinion.

18. Michael Sandel notes that the range of choice open to an individual, as presented by liberal theory, is not pretermitted or circumscribed. Sandel comments on those moral or religious ties that circumscribe the individual's range of action for reasons unrelated to choice. See Michael Sandel, "Review of John Rawls, *Political Liberalism*," 107 *Harvard Law Review* 1765, 1769–70 (1994).

19. One of the primary justifications for continuing the VRA despite the fact that virtually no one is being denied the right to vote is the importance of encouraging and promoting the idea of self-governance in groups formerly excluded from political power. This often takes the form of majority-minority districts. Professor Lani Guinier calls recent Supreme Court opinions "impoverished" for failing to connect minority community representation to "a more general understanding of representative democracy." Lani Guinier, "[E]racing Democracy: The Voting Rights Cases," 108 *Harvard Law Review* 109, 118 (1994).

20. Racial and partisan characteristics are difficult to disentangle. It is not clear, for example, that creating more black districts results in a more liberal assembly. It may increase Republican seats as safe Democrat seats are split to form majority-minority

districts. Nonetheless, creating more black districts increased the descriptive presence of blacks in legislatures in the South, where they were previously excluded. See Richard Pildes, "The Politics of Race. Review of *Quiet Revolution in the South*, edited by Chandler Davidson and Bernard Grofman," 108 *Harvard Law Review* 1359, 1376–80 (1995).

21. In the context of racially polarized voting, resemblance may mean simply "who most looks like me." The unstated implication is that in the context of race, the resemblance test is a reliable proxy for determining who shares the electors' experiences and political views. Of course, some electors do not feel they will be well represented no matter who the winning candidate is. They may choose not to vote, vote for an undesirable alternative, or spoil their ballot. Other electors may make mistakes. Still others may have no clear idea of their interests or of the candidates. Not all electors are engaged in the reasoned process of matching their interests to the appropriate candidate.

22. The legal claim is racially descriptive. Under Section 2 of the VRA, blacks and language minorities can make out a cause of action by, among other things, simply comparing the number of minorities among officeholders with their percentage in the general population. This is known as the results test.

23. *New Expanded Webster's Dictionary* (Taunton, Mass.: World Book Marketing, 1989), 44.

24. I refer to Sections 2 and 5 of the VRA. Other aspects of fair representation to be considered include arithmetic proportionality of districts as guaranteed by *Wesberry* v. *Sanders* and *Reynolds* v. *Sims*, and the antiracial gerrymandering principle articulated in *Shaw* v. *Reno*, 125 L.Ed.2d 511, 113 S.Ct. 2831 (1993), and *Gomillion* v. *Lightfoot*.

25. Aleinikoff and Issacharoff, "Race and Redistricting," 588. They argue for a legal standard that is race-conscious and politically legitimate rather than the *status quo*, which "is politics pure, fraught with the capacity for self-dealing and cynical manipulation."

26. *Chisom* v. *Roemer*, 111 S.Ct. 2354 (1991).

27. Under Section 2 of the VRA, plaintiffs are not required to demonstrate intent to discriminate but can prove vote dilution by demonstrating a denial or abridgment of the right to vote on account of race by a totality of the circumstances. Ibid., 2363.

28. One might say the interpretation in *Chisom* v. *Roemer* was in the spirit of the VRA as it evolved during the 1970's and 1980's. On the other hand, the spirit of the VRA underwent a metamorphosis in the 1990's, and *Chisom* v. *Roemer* might now be seen as delimiting the reach of the VRA.

29. *Chisom*, 111 S.Ct. at 2366.

30. I say "not surprisingly" because Pitkin was able to write an entire book about or related to the subjects of representatives and representation. The Supreme Court has split badly in recent cases involving representation.

31. Hannah Pitkin, *The Concept of Representation* (Berkeley: University of California Press, 1967), 2369, 2375.

32. Abrams, "Relationships of Representation," 1411, 1412. Abrams stresses the relationship of governance between a representative and her constituency. Representation encompasses more than merely voting. It is a process of interaction and accountability. I do not mean to suggest Abrams, Guinier, Karlan, and others who advocate increased minority representation embrace the majority-minority district as the best remedy for minority vote dilution. Often variants of proportional representation are put forth as better alternatives. But, given the current system, the majority-minority district is the vehicle used to increase minority representation.

33. Abrams sketches out the relation of the representative and the voter. It is one that starts with the election. Karlan discusses the status of blacks as a marginalized

faction viewing the electoral process differently than the majority faction. Abrams, "Relationships of Representation," 1418; Pamela Karlan, "The Rights to Vote: Some Pessimism About Formalism," 71 *Texas Law Review* 1705, 1738–40 (1993).

34. Abrams, "Relationships of Representation," 1431.

35. Pamela Karlan, Lani Guinier, and Melissa Williams, among others, cite Pitkin's *The Concept of Representation* as the foundational text on the subject of representation.

36. Pitkin, *The Concept of Representation*, 2.

37. "The authorization view stresses only the representative's capacity to bind others, not his obligations to conform to some external standard or act in accord with special considerations." Ibid., 49.

38. Ibid., 57.

39. Lani Guinier, *Tyranny of the Majority* (New York: Free Press, 1994), 36–37. Guinier notes that "[E]ven a mildly sympathetic white official will not dependably consider black interests if that individual must also accommodate the more dominant views of white constituents."

40. Pitkin, *The Concept of Representation*, 61.

41. Ibid., 62.

42. Ibid., 61.

43. Ibid., 87, 89.

44. Ibid., 144.

45. Some things, such as party organization and the seniority system, are beyond the representative's control. On the other hand, they offer avenues to exploit institutional power.

46. "The activity of representing as acting for another must be defined in terms of what the representative does and how he does it, or in some combination of these two considerations." Pitkin, *The Concept of Representation*, 142–43, 144. The behavior of the representative can be used to describe him.

47. As Pitkin puts it, "What the representative must do is act in his constituents' interests, but this implies that he must not normally come into conflict with their will when they have an express will. But this prohibition is not equivalent to saying that he represents only when he acts in accord with their actual, conscious wishes. Quite the contrary: leadership, emergency action, action on issues of which the people know nothing are among the important realities of representative government. They are not deviations from true representation, but its very essence. It is often for that very purpose that people choose representatives." Ibid., 154, 164.

48. "Your representative owes you, not his industry only, but his judgment; and he betrays, instead of serving you, if he sacrifices it to your opinion." Edmund Burke, "Speech to the Electors of Bristol," in B. W. Hill, ed., *Edmund Burke on Government, Politics and Society* (New York: International Publications Service, 1976), 157.

49. Pitkin, *The Concept of Representation*, 169, 170, citing Edmund Burke, "Reflections on the Revolution in France," in Ross Hoffman and Paul Levack, eds., *Burke's Politics* (New York: Alfred Knopf, 1949), 305, 316; Francis Canavan, *The Political Reason of Edmund Burke* (Durham, N.C.: Duke University Press, 1960), 143.

50. Pitkin, *The Concept of Representation*, 173.

51. See Lani Guinier, *Tyranny of the Majority*, 36–37. Guinier argues that virtual representation is not as legitimate as direct representation. She writes, "Virtual representation theory is not appropriate if the interests of a racial minority are not necessarily fungible with those of the 'actual' representatives or of their white constituents. For example, blacks, as a poor and historically oppressed group, are in greater need of government-sponsored programs and solicitude, which whites often resent and vigorously oppose. Even a mildly sympathetic white official will not

dependably consider black interests if that individual must also accommodate the more dominant views of white constituents." Ibid., 37.

52. Ibid.

53. It is important to historicize notions of representation. For example, Burke's views reflect his time and, in comparison with the contemporary United States, a racially homogeneous nation.

54. Pitkin, *The Concept of Representation*, 183, 187, citing Edmund Burke, "Letter to Langriche," in *Burke's Politics*, 28.

55. Edmund Burke, "On American Taxation," in *Edmund Burke on Government, Politics and Society*, 151. There is a related question as to whether an interest is represented in a legislative body if its representatives lack influence. In part, this concern goes to representative competence, a judgment not readily amenable to legal standards except in the most general sense of meeting statutory and constitutional qualifications for holding office.

56. Pitkin, *The Concept of Representation*, 170, 183, 187, 188.

57. Ibid., 183.

58. Ibid., 171, relying in particular on "Speech to the Electors of Bristol," in *Burke's Politics*, 116.

59. Ibid., 168–88.

60. It was still the case that Madison understood how important groups were in the process of representation. He spent a considerable amount of effort attempting to account for the power of groups or factions in *The Federalist* and the United States Constitution.

61. Representation was based on the model of an autonomous, rational individual as the foundation of the political community. Pitkin, *The Concept of Representation*, 190.

62. Ibid., 193, 195.

63. James Madison, "Federalist No. 10," in *The Federalist*, 55.

64. Ibid., 54

65. Many of the original thirteen colonies were havens for religious minorities. For instance, Massachusetts, Maryland, Pennsylvania, and Rhode Island were founded as places for particular groups to worship freely, as they could not elsewhere. Of course, tolerance for some religious beliefs did not mean universal tolerance. Some colonies replicated the religious intolerance they had struggled to escape. Pitkin argues that religion was until historically recently the major political cleavage for many countries in the West.

66. Local prejudices were not interests. The general good guided deliberation. A true interest was not inimical to the common good. See Edmund Burke, "Speech to the Electors of Bristol," in *Edmund Burke on Government, Politics, and Society*, 158.

67. Factions were represented at the same time they were constrained from dominating the representative process and thereby harming the national interest. Promoting or increasing the number of factions had the effect of decreasing the possibility of one interest's dominating politics.

68. Madison, "Federalist No. 10," in *The Federalist*; Alexis de Tocqueville, *Democracy in America*, Richard D. Heffner, ed. (New York: Mentor Books, 1956); and Guinier, *Tyranny of the Majority*, express similar concerns as to the danger of an unmediated majority, though they write in and describe dissimilar contexts.

69. Pitkin, *The Concept of Representation*, 183, 195, 196; and Madison, "Federalist No. 10," in *The Federalist*.

70. Adams writes that it is "inconsistent with the spirit of the common law and of the essential fundamental principles of the British constitution that we should be subject to any tax imposed by the British Parliament, because we are not represented in that assembly in any sense, unless it be by a fiction of law." John Adams, "Instructions of the

Town of Braintree to Their Representative," in George A. Peek, Jr., ed., *The Political Writings of John Adams* (New York: Liberal Arts Press, 1954), 23.

71. Madison, "Federalist No. 10," in *The Federalist*, 59–60.

72. Not much has changed. The poor do not get elected because elections require money, and to be poor in a capitalist society means, to some extent, that one has failed. Women and blacks are elected, but in far fewer numbers than their percentage of the population.

73. "Representation is thought a substitute for direct participation, a far preferable substitute." Pitkin, *The Concept of Representation*, 191.

74. Ibid., 188.

75. Ibid., 190. Of course, Madison and others acknowledge class, race, and sex differences. So do we. The measure of our political morality is how we draw the distinctions between races, sexes, and classes. It is baffling to expect those who preceded us by 200 years to have the prescience to reach for our measure.

76. Where at least percent of the population is a racial or language minority, the VRA governs electoral practices and procedures. This law covers a vast and diverse election process where different types of representatives are elected and perform different functions. 42 U.S.C. sec. 1973 (1988).

77. See Guinier, "[E]racing Democracy," 118; and Abrams, "Relationships of Representation," 1418.

78. We may ask, How is any representation direct in a representative democracy? The representative stands for his constituency and between the state and his constituency. He represents and displaces them. They are in the legislature virtually, through his practice. In one sense, the representative directly represents the constituency. They elect him. But in deliberation, they are no more than virtually represented. The constituency that the representative represents is present only insofar as he approximates their interests and understands their plaints.

79. Guinier, *Tyranny of the Majority*, 133. Edmund Burke used the term "direct" to refer to those representatives who directly represented their constituency by dint of election. Guinier uses the nomenclature "actual" to refer to direct representatives who also share the experiences and interests of their constituency. She uses the example of blacks. Blacks have a particular interest that is actually represented when blacks are able to elect black representatives.

80. Were not all these conditions met, the representative might still be said to represent. However, it would no longer be the type of democratically authorized representation that we liberals have come to view as peculiar to our notion of democracy.

81. Stanley Fish, "Change," in his *Doing What Comes Naturally* (Durham, N.C.: Duke University Press, 1989) 141–60. Fish argues that discourse, the practice of a particular interpretive community, conserves and changes that community. There is no outside text or outside practice a member of an interpretive community can appeal to in order to ground the truth claims of her rhetoric or to stop the reinterpretation of those claims.

82. Pitkin describes the construction of effective representation in these terms: "[p]olitical representation is primarily a public, institutionalized arrangement involving many people and groups. . . . Representation should present a continuing but not hopeless challenge: to construct institutions and train individuals in such a way that they engage in the pursuit of the public interest, the genuine representation of the public; and, at the same time, to remain critical of those institutions and that training, so that they are always open to further interpretation and reform." Pitkin, *The Concept of Representation*, 221, 238, 240.

83. Issacharoff is troubled by politics intruding into districting. He advocates

computer-automated redistricting. Samuel Issacharoff, "Judging Politics: The Elusive Quest for Judicial Review of Political Fairness," 71 *Texas Law Review* 1643, 1697 (1993).

84. Karlan, "The Rights to Vote," 1733.

85. Aleinikoff and Issacharoff, "Race and Redistricting," 588.

86. The question remains since *Baker* v. *Carr*: How political must the Supreme Court become in this area? See *Baker* v. *Carr*, 369 U.S. 186 (1962) (Frankfurter, J., dissenting).

87. Issacharoff, "Judging Politics," 1762, decries "self-serving manipulation" of the districting process. It has become "a constitutional guarantee of sinecure for the pre-existing power base" of incumbents.

88. "Leaving strictly legal terminology aside . . . an agent is someone who 'does the actual work.'. . . When we call a man someone's agent we are saying that he is the tool or instrument by which the other acts. . . . When we call him a representative, on the other hand, we are saying not so much that he is a part or tool of the corporation as that the entire corporation is present in him." Pitkin, *The Concept of Representation*, 125, 122–25.

89. This is particularly true when we consider that the VRA explicitly means to alter the districting process by promoting the ability of minorities to elect candidates of their own choice. The fact that a law is in accord with our notion of the good does not make it any less political. It is simply part of the institutions and practices of our political community and will be manipulated by political agents, citizens, to gain political advantage.

90. Issacharoff succumbs to a belief in an apolitical standard, which is guided by principle and aided by technology, to save the apportionment process from politics. Issacharoff, "Judging Politics," 1703.

91. A vision uninfected by bias.

92. With respect to representation, difference politics creates the possibility for justice through the promotion of increased racial and ethnic diversity in electoral bodies.

93. "Partial" is defined as "belonging to or affecting a part only; not general; biased to one party; having a fondness." *New Expanded Webster's Dictionary*, 243.

94. For instance, Samuel Issacharoff wishes the courts to "leave behind the noxious doctrine of post facto judicial review of political fairness." "Judging Politics," 1703. Pildes and Niemi urge us to separate impulses from judicial doctrine and adopt a quantitative model of compactness for redistricting. Richard Pildes and Richard Niemi, "Expressive Harms, 'Bizarre Districts,' and Voting Rights: Evaluating Election-District Appearances After *Shaw* v. *Reno*," 92 *Michigan Law Review* 483 (1993).

95. I argue in Chapter 3 that this is not an altogether fantastic characterization of some reapportionment and redistricting practices under the VRA, the very piece of legislation passed to remedy antidemocratic practices that struck at the legitimacy of the political process. See Abigail Thernstrom, *Whose Votes Count?* (Cambridge, Mass.: Harvard University Press, 1987), 243; Carol Swain, *Black Faces, Black Interests* (Cambridge, Mass.: Harvard University Press, 1993), 200–205. Justice Thomas describes majority-minority districts created under the VRA as "political homelands." *Holder* v. *Hall*, 114 S.Ct. 2581, 2618 (1994) (Thomas, J., concurring in the judgment).

96. See Wendy Brown-Scott, "The Communitarian State," 107 *Harvard Law Review* 1209 (1994) arguing that communitarianism must be modified from a race-conscious perspective in order to be just. She proposes the eradication of racism; depriviledging whiteness; revamping civic institutions; relaxing the private–public distinction; and requiring the dominant community to accept responsibility for enslaving and subordinating people of color. Ibid., 1217, 1222–27. Also of relevance are Adeno Addis,

"Individualism, Communitarianism, and the Rights of Ethnic Minorities," 67 *Notre Dame Law Review* 615, 648–58 (1991); and Taibi, "Race Consciousness, Communitarianism, and Banking Regulation," 1992 *University of Illinois Law Review* 1103–6.

97. For a comprehensive summation of collective identities in our social and political institutions, see Amy Gutmann, "Introduction," in Amy Guttman, ed., *Multiculturalism: Examining the Politics of Recognition* (Princeton: Princeton University Press, 1994), 3–24.

98. Ibid., 6–8.

99. Here are exceptions. Consider law professor Mary Ann Glendon of Harvard, whose book *Rights Talk* is discussed herein. She is associated with the political right and is a leading communitarian theorist. See Sanford Levinson, "Book Review: Mary Ann Glendon, *A Nation Under Lawyers: How the Crisis in the Legal Profession Is Transforming American Society*," 45 *Journal of Legal Education* 143, 147–48 (1995). Conversely, Lani Guinier embraces liberal politics while advocating specific measures to achieve a political good characterized by her sense of group equality. It is hard to determine whether Guinier's objection is political, philosophical, or both when she alleges that the Reagan administration unduly politicized the enforcement of the VRA. Guinier, *The Tyranny of the Majority*, 21–40.

100. Lani Guinier, "Groups, Representation, and Race-Conscious Districting: A Case of the Emperor's Clothes," 71 *Texas Law Review* 1589, 1618, 1622, 1623 (1993); Abrams, "Relationships of Representation," 1426 (1993).

101. For Guinier, actual representation of blacks occurs when the representative is democratically elected shares the racial characteristics of her constituency.

102. Abrams, "Relationships of Representation," 1431.

103. Henry Louis Gates, Jr., "Let Them Talk," *The New Republic*, 20–27 September 1993: 46.

104. Certainly the VRA, which designates certain racial and language minorities as legally significant, helps us discern those politically important aspects of social situatedness.

105. Carol Swain, *Black Faces, Black Interests*, 21–23.

106. "Perfect accuracy of correspondence is impossible. This is true not only of political representation but also of representational art, maps, mirror images, samples and miniatures. So it is always a matter of what information we need, what features are to be reproduced and what will be significant. . . . In a general sense, we are very much aware that politically significant characteristics vary with time and place, and that the doctrines about them vary as well—consider religious affiliation. . . . The nation is not like a geographic area to be mapped—solidly there, more or less unchanging, certainly not changed by the map making process. . . . Descriptive representation is obviously relevant to political life, yet it is again only a partial view, and therefore deceptive in areas where it does not apply. We need only remind ourselves of some of the things it cannot do, aspects of political and other representation which it neglects. . . . At most a descriptive view of representation might be held to account for whether he has given accurate information about the constituents; and here selection by random sampling might well be more effective than elections. . . . If we restrict representing to the descriptive view, to a giving of information, then we cannot account for the other, conflicting ways in which the concept is used and we cannot explain how a governing executive represents." Pitkin, *The Concept of Representation*, 87, 89, 90, 91.

107. Daniel D. Polsby and Robert D. Popper, "Ugly: An Inquiry into the Problem of Racial Gerrymandering Under the Voting Rights Act," 92 *Michigan Law Review* 652, 666 (1993). See Pitkin, *The Concept of Representation*, 60. Adams's description of the legislature continues, "it should think, feel, reason and act like them. That it may be the

interest of this assembly to do strict justice at all times, it should be an equal representation, or, in other words, equal interests among the people should have equal interests in it." *The Political Writings of John Adams*, 86.

108. Adams argued that an aristocracy could represent as well as an elected assembly. Pitkin, *Concept of Representation,* 60–61, n.2 citing John Adams, "Defense of the Constitution of Government of the United States of America," in *The Works of John Adams* (Boston: Little, Brown, 1956), 284. In addition, Adams, *Political Writings*, 86.

109. Pitkin criticizes the portrait metaphor of proportional representation in the following manner. "The critics charge that a proportional system atomizes opinion, multiplies political groupings, increases the violence of faction, and prevents the formation of a stable majority. . . . They have not, but should, challenge the view of what representation means.   Yet representation does not have to be defined in terms of resemblance or correspondence. A representative must first of all be capable of effective action. . . . The history of art criticism demonstrates that artistic representation has always been a matter of style and convention, as well as of skill. A painting is not a photograph, and even photographs are not much like the objects they depict. Even in paintings of the most painstaking accuracy, the artist does not reproduce reality, but combines paint in complex ways on canvas. This is something an artist has to learn to do and a viewer has to learn to read." Pitkin, *The Concept of Representation*, 64, 65, 66.

110. Ibid., 187–88.

111. See Guinier, "[E]racing Democracy"; and Douglas Amy, *Real Choices/Real Voices* (New York: Columbia University Press, 1993), 106–11, 128–30.

112. There is an uncomfortable alliance between the Republican Party and minority officeholders and aspirants. Aleinikoff and Issacharoff, "Race and Redistricting," 589. Republican candidates may have benefited from the creation of majority-minority districts.   Some have asserted that maximizing Democratic electoral success meant creating no majority-minority districts. Pildes, "The Politics of Race," 1380–81, citing Bernard Grofman, Robert Griffin, and Amihai Glazer, "The Effect of Black Population on Electing Democrats and Liberals to the House of Representatives," 17 *Legislative Studies Quarterly* 365, 374 (1992).

113. Multi-member districts that are not racially discriminatory are acceptable.

114. Amy, *Real Choices*, 1–9; Karlan, "Maps and Misreadings: The Rule of Geographic Compactness in Racial Vote Dilution Litigation," 24 *Harvard Civil Rights–Civil Liberties Law Review* 173, 221 (1989); Lani Guinier, "The Representation of Minority Interests: The Question of Single-Member Districts," 14 *Cardozo Law Review* 1135, 1136 (1993).

115. Of course, this is circular reasoning, since gerrymandering requires boundaries. Doing away with or decreasing the number of political boundaries by definition lessens gerrymandering. Amy, *Real Choices*, 21–139.

116. A notable example is the National Front of France, headed by Jean Marie le Pen.

117. See Madison, "Federalist No. 48," in *The Federalist* for his views regarding the division and mediation of political power.

118. See Pildes, "The Politics of Race," 1365–76, for a discussion on the continuing pervasiveness of race in the South, where Section 5 and Section 2 of the Voting Rights Act transformed substantive black representation.

119. *Thornburg* v. *Gingles*, 478 U.S. 30, 62 (1986).

120. Amy, *Real Choices*, 21–24; Guinier, "The Representation of Minority Interests," 1137 (1993).

121. Polsby and Popper, "Ugly," 669, citing Rein Taagepera and Matthew Soberg Shugart, *Seats and Votes: The Effects and Determinants of Electoral Systems* (New

Haven: Yale University Press, 1989), 184–98.

122. See Abrams, "Relationships of Representation," 1418, on the link between governance and voting.

123. Guinier, "The Representation of Minority Interests," 1137.

124. Pamela Karlan, "All Over the Map: The Supreme Court's Voting Rights Trilogy," 1993 *Supreme Court Review* 245, 260–68 (1993); Neither Justice Thomas nor Justice Scalia subscribes to the results-oriented concept of vote dilution advocated by Karlan; they advance a narrower conception of what standard, practice, or procedure is covered by the Voting Rights Act. See *Holder* v. *Hall*, 129 L.Ed.2d 687, 702 (1994).

125. Polsby and Popper, "Ugly," 668.

126. Ibid., 671.

127. Guinier recognizes this and has criticized the use of majority-minority districts on accountability and authorization grounds. They may provide only "symbolic" representation. Guinier, "The Representation of Minority Interests," 1157–62.

128. Iris Marion Young, *Justice and the Politics of Difference* (Princeton: Princeton University Press, 1990), 10.

129. See Justice O'Connor's opinion in *Shaw* v. *Reno*, 125 L.Ed.2d 511 (1993); and Justice Kennedy's opinion in *Johnson* v. *DeGrandy*, 129 L.Ed.2d 775 (1994).

130. Young, *Justice and the Politics of Difference*, 43–44.

131. For commentary on race, the VRA and majority-minority districting, see Guinier, "The Representation of Minority Interests" (1993); Bernard Grofman, "Would Vince Lombardi Have Been Right if He Said: 'When It Comes to Redistricting, Race Isn't Everything, It's the Only Thing'?" 14 *Cardozo Law Review* 1237 (1993); Issacharoff, "Polarized Voting and the Political Process," 90 *Michigan Law Review* 1833 (1992); and Katherine Butler, "Reapportionment, the Courts and the Voting Rights Act: A Resegregation of the Political Process?" 56 *University of Colorado Law Review* 58 (1984).

132. An expansive reading is sometimes referred to as a reading "in the spirit of" the VRA, as opposed to one that apparently restricts itself to the bare language. A determination of whether a reading is expansive, literal, or in the spirit reflects the interpretive prejudices we bring to the reading and the interpretive community of which we are a part.

133. Young, *Justice and the Politics of Difference*, 157–68. Andrew Kull argues that the color-blind vision has not been and is not constitutional doctrine. In fact, color-blind rhetoric has not commanded a majority of the Supreme Court. Young's argument with respect to color-blindness is overstated if one subscribes to Kull's reading of legal history. Andrew Kull, *The Color-Blind Constitution* (Cambridge, Mass.: Harvard University Press, 1992).

134. "Feminist scholars have pointed out that the unencumbered individual is invariably male." Margaret Thornton, *The Liberal Promise: Anti-Discrimination Legislation in Australia* (Oxford: Oxford University Press, 1990), 8.

135. Concurrent with physical separation may be the phenomena of raised consciousness that produces a psychological solidarity with group identity. Ibid., 248. "The politics of group assertion takes as a basic principle that members of oppressed groups need separate organizations that exclude others, especially those from more privileged groups. Separate organization is probably necessary in order for these groups to discover and reinforce the positivity of their specific experience, to collapse and eliminate double consciousness." Young, *Justice and the Politics of Difference*, 167.

136. Ibid., 174.

137. Ibid., 185.

138. Ibid., 187.

139. Proponents of communal rights may discount the difficulty of putting such a plan into practice. "The danger of rights for collective entities is that they may operate as a means of entrenching the *status quo* of the dominant group as has happened with attempts to preserve racial entities. . . . there is also the problem of how one might conceptualize collective rights in a non-universalistic way." Ibid., 253.

140. Social scientists and biologists use the term "race" cautiously. Its political overtones can drown its efficacy as a category. Ibid., 47.

141. K. Anthony Appiah, "Identity, Authenticity, Survival," in Amy Gutmann, ed., *Multiculturalism: Examining the Politics of Recognition* (Princeton: Princeton University Press, 1994).

142. Young, *Justice and the Politics of Difference*, 5.

143. Melissa Williams, "Voice, Trust and Memory: Marginalized Groups and the Failings of Liberal Representation" (Ph.D. diss., Harvard University, 1993), 7. Changing social conditions or the majority's interpretations of history cannot challenge this claim.

144. Ibid., 25.

145. Ibid., 27.

146. Madison, "The Federalist No. 10," in *The Federalist*.

147. This reasoning is remarkably similar to the tone of the 1982 amendments to the VRA, particularly Section 2.

148. Pitkin reminds us there is no one theory of representation, and it remains something that political communities debate.

149. One of the more controversial decisions in this area, and one with which Williams vehemently disagrees is *City of Richmond* v. *Croson*, 109 S.Ct. 706, 727 (1989) where the Court, certainly a liberal institution, struck down preferences for blacks in Richmond on the basis of the Equal Protection Clause. Also consider *Adarand* v. *Pena,* 515 U.S. 200 (1995) (extending *Croson* to federal minority business set-aside programs) and *Hopwood* v. *Texas,* 84 F.3d 720 (1996) (group preferences and law school admissions).

150. Williams argues that "whereas liberal representation generally conceives of intergroup competition as salutary, members of marginalized groups tend to regard competition as inimical to their most fundamental political interests." Williams, "Voice, Trust and Memory," 93–95.

151. *Shaw* v. *Reno,* 125 L.Ed.2d 511 (1993); and *Gomillion* v. *Lightfoot.*

152. Melissa Williams, "Voice, Trust and Memory," 97–99. For liberal conceptions of equality, see John Rawls, *A Theory of Justice* (Cambridge, Mass.: Harvard University Press, 1971), 73; Isaiah Berlin, "Equality," in his *Concepts and Categories* (New York: Viking Press, 1979), 93. Some of the strongest critiques of liberal regimes focus on a substantive lack of equality, particularly material equality, among citizens. Anatole France noted, "The law, in its majestic equality, forbids all men to sleep under bridges, to beg in the streets, and to steal bread—the rich as well as the poor." Likewise, Proudhon remarked, "Property is theft."

153. How might this affect claims for equal representation by ethnic and racial minorities? By considering all individuals, despite their status, as equal political agents. "Difference exists but plays no role in the allocation of civil and political rights. Nor when there is equal opportunity does social difference affect competition for the scarce social goods mentioned above." Williams, "Voice, Trust and Memory," 102–3. Determining unequal opportunity is an exercise in regress; we cannot draw the line even at birth, since history precedes the individual.

154. Williams uses the phrase "difference politics," which is analogous to how I employ the term "race-conscious communitarianism."

155. In fact, this was part of the impetus behind the VRA.

156. Williams, "Voice, Trust and Memory," 135.

157. Young, *Justice and the Politics of Difference*, 185; Melissa Williams, "Voice, Trust and Memory," 304–5.

158. Charles Taylor, "The Politics of Recognition," in Amy Gutmann, ed., *Multiculturalism: Examining the Politics of Recognition* (Princeton: Princeton University Press, 1994), 32.

159. Ibid., 33.

160. Ibid., 36.

161. Ibid., 31.

162. See Martha Minow, *Making All the Difference* (Ithaca, N.Y.: Cornell University Press, 1990), 78.

163. Margaret Thornton notes that "discrimination is an essentially contextual concept whose application to specific phenomena is always in dispute because its meaning is shaped by changing human desires and attitudes towards things . . . and changing social forms." Thornton, *The Liberal Promise*, 2.

164. Taylor, "The Politics of Recognition," 34.

165. Ibid., 36.

166. Ibid., 37–38; Thornton, *The Liberal Promise*, 54: "Multiculturalism as an ideology argues that national unity arises from tolerated diversity."

167. Thornton, *The Liberal Promise*, 101, 203.

168. The color-blind application of the laws is closely linked with another concept: the rule-of-law. Under the rule-of-law, the law is applied objectively. The passions and prejudices of men do not influence it. It guarantees equal treatment to all who come before the law regardless of their status.

169. Taylor, "The Politics of Recognition," 39.

170. Thornton warns that there has been an unwillingness "to accept the existence of societal, structural or systematic discrimination." Thornton, *The Liberal Promise*, 71.

171. "While liberal ideology upholds the values of individualism, equality and community, the legal order is able to obscure the prevailing relations of inequality, domination and alienation. By treating all persons as equal, the legal order helps mask their inequality." Ibid., 14.

172. Taylor, "The Politics of Recognition," 40.

173. The liberal ideal, Taylor asserts, "insists on uniform application of the rules defining these rights, without exception, and (b) it is suspicious of collective goals. . . . it can't accommodate what the members of distinct societies really aspire to, which is survival. This is (b) a collective goal, which (a) inevitably will call for some variations in the kinds of law we deem permissible from one cultural context to another, as the Quebec case clearly shows." Ibid., 61, 57.

174. Appiah, "Identity, Authenticity, Survival," 159.

175. "It is familiarly thought that the bureaucratic categories of identity must come up short before the vagaries of actual people's lives. But it is equally important to bear in mind that a politics of identity can be counted on to transform the identities on whose behalf it ostensibly labors. Between the politics of recognition and the politics of compulsion, there is no bright line." Ibid., 163.

176. Ibid., 155–56.

177. Thornton, *The Liberal Promise*, 63.

178. Pitkin, *The Concept of Representation*, 209.

179. "To allow such a move is to undercut the central liberal commitment to the freedom and autonomy of individual citizens, for it allows the state to ascribe political beliefs and preferences to individuals on the grounds of their group membership, rather than preserving a system that gives them the freedom to express their views on an

individual basis." Williams, "Voice, Trust and Memory," 142.

180. "The commitment to political equality, viewed through the lens of deliberative democracy, bans large disparities in the political influence held by different social groups." Cass Sunstein, *The Partial Constitution* (Cambridge, Mass.: Harvard University Press, 1993), 138.

181. This is elucidated in Section 2 of the VRA.

CHAPTER 2: RHETORIC AND THE APPEARANCES OF REPRESENTATION

1. I conceive of the "legal community" in broad terms. It includes, obviously, judges, lawyers, and law professors. It also includes others who comment on and affect the legal community's practices, such as political scientists, sociologists, historians, and journalists.

2. Later in the chapter, I discuss the effectiveness of storytelling as a rhetorical device and explain how it is explicitly employed by advocates of difference politics as a stratagem to promote a particular political agenda.

3. This is thought to be central to storytelling or discourse in the margins.

4. The vitality of our colonial patrimony does not make the use of the "Founding Fathers" less mythic. The "Founding Fathers" are, in part, persuasive of the historical antecedents to which we are privy.

5. There is no reason why archetypal legal argumentation cannot employ rational argumentation and tell a passionate myth. Some of the most effective legal arguments weave the two together so that it is hard to tell where the law stops and the passion and myth begin. See *Shaw* v. *Barr (Reno)*, No. 92-357, "Appellants' Brief on the Merits" (1992).

6. They also fought for it in the legislatures.

7. The Court's uneasiness with racial classifications in recent VRA cases, such as *Shaw* v. *Reno*, 125 L.Ed.2d 511, 113 S.Ct. 2831 (1993), and *Miller* v. *Johnson*, 132 L.Ed.2d 762, 1995 U.S. LEXIS 4462 consistent rulings in other areas of the law, and forfends a final decision as to how racial classifications may be used. See *Piscataway* v. *Taxman*, 91 F.3d 1547, 117 S.Ct. 2506 (1997) (subsequently settled by cash payment from civil rights groups to avoid a Supreme Court ruling on Title VII); *Hopwood* v. *Texas*, 84 F.3d 720 (1996) (law school admissions); and California's much discussed Proposition 209 (restricting group preferences).

8. In Chapter 3, I illustrate Supreme Court rhetoric in the context of representation jurisprudence by examining the language of Supreme Court opinions. I argue that Supreme Court justices employ either liberal or communitarian rhetoric, and sometimes both, when deciding reapportionment cases. The questions that a justice asks and the answers that a justice frames differ when a justice employs liberal as opposed to communitarian oratory.

9. Tropes are figures of speech. Tropes work because there is the belief that some words work literally or give a plain meaning. When tropes work effectively, we no longer recognize them as figures of speech. They read literally. Functioning as tropes, they are no longer tropes. Depending on the reader, "equal protection" and "right" may or may not function as tropes.

10. They disguise assumptions insofar as it is not always rhetorically effective to announce assumptions directly nor is the speaker necessarily conscious of his or her assumptions.

11. Here "story" refers to all types of legal narratives: the parties' briefs, law review articles, and appellate court decisions. Something is extra-textual or prelegal when it

justifies the decision exterior to the interpretive dispute.

12. The interpretive community that uses particular words and phrases in the context of fair representation—*e.g.*, "equitable," "fair," or "compact"—understands these words within a range of meaning that characterizes that community.

13. I use the term "authenticate" to mean proving something to be genuine or authoritative. Authors authorize. They prove the circumstances within which their discourses evoke meaning.

14. That is, members of an interpretive community have a rough idea of the limits of a sensible argument. Yet, these limits change. The standards of the community change, and they change through debate within the community over the interpretive limits of the words and phrases members use to form their arguments.

15. Here, "metalanguage" refers to the logic of language, a superlanguage, uninfected with uncertainty that misleads the reader and author as to authentic meaning.

16. Descriptions are rhetorical in that they are open to more than one interpretation. Our interpretations are contingent upon how we find the words, the interpretive community of which we are a part, and ambiguity in elocution.

17. Something is a subtext when it is not originally read. A subtext reveals new meanings that we see because figurative, as opposed to literal, discourse becomes apparent. The number of subtexts is limited only by our imagination. The distinction between what is text and subtext changes as we discriminate among meanings that were not previously apparent.

18. For instance, a Supreme Court decision such as *Shaw* v. *Reno* is a narrative about districting in North Carolina. It is also a narrative about the tension between the conservative and liberal factions on the Court and the larger struggle over the limits of affirmative action. *Shaw* v. *Reno* is also a narrative about fair representation within a particular politico-historical context. Just as there may be many subtexts, so there are also many narratives told within any particular text.

19. It persuades at the level at which we recognize a narrative as a particular written or spoken form though we may remain unpersuaded at the level of agreeing with the speaker or author.

20. Pierre Bourdieu, *Outline of a Theory of Practice* (Cambridge: Cambridge University Press, 1977), 164–65.

21. I do not, of course, argue against the promotion of racial and ethnic equality. But it is one thing to work toward it and another to believe that the way you follow delimits other conceptions of racial and ethnic equality. In the end, the promotion of racial and ethnic equality is pure politics. By presenting the quest as a transcendent truth, some may attempt to limit the debate or sacralize the terms of the debate.

22. Joanne Kovacich, "The Impact of Law and Policy on the Social Construction of 'Culture,'" paper presented at the *Law and Society Association* annual conference (1994); Ian F. Haney Lopez, "The Social Construction of Race: Some Observations on Illusion, Fabrication, and Choice," 29 *Harvard Civil Rights–Civil Liberties Law Review* 1 (1994).

23. Here "objective" is used to mean "static." When things are not dynamic, their presentment remains in doubt. We might doubt whether such an objectivity is recognizable.

24. For instance, Section 2 of the VRA affords minority voters "the opportunity to elect candidates of their own choice." As interpreted, it means minority voters are expected to elect candidates from their ethnic group and that certain remedies will be put into place to ensure that this happens. The interpretation of this phrase may change as our understanding of minority voters and opportunity, not to mention choice and representation, fits different political conditions.

25. Naming something a "gerrymander" reflects a political determination, though

the rhetoric of science and the law may be employed.

26. See Jacques Derrida, "Force of the Law: The Mystical Foundations of Authority," in David G. Carlson, Drucilla Cornell, and Michael Rosenfeld, eds., *Deconstruction and the Possibility of Justice* (New York: Routledge, 1992), 190.

27. Code words are figures of speech, (*i.e.*, tropes). For instance, "diversity" does not refer to just any heterogeneous conglomeration. In representation, "diversity" refers to certain minorities and minority candidates.

28. Of course, how we recognize diversity is as important as the recognition.

29. Amy Gutmann, "Introduction," in Gutmann, ed., *Multiculturalism: Examining the Politics of Recognition* (Princeton: Princeton University Press, 1994), 3–4.

30. Not all diversity is recognized. Promoting diversity among publicly elected officials means discriminating among possible types of diversity. The VRA promotes racial and language minority diversity. It does not promote diversity of officials in terms of disabilities, sexual diversity, sexual preference, wealth, or religion.

31. See Martha Minow, *Making All the Difference* (Ithaca, N.Y.: Cornell University Press, 1990), for an optimistic view of inclusive diversity.

32. Recognizing diversity is not necessarily illiberal. For Amy Gutmann, if we treat a "secure cultural context" as a basic prerequisite for exercising civil and political liberties, then departing from neutrality in the name of recognizing diversity is not necessarily at odds with "rule-of-law" liberalism. Gutmann, "Introduction," 4–5.

33. How does one establish which claims are authoritative and provoke the law into action?

34. Robin West, "The Supreme Court, 1989 Term—Foreword: Taking Freedom Seriously," 104 *Harvard Law Review* 43 (1990).

35. K. Anthony Appiah, "Identity, Authenticity, Survival: Multicultural Societies and Social Reproduction," in Amy Gutmann, ed., *Multiculturalism: Examining the Politics of Recognition* (Princeton: Princeton University Press, 1994), 153.

36. Ibid., 155.

37. Labels such as "critical race theory" and "race-conscious communitarianism" run the risk of overgeneralizing. It is not the case that all critical race theorists subscribe to a communitarian political theory. On the other hand, many critical race theorists are race-conscious communitarians and may view race-conscious communitarianism as an effective tool to accomplish the goals of their critical race politics.

38. The sanctified voice grounds the truth claims of the speaker. Voicing an alternative liturgy risks apostasy. With this mechanism in place, the group can police its boundaries. The authenticity of the voice is thereby sacrelized. Sacredness depends upon the essentialization of group boundaries. Uncovering the rhetorical structure of the truth claim casts the truth claims of the speaker into doubt. See Stanley Fish, "Rhetoric," in his *Doing What Comes Naturally* (Durham, N.C.: Duke University Press, 1989), 490–94.

39. The minority representative is one whose rhetoric is informed by membership in a marginal collectivity. Identity informs his or her situatedness. The person voices the perspective of the collectivity. A minority representative is a group member elected by the group to voice its needs, experiences, and perspective.

40. See Richard Delgado and Jean Stefanic, " 'Critical Race Theory': An Annotated Bibliography," 79 *Virginia Law Review* 461 (1993), citing Robin D. Barnes, "Race Consciousness: The Thematic Content of Racial Distinctiveness in Critical Race Scholarship," 103 *Harvard Law Review* 1864 (1990); John Calmore, "Critical Race Theory, Archie Shepp and Fire Music: Securing an Authentic Intellectual Life in a Multicultural World," 65 *Southern California Law Review* 2129 (1992); and John Calmore, "Exploring the Significance of Race and Class in Representing the Black Poor,"

61 *Oregon Law Review* 201 (1982).

41. For instance, Justice Clarence Thomas and Professor Shelby Steele were singled out for their opposition to the current form of affirmative action. Commentators characterized them as conservative and not representative of the black community. See Richard Delgado, "Rodrigo's Third Chronicle: Care, Competition, and the Redemptive Tragedy of Race," 81 *California Law Review* 387, 411 n115 (1993); Samuel Starks, "Note: Understanding Government Affirmative Action and *Metro Broadcasting, Inc.*," 1991 *Duke Law Journal* 933, 967 n211 (1992); Monica Evans, "Stealing Away: Black Women, Outlaw Culture, and the Rhetoric of Rights," 28 *Harvard Civil Rights–Civil Liberties Law Review* 263, 285 (1993); and Barbara Stark, "Postmodern Rhetoric, Economic Rights and an International Text: 'A Miracle for Breakfast,' " 33 *Virginia Journal of International Law* 433, 447 (1993).

42. M. M. Slaughter, "The Multicultural Self," 14 *Cardozo Law Review* 885 (1993).

43. Robin West, "Toward a First Amendment Jurisprudence of Respect: A Comment on George Fletcher's Constitutional Identity," 14 *Cardozo Law Review* 759, 762 (1993).

44. Opposed to dominant or conventional legal scholarship, voice scholarship expresses the concerns and viewpoints of the Other. Arthur Austin, "Deconstructing Voice Scholarship," 30 *Houston Law Review* 1671, 1673 (1993), citing Stephanie B. Goldberg, "The Law, a New Theory Holds, Has a White Voice," *New York Times*, 17 July 1992, A23. For an archetype of voice scholarship, see Patricia J. Williams, "Alchemical Notes: Reconstructing Ideals from Deconstructed Rights," 22 *Harvard Civil Rights–Civil Liberties Law Review* 401, 409 (1987). The Other, whether defined by sex, religion, ethnicity, race, or sexual preference, "suffered historical under-representation and silencing in the law schools." Austin, "Deconstructing Voice Scholarship," 1672.

45. "The assumption that the works they create transparently convey the authentic, unmediated experience of their social identities, though officially renounced, has crept quietly in through the back door." Austin, "Deconstructing Voice Scholarship," 1673, citing Henry L. Gates, Jr., "Authenticity, or the Lesson of Little Tree," *New York Times Book Review*, 24 November 1991, 1. "Social space" refers to those sets of institutions and collective representations that allow for and situate the individual in social life. See Lucie E. White, "The Legacy of *Goldberg* v. *Kelly:* A Twenty Year Perspective: *Goldberg* v. *Kelly* on the Paradox of Lawyering for the Poor," 56 *Brooklyn Law Review* 861 (1990).

46. The outsider's voice articulates politico-legal criticisms while telling the story of marginality.

47. Kathryn Abrams, "Relationships of Representation in Voting Rights Act Jurisprudence," 71 *Texas Law Review* 1409, 1431–33 (1995).

48. Race and sex are not the only means by which to claim marginal status. Foremost, the rhetoric of otherness involves making a politico-historical assertion about individual and group situatedness.

49. Austin, "Deconstructing Voice Scholarship," 1674, citing Randall Kennedy, "Racial Critiques of Legal Academia," 102 *Harvard Law Review* 1745, 1759 (1989).

50. Ironically, the VRA, a law deliberated and passed by a series of privileged, white, male Congresses, is the very model of dominant rhetoric.

51. By "privileged discourse" I mean, for example, that mode of expression that is heard by the courts as evincing a lawyerly argument. In theory any defendant in a criminal trial could defend himself. This is most often foolhardy. The reason for this, beyond the superior resources of the attorney, is that an attorney speaks in a lexicon that makes use of a legal taxonomy the court understands. The defendant most often does not. Hence, the attorney speaks a privileged discourse.

52. Iris Marion Young, *Justice and the Politics of Difference* (Princeton: Princeton University Press, 1990), 117.   Young wishes to escape the rhetoric of rational argumentation for something unsullied and pure. It is this I call "antirhetoric." It is not vulnerable to reinterpretation or co-optation by rational discourse.   It remains free, mythic, passionate, and poetic.

53. Ibid., 157–58. What we lack are an emancipatory politics and a new standard of equality.

54. These maladies include arbitrary social status distinctions, an ambiguous standard of equality contingent on social group status, and circumvention of the individual by social group membership.

55. Mary Ann Glendon, *Rights Talk* (Toronto: Macmillan, 1991). She distinguishes between communitarian and liberal rights talk.

56. Ibid., 67.

57. Ibid., 75.

58. The nature of what we mean by "social" is abstracted from our personal practices. No specific type of community intrinsically corresponds to "social" despite the familiar incantation about the social construction of human existence.

59. *Baker* v. *Carr*, 369 U.S. 186, 272 (1962); *Wesberry* v. *Sanders*, 376 U.S. 1 (1963); *Miller* v. *Johnson*, 132 L.Ed.2d 762 (1995); and *Johnson* v. *DeGrandy*, 129 L.Ed.2d 775 (1994).

60. Glendon, *Rights Talk*, 75.

61. *Reynolds* v. *Sims*, 377 U.S. 533, 621–25 (1964) (Harlan, J., dissenting).

62. For example, see *Fullilove* v. *Klutznick*, 448 U.S. 448, 65 L.Ed.2d 902, 100 S.Ct. 2758 (1980) (Minority Business Enterprise set-asides); *Asian Americans for Equality* v. *Koch*, 129 Misc.2d 67, 492 N.Y.S.2d 837 (1985) (minority housing in Chinatown); and *Morse* v. *Republican Party of Virginia*, 1996 U.S. LEXIS 2164, *10 (association rights of Republican Party v. individual right to vote absent barriers such as a poll tax). Recognition of communal interests is ubiquitous in the law. However, this does not mean that every communal interest is voiced or that a particular communal interest will enjoy success in court. Also, Justices Kennedy and Breyer in *Abrams* v. *Johnson*, 1997 WL 331802, manipulated liberal and communitarian versions of the polity in their opinions.

63. It asserts and conserves the state as the font of political authority. Moreover, it negotiates the relationship of the state to the people and articulates a hierarchy among the branches of government.

64. *Shaw* v. *Reno*, 125 L.Ed.2d 511 (1993) (redistricting and vote dilution).

65. The VRA promotes the representation of communities excluded from political office in many parts of the country.

66. See Bourdieu, *Outline of a Theory of Practice*.

67. See John Hart Ely, *Democracy and Distrust* (Cambridge, Mass.: Harvard University Press, 1980), 135–79 on "the representation reinforcing role," of the United States Supreme Court. The Court may act in a counter-majoritarian fashion to promote the participation and representation of excluded minorities in the political community. This counter-majoritarian role is not antidemocratic, but necessary when the majority acts to make impossible the representation of whole classes of people. The Court attempts to keep the political community from degenerating when majorities choke off the channels of political participation.

68. See Joel B. Grossman and Richard Wells, *Constitutional Law and Judicial Policy Making*, 3d ed. (New York: Longman, 1989), 286.

69. *Frontiero* v. *Richardson*, 411 U.S. 677 (1971) (sex); *City of Cleburne* v. *Cleburne Living Centers Inc.*, 473 U.S. 432 (1985) (mental retardation); *Bowers* v. *Hardwick*, 478 U.S. 186 (1986) (sexual orientation); *San Antonio Independent School*

District v. *Rodriguez*, 411 U.S. 1 (1973) (wealth).

70. For instance, the VRA recognizes blacks and certain language minorities as groups in need of special protection.

71. Madison and Hamilton warned about the tendency of factions to divide the political community. See James Madison, "Federalist No. 10," and Alexander Hamilton, "The Federalist No. 9," in *The Federalist* (New York: Modern Library, 1960).

72. For a historical description of the longing for a color-blind constitution, see Andrew Kull, *The Color-Blind Constitution* (Cambridge, Mass.: Harvard University Press, 1992), 164.

73. John Dunne, "Remarks," in "Redistricting in the 1990s: The New York Example," 14 *Cardozo Law Review* 1119, 1122–23 (1993). On the necessity of race-conscious redistricting where racial bloc voting has been a historical fact.

74. Actions we find to be unfair or unwarranted are often those that affect us adversely.

75. Niccolo Machiavelli, *The Prince*, in *The Prince and the Discourses*, Luigi Ricci, trans. (New York: Random House, 1940), 62. Machiavelli speaks of a prince exercising state power. The construction and maintenance of legal taxonomies are applications of state power.

76. They are artifices. By definition these strike us as unnatural and draw our notice.

77. I use "unnatural" to mean power appropriations that appear brazen and unnecessary. Niccolo Machiavelli, *The Prince*, 56–57, 63–77.

78. Some categories, such as property ownership, are likely to be familiar to those who employ the law.

79. Promoting diversity of public officials is problematic for political liberals. The goal of increasing the number of blacks, women, and Hispanics in public office has cost the Democratic party political power. One of the reasons for the oddly shaped electoral district in North Carolina that gave rise to the challenge in *Shaw I* was the desire to protect Democratic incumbents and increase the number of black representatives.

80. Marc Galanter, "Why the Haves Come Out Ahead: Speculations on the Limits of Legal Change," 9 *Law and Society Review* 95–160 (1974). Empirical research demonstrates that the institutional players, the repeat players, tend to come out ahead.

81. Gregory Caldeira, "Litigation, Lobbying and the Voting Rights Act," in Bernard Grofman and Chandler Davidson, eds., *Controversies in Minority Voting* (Washington, D.C.: Brookings Institution, 1992), 242.

82. Hannah Pitkin, *Wittgenstein and Justice* (Berkeley: University of California Press, 1972), citing Sheldon S. Wolin, *Politics and Vision* (Boston and Toronto: Little, Brown, 1960), 43. Lani Guinier describes three succeeding generations of VRA litigation. Guinier, *The Tyranny of the Majority* (New York: Free Press, 1994), 48.

83. Bernard Grofman, "Would Vince Lombardi Have Been Right if He Said: 'When It Comes to Redistricting, Race Isn't Everything, It's the Only Thing'?" 14 *Cardozo Law Review* 1237, 1244 (1993).

84. *Shaw* v. *Barr (Reno)*, No. 92-357, "Appellants' Brief on the Merits" (1992), 29–32.

85. T. Alexander Aleinikoff and Samuel Issacharoff, "Race and Redistricting: Drawing Constitutional Lines After *Shaw* v. *Reno*," 92 *Michigan Law Review* 588, 591 (1993).

86. *Shaw* v. *Barr (Reno)*, "Appellants' Brief on the Merits," 29.

87. *Jacobellis* v. *Ohio*, 378 U.S. 184 (1964).

88. See Pamela Karlan, "End of the Second Reconstruction? Voting Rights and the Court," *The Nation*, 23 May 1994, 698–700. Karlan can be criticized for asking the

Court to look past appearances and into the reality of the situation. But the reality of the situation must also appear to us and be interpreted. And even if it is all appearances, the Court still must give the impression that it is looking past how things look and into how things really are.

89. For a confused Court aware that it is stepping into increasingly muddy waters see *Shaw* v. *Hunt*, 1996 U.S. LEXIS 3880; and *Bush* v. *Vera* 1996 U.S. LEXIS 3882.

90. "*Shaw* might be read as merely 'cueing' states to the need to comply with the Equal Protection Clause when making districting decisions." It might be conceived as "a shot across the bow" to all parties involved in the districting process. It is a means to get the attention of the various interested participants. Aleinikoff and Issacharoff, "Race and Redistricting," 603.

91. Ibid., 604.

92. The Court derives some institutional authority because it is not perceived to be as infected with politics as the executive and legislative branches. Moreover, judges lack the specific expertise and local knowledge to get involved with reapportionment. Getting the courts involved in this process unnecessarily politicizes the courts and endangers their institutional authority. Frankfurter and Harlan in *Baker* v. *Carr*, 362 U.S. 186, 272 (1962 (Frankfurter, J., dissenting); *Baker* v. *Carr*, at 334 (Harlan, J., dissenting); and Harlan in *Reynolds* v. *Sims*, 377 U.S. 533, 598 (1964) (Harlan, J., dissenting) criticized the Supreme Court's entry into the reapportionment process, recognizing that apportionment reflects legislative judgment.

93. He was not considering the issue of race because this was not the issue in *Baker*.

94. See Robert G. McCloskey, "The Supreme Court, 1961 Term—Foreword: The Reapportionment Case," 76 *Harvard Law Review* 54 (1962).

95. In fact, the Court's recent decision has been castigated as "judicial activism," as opposed to thoughtful "judicial restraint." David Kairys, "Conference: The Supreme Court, Racial Politics, and the Right to Vote: *Shaw* v. *Reno* and the Future of the Voting Rights Act," 44 *American University Law Review* 1, 11 (1994).

96. The Supreme Court may come into conflict with the Attorney General and the President.

97. Richard Pildes and Richard Niemi, "Expressive Harms, 'Bizarre Districts,' and Voting Rights: Evaluating Election-District Appearances After *Shaw* v. *Reno*," 92 *Michigan Law Review* 483, 507 (1993).

98. Authentic collective understandings refer to those beliefs around which Pildes and Niemi believe there is a consensus. These beliefs are "solid" enough to guide the Court through the shoals of constitutional interpretation. The existence of these beliefs for Pildes and Niemi, I believe, enables them to advocate a particular rhetorical strategy while disclaiming political motive.

99. Pildes and Niemi, "Expressive Harms," 508.

100. An expressive harm "expresses" a policy that harms the political community. For instance, the 12th Congressional District in *Shaw* expressed the necessity of segregating blacks from whites in order to increase black representation. Does the story of the expressive wrong speak to us? If it does, why? If it does not, why not? Because debates over democracy and race inspire strong partisan responses, it is likely that these stories of majority-minority districts will continue to speak to us.

101. New York State has a large population in comparison with most states, but much of that population is concentrated in New York City. The population of New York State is not distributed evenly.

102. Pildes and Niemi, "Expressive Harms," 528.

103. If compactness differs from context to context, the Court will seem inconsistent. But the Court may be taking into account the very local differences that

make a jurisdiction politically meaningful.

104. Pildes and Niemi, "Expressive Harms," 528.

105. The aesthetics of the 12th Congressional District in *Shaw I*—it was serpentine—was a major part of the controversy.

106. Terry Eagleton, *The Ideology of the Aesthetic* (Cambridge, Mass.: Blackwell, 1990).

107. *Dillard* v. *Baldwin County Board of Education*, 686 F.Supp. 1459, 1465 (M.D. Ala. 1988).

108. We could describe this ideal, depending on our viewpoint, as symmetrical or beautiful.

109. Pildes and Niemi, "Expressive Harms," 567.

110. The important point to take away from these figures is that if we are to apply a standard of compactness when determining the legality of a district, majority-minority districts will be adversely affected in comparison with white districts. The VRA, as interpreted, results in a disproportionate number of "extremely noncompact" districts to facilitate the election of minority candidates. These noncompact majority-minority districts are concentrated in just a few states. Over 75 percent of extremely noncompact districts are in Florida, Louisiana, New York, North Carolina, and Texas. Pildes and Niemi, "Expressive Harms," 567. All of these states have substantial minority populations and are covered, in part, by Section 5.

111. Aleinikoff and Issacharoff, "Race and Redistricting," 605. Internal citations omitted.

112. In fact, O'Connor recognized that race was the primary issue in *Shaw I*. A tenet of critical race theory is that law and politics are thoroughly imbued with considerations of race. We can hardly think legally and politically without thinking racially. This insight is irrefutable, which makes it so useful.

113. See *Miller* v. *Johnson*, 132 L.Ed.2d 762 (1995).

114. See *Shaw* v. *Hunt*, 861 F. Supp. 408 (E.D.N.C. 1994). This district was later found unconstitutional in *Shaw* v. *Hunt*, 1996 U.S. LEXIS 3880.

115. The idea is that a joke is funny up to a point. After that point, it ceases to be funny and may be insulting. In the area of fair representation, certain arguments for fair representation may strike us as reasonable if not persuasive. After a certain point, they are no longer reasonable and inspire strong opposition.

116. Aleinikoff and Issacharoff, "Race and Redistricting," 609.

117. See Jacques Derrida, who historicizes and politicizes the *"res publica"* in his critique of Francis Fukuyama's *The End of History and the Last Man*. Derrida, *Specters of Marx* (New York: Routledge, 1994), 79.

118. Aleinikoff and Issacharoff, "Race and Redistricting," 611.

119. *Shaw* v. *Barr (Reno)*, "Appellants' Brief on the Merits," 31.

120. Aleinikoff and Issacharoff, "Race and Redistricting," 611.

121. It is difficult to separate rhetoric from the phenomena it purports to describe. I do not claim this is possible. I merely assert that our description changes that which we describe.

CHAPTER 3: CASE ANALYSES OF FAIR REPRESENTATION ANTE *SHAW* v. *RENO*

1. Kenneth Burke speaks of the rhetoric of motive and the grammar of motive. Generally, he explicates motive as desire, the engine. Liberal and communitarian narratives found in Supreme Court opinions attempt to account for race in the jurisprudence of representation, but the opinions never capture the motives of the cases in

such a manner as to end further litigation of the subject. See Kenneth Burke, *Language as Symbolic Action* (Berkeley: University of California Press, 1968), 480–506.

2. Factions of all types: political; religious; racial; and otherwise.

3. The Supreme Court first articulated the one person, one vote standards in *Gray* v. *Sanders*, 372 U.S. 368 (1963) and *Wesberry* v. *Sanders*, 376 U.S. 1 (1964).

4. *Reynolds* v. *Sims*, 377 U.S. 533, 559 (1964).

5. Ibid.

6. Ibid., 559–60, citing *Wesberry* v. *Sanders*.

7. Isaiah Berlin, "Two Concepts of Liberty," in Michael Sandel, ed., *Liberalism and Its Critics* (New York: New York University Press, 1984), 22–23.

8. Friedrich Hayek, "Equality, Value, and Merit," in Michael Sandel, ed., *Liberalism and Its Critics* (New York: New York University Press, 1984), 80.

9. Even if we encode a nonhierarchical legal system, whatever this might mean, it becomes decidedly hierarchical as society changes. There is simply not a social reality out there shorn of interpretation, and law, for the law to decipher and codify.

10. *Reynolds*, 377 U.S. at 542–43.

11. Ibid., 546.

12. Ibid., 554.

13. Ibid., 555.

14. Ibid.

15. Ibid., 558.

16. Ibid., 567 (internal citation omitted).

17. See generally, James Madison, "Federalist No. 10," in *The Federalist* (New York: Modern Library, 1960).

18. Parts of social reality became things. Hence, ethno-racial groups were not only more or less ill-defined political factions whose membership was in constant flux, but actual things, hard to the touch that could subsequently be used by lawyers. An artifact is, according to *Webster's,* an object made by man with a view for future use. In the context of voting rights and fair representation, "artifact" aptly refers to divisions in the law used to make sense of the political community. *Webster's New Universal Unabridged Dictionary* (New York: Barnes & Noble, 1989), 84.

19. As discussed in Chapter 1, Hannah Pitkin argued that the main cleavage in Western societies was religion. Our senses of faction and representation change. Hannah Pitkin, *The Concept of Representation* (Berkeley: University of California Press, 1967), 60–91. It still is the case that religion is a divisive force.

20. Daniel Polsby and Robert Popper, "Ugly: An Inquiry into the Problem of Racial Gerrymandering Under the Voting Rights Act," 92 *Michigan Law Review* 652, 654 (1993). Racial gerrymandering occurs where more than one race competes for political power in a racially polarized environment. The difference here is that gerrymander occurs under the color of the VRA, particularly Section 2.

21. *Reynolds*, 377 U.S. at 561, citing *Wesberry*, 376 U.S. 1, 8 (1964).

22. Ibid., 579.

23. See Andrew Kull, *The Color-Blind Constitution* (Cambridge, Mass.: Harvard University Press, 1992) for an excellent exegesis on the subject of the "color-blind" Constitution and how the notion of color-blindness has and has not been appropriated by various Supreme Court Justices.

24. In the context of fair representation, the notion of equality plays a central role. For instance, equal protection jurisprudence is enlisted to determine some aspects of vote dilution claims or remedies. Likewise, under the VRA, fair and equitable representation presumes equal access to the ballot, rough equality of result, and equal worth of the vote.

25. This is not to argue that to some, blindness means no recognition of race and

ethnicity.

26. This is true in some but not all circumstances. The VRA is blind to sex but not to race. In Chapter 4, I discuss the Court's uneasiness with race-consciousness in *Miller* v. *Johnson* and *Shaw* v. *Reno*.

27. I do not contend that Harlan identified himself as a communitarian, but that his opinion was consistent with philosophical communitarianism.

28. *Reynolds*, 377 U.S. at 622 (Harlan, J., dissenting).

29. Ibid., 623–24.

30. *Baker* v. *Carr*, 369 U.S. 186, 209 (1962).

31. *Colgrove* v. *Green*, 328 U.S. 549, 556 (1946). See generally Larry Alexander, "Lost in the Political Thicket," 41 *Florida Law Review* 563 (1989).

32. Bernard Grofman, "Would Vince Lombardi Have Been Right if He Said: 'When It Comes to Redistricting, Race Isn't Everything, It's the Only Thing'?" 14 *Cardozo Law Review* 1237, 1268–69 (1993).

33. In other words, it was meant to protect the individual black's right to vote. William Gillette, *The Right to Vote* (Baltimore: Johns Hopkins University Press, 1969), 12.

34. *South Carolina* v. *Katzenbach*, 383 U.S. 301, 342 (1966).

35. Discrimination is not the same thing as retrogression, though discrimination may be used as evidence of retrogression. For example, discrimination originally meant denying blacks the right to vote in the South and in a few other parts of the country. It also contemplated numerical disproportionality in the weight of votes across a particular jurisdiction. Discrimination was later found in electoral mechanisms such as multi-member or at-large districts enacted for the purpose, or with the effect, of keeping blacks out of political office. Electoral practices that decrease the opportunities of minorities to elect minorities may violate the nonretrogression principle.

36. Katherine Butler, "Reapportionment, the Courts and the Voting Rights Act: A Resegregation of the Political Process?" 56 *University of Colorado Law Review*, 58–65 (1984).

37. Lani Guinier argues that this promotion of legislative diversity was based on four principles: (1) they are authentic psychological and cultural role models; (2) their election mobilizes black voter participation; (3) their election reduces electoral polarization by transforming cross-racial contact from the anonymity and ignorance of the ballot box to the intimacy and expertise of the legislature; and (4) black representatives respond to the needs of all their constituents, including blacks. Lani Guinier, "The Triumph of Tokenism," in her *The Tyranny of the Majority* (New York: Free Press, 1994), 41.

38. Kull, *The Color-Blind Constitution*, 211.

39. Abigail Thernstrom, *Whose Votes Count?* (Cambridge, Mass.: Harvard University Press, 1987), 49–51.

40. Kull, *The Color-Blind Constitution*, 118. Kull argues that the Court's treatment of race in the context of the VRA is consistent with Justice Brown's opinion in *Plessy* v. *Ferguson*, 163 U.S. 537 (1896).

41. When the Court applies strict scrutiny to race-conscious legislation, it evaluates what is reasonable in terms of "compelling state interests" and "narrowly tailored means." Some race-conscious legislation strikes a chord with such historical resonance that the boundaries of what is reasonable become quite narrow.

42. If legislation employs racial categories that adversely affect a historically discriminated-against racial group, the Court will normally apply strict scrutiny to determine its constitutionality. *San Antonio Independent School District* v. *Rodriguez*, 411 U.S. 1, 16–22 (1973). The legislation creates the conditions by which it is judged

and recognized.

43. Another form of discrimination may be how the census is actually tallied. The census tends to undercount the poor and members of some minority groups. Steven Holmes, "Plans for the 2000 Census Are Challenged on 2 Fronts," *New York Times*, 6 June 1996, A14. The use of ethnic and racial categories in the census may perpetuate a race-conscious description of the political community.

44. Affirmative action has been attacked as discriminatory and unconstitutional. See *Adarand* v. *Pena*, 515 U.S. 200 (1995) (percentage of minority contracts); *Hopwood* v. *Texas*, 84 F.3d 720 (1996) (law school admissions); and *Piscataway* v. *Taxman*, 91 F.3d 1547, 117 S.Ct. 2506 (1997) (minority teacher retention).

45. Kull, *The Color-Blind Constitution*, 121. Harlan opposed government classifications; he also agreed that whites were superior to Negroes.

46. *Plessy*, 163 U.S. at 559 (Harlan, J., dissenting).

47. This was meant to be an aspiration rather than a description by Harlan. When he was writing, the Constitution denied women suffrage. But even if we accept that the Constitution attempted to be color-blind, society was not. The Civil War was a fresh memory, and Northern troops had only recently been pulled out of the South. By *Plessy*, white supremacists were already wresting control of the Southern state legislatures from the freedmen, scalawags, and carpetbaggers. However, it is hard to make the case that Harlan stood, from an interpretive standpoint, on firm ground. The 13th, 14th, and 15th Amendments did take race into account, were culturally specific to American slavery and the Civil War, and attacked the antebellum social and political framework of the American South.

48. Cass Sunstein, *The Partial Constitution* (Cambridge, Mass.: Harvard University Press, 1993), 78–79.

49. Kull, *The Color-Blind Constitution*, 146.

50. U.S. Department of Labor, Office of Policy Planning and Research, *The Negro Family: The Case for National Action* (March 1965), in Kull, *The Color-Blind Constitution*, 184–85.

51. Abigail Thernstrom, *Whose Votes Count?* 124–26.

52. *Fortson* v. *Dorsey*, 379 U.S. 433, 439 (1965). This was a 14th Amendment case considering the constitutionality of Georgia's state Senate districts.

53. *Allen* v. *State Board of Elections*, 393 U.S. 544 (1969). This was a VRA case that consolidated suits involving Mississippi and Virginia.

54. Ibid., 565.

55. States covered by the nonretrogression principle in Section 5 of the VRA are, for the most part, Southern states, which denied blacks the right to vote. Section 5 was expanded to cover parts of the North where voter participation among minorities had been low during the 1968 elections. Under the VRA, any change in voting practice or procedure by these states must be precleared with the Justice Department or, alternatively, these states may seek a declaratory judgment from the District Court of the District of Columbia.

56. *Allen*, 393 U.S. at 597 (Black, J., dissenting).

57. Self-identification allows the state to claim it is simply legalizing predefined social categories. However, laws and society, the state and social groups, influence with which social groups the individual self-identifies. This is individual agency of a sort, but it is not a sort devoid of legal, political or social influence.

58. Pamela Karlan, "Maps and Misreadings: The Role of Geographic Compactness in Racial Vote Dilution Litigation," 24 *Harvard Civil Rights–Civil Liberties Law Review* 173, 176 (1989), citing *Whitcomb* v. *Chavis*, 403 U.S. 124, 142 (1971).

59. *Whitcomb* v. *Chavis*, 403 U.S. 124, 158–59 (1971).

60. *White* v. *Regester*, 412 U.S. 755, 766 (1973).

61. Thernstrom, *Whose Votes Count?* 150.

62. *Whitcomb*, 403 U.S. at 149.

63. For instance, only two blacks had been elected to the Texas State House of Representatives from Dallas County. *White*, 412 U.S. at 756.

64. Ibid., 756.

65. *City of Richmond* v. *United States*, 422 U.S. 358, 370–71 (1975).

66. *Beer*, 425 U.S. 130, 141 (1976).

67. Thernstrom, *Whose Votes Count?* 51–53.

68. Lani Guinier, *The Tyranny of the Majority*, 119–56.

69. Thernstrom, *Whose Votes Count?* 137–91.

70. Social justice is not prepolitical or prelegal. Yet, the task of the reapportioner is to appear to be as apolitical as possible. This means drawing electoral districts, which reflect those political distributions that are so accepted, so much a part of the background, in a way that patterns of dominance and submission are submerged. When the reapportioner departs from this order suddenly or explicitly, she reveals forgotten anomalies.

71. In this sense, we may say that social justice is not objective, although we may, and do, objectify our notions of it.

72. See Jennifer Hochschild, *What Is Fair? American Beliefs About Distributive Justice* (Cambridge, Mass.: Harvard University Press, 1981).

73. Kenneth Burke, *A Rhetoric of Motives* (New York: George Braziller, 1955), 23–27.

74. *United Jewish Organizations of Williamsburg, Inc.* v. *Carey*, 430 U.S. 144 (1977).

75. The recognition and aggregation of minorities under the VRA remains a substantially debated issue. See Katherine Butler and Richard Murray, "Minority Vote Dilution Suits and the Problem of Two Minority Groups: Can a 'Rainbow Coalition' Claim the Protection of the Voting Rights Act?" 21 *Pacific Law Journal* 619 (1990).

76. T. Alexander Aleinikoff and Samuel Issacharoff, "Race and Redistricting: Drawing Constitutional Lines After *Shaw* v. *Reno*," 92 *Michigan Law Review* 588, 594 (1993), citing *UJO*, 430 U.S. at 165 (opinion of White, J.).

77. In this case, Hasidic identity in the field of ethno-legal group valuation occupied a subordinate legal position to that of blacks. The Hasidim were not as politically or legally salable as were blacks.

78. It is hard to argue that race is socially constructed while maintaining a definition of the racial group that stands outside of interpretation. It is a question of choosing between mutually incompatible understandings of group constitution. For a remarkably different appraisal, see Aleinikoff and Issacharoff, "Race and Redistricting," 597.

79. Guinier, *Tyranny of the Majority*, 138. As I understand her argument, Guinier misinterprets Hannah Pitkin as somehow arguing that descriptive characteristics are a readable guide to how a representative will perform.

80. Pitkin, *The Concept of Representation*, 174, citing Edmund Burke, *Burke's Politics* (internal citations omitted).

81. Carol Swain, *Black Faces, Black Interests* (Cambridge, Mass.: Harvard University Press, 1993) 34–37.

82. Alexander Yanos, "Note: Reconciling the Right to Vote with the Voting Rights Act," 92 *Columbia Law Review* 1810, 1852 n232 (1992); Abigail Thernstrom, "More Notes from a Political Thicket," 44 *Emory Law Journal* 911, 934–35 (1995).

83. Congresswoman Barbara Jordan, upon enactment of the VRA, noted that it was strong medicine. For its invasiveness of state practices, the VRA was a special piece of

legislation. Cited in Thernstrom, *Whose Votes Count?* 53.

84. Pamela Karlan and Daryl Levinson, "Why Voting Is Different," 84 *California Law Review* 1201 (1996).

85. Lani Guinier, "No Two Seats: The Elusive Quest for Political Equality," 77 *Virginia Law Review* 1413 (1991).

86. *Metro Broadcasting, Inc.* v. *FCC*, 497 U.S. 547, 621 (1990) (O'Connor, J., dissenting).

87. Glenn C. Loury distinguishes among more and less extreme versions of and justifications for affirmative action. Loury, "The Conservative Line on Race," *Harper's*, November 1997, 144–54 reviewing Stephan Thernstrom and Abigail Thernstrom, *America in Black and White: One Nation, Indivisible* (New York: Simon & Schuster, 1997).

88. This redistricting resulted from reapportionment after the 1990 census. The conflict culminated in *Johnson* v. *DeGrandy*, 129 L.Ed.2d 775 (1993).

89. Ibid. It was argued in the brief of the Florida State NAACP that when black and Hispanic interests conflict, the Court should favor black interests.

90. Aleinikoff and Issacharoff, "Race and Redistricting," 631 quoting Larry Rohter, "A Black-Hispanic Struggle Over Florida Redistricting," *New York Times*, 30 May 1992, A6, quoting State Rep. James C. Burke.

91. Alexander Bickel, *The Morality of Consent* (New Haven: Yale University Press, 1975), 133.

92. Ibid., 133.

93. Alexander Bickel, *The Supreme Court and the Idea of Progress* (New York: Harper and Row, 1970), 81–87.

94. Consider the practice of law at the level of the Supreme Court. Cases are argued only after having filtered through an arduous appellate process. The issues that reach the Court are narrowly defined to fit into legal categories, though of course these categories can expand and contract. Nonetheless, everything is done according to a very specific procedure. When the Court does decide a case, and issue a written decision, it makes law. Of course, the decision is open to further interpretation by litigants, the Court, and other branches of government. The point is that the law is made in a particular fashion and that process serves to legitimate the law. The Clerk of the Supreme Court now has a packet for parties who wish to petition the Court *via* a *writ of certiorari*. This packet explains how the litigant is to prepare her petition and leaves few potential questions of form unanswered.

95. Consider the right of convicted felons to a "direct appeal." This is guaranteed by statute and by constitutional case law. In Wisconsin, felons may ask the trial court and the state appellate court to consider post-conviction motions or appeals pursuant to sec. 809.30, Wis. Stats. The direct appeal is necessary to check the power of the state. It also guards against incompetent or ineffective trial counsel. Finally, it may be a means to overturn the decision of a judge who has abused his or her discretion or simply misapplied the law. The direct appeal gives the appearance of evening the playing field for the convicted. In practice, the direct appeal may not operate so effectively and it is vulnerable to many of the same political and human pressures that pervade the trial court.

96. John Hart Ely, *Democracy and Distrust* (Cambridge, Mass.: Harvard University Press, 1980), 101–4.

97. *Mobile* v. *Bolden*, 446 U.S. 55 (1980).

98. Stewart stressed the necessity of showing purposeful discrimination and not relying merely on the effects of systematic patterns of failure. *Mobile*, 446 U.S. at 71 (opinion of Stewart, J.).

99. Ibid., 63.

100. Ibid., 446 U.S. at 83 (Stevens, J., concurring in judgment).

101. Ibid., 88.

102. *Rogers* v. *Lodge*, 458 U.S. 613 (1982).

103. "Necessarily, an invidious discriminatory purpose may often be inferred from the totality of the relevant facts." Ibid., 617.

104. Ibid., 623.

105. Section 2(b) of the VRA as amended in 1982. 42 U.S.C. sec. 1973.

106. This assumes that we can imagine a totality where race is not a factor or where race is used as we believe it ought to be used.

107. Electoral results are clear and clean-cut measurements for federal courts examining the legality of electoral practices.

108. Richard Pildes and Richard Niemi, "Expressive Harms, 'Bizarre Districts,' and Voting Rights: Evaluating Election-District Appearances After *Shaw* v. *Reno*," 92 *Michigan Law Review* 483, 486 (1993).

109. *Karcher* v. *Daggett*, 462 U.S. 725 (1983).

110. Ibid., 743.

111. Ibid., 740–44.

112. Ibid., 462 U.S. at 752, 762 (Stevens, J., concurring).

113. *Thornburg* v. *Gingles*, 478 U.S. 30 (1986).

114. Ibid., 50–51.

115. Ibid., 35.

116. Ibid., 63, 68, 76.

117. Ibid., 80.

118. Ibid., 478 U.S. at 96 (O'Connor, J., dissenting).

119. Polsby and Popper, "Ugly," 657.

120. Guinier, *Tyranny of the Majority*, 157–82. Guinier contrasts her own views, as a party to the litigation in *Thornburg*, with the color-blind solution advanced by Solicitor General Charles Fried.

121. Polsby and Popper, "Ugly," 659.

122. *Growe* v. *Emison*, 113 S.Ct. 1075 (1993).

123. Polsby and Popper, "Ugly," 659.

124. Lani Guinier, "The Representation of Minority Interests: The Question of Single-Member Districts," 14 *Cardozo Law Review* 1135, 1172 (1993).

125. *Davis* v. *Bandemeer*, 478 U.S. 109, 119 (1986).

126. Ibid., 124.

127. Ibid., 156, citing *United Jewish Organizations of Williamsburg, Inc.* v. *Carey*, 430 U.S. at 171, n.1 (Brennan, J., concurring).

128. Pildes and Niemi, "Expressive Harms," 489.

129. *Houston Lawyers' Assn.* v. *Attorney General of Texas*, 111 S.Ct. 2376 (1991), and *Chisom* v. *Roemer*, 111 S.Ct. 2354 (1991).

130. *Houston Lawyers' Assn*, 111 S.Ct. at 2379.

131. *Chisom*, 111 S.Ct. at 2359.

132. Ibid., 2361.

133. Lawyers argue as to whether a contract is to be read narrowly or expansively. When they say narrowly, they commonly mean something close to literally. It means what it says. The problem is, if it meant what it says and all parties knew it, they would not have this dispute. Likewise, when they say broadly, they mean something like, "Let us see if this interpretation reflects the spirit of the agreement." The problem is that they may not agree on the spirit of a particular agreement. There will be subsequent litigation meant to return the interpretation of the agreement to what it really means or simply says. This is often the refrain heard from Justices Scalia and Thomas in the area of fair

representation.

134. *Chisom*, 111 S.Ct. at 2366.

135. Ibid., 2368.

136. Ibid., 2369 (Scalia, J., dissenting).

137. Ibid., 2374, 2375.

138. *Presley* v. *Etowah County Commission*, 112 S.Ct. 820 (1992), was considered wrongly decided by many voting rights activists. See Kathryn Abrams, "Relationships of Representation in Voting Rights Act Jurisprudence," 71 *Texas Law Review* 1409, 1412 (1995).

139. The relevant standard, absent intervening changes, was those practices in existence on 1 November 1964.

140. After the election of the black commissioner to a "Common Fund Resolution" was passed by four holdover white commissioners that reduced the power of the county commissioners. This altered the practice of allowing each commissioner the authority to determine how to spend road funds within his district.

141. *Presley,* 112 S.Ct. at 829, 832.

142. Ibid., 833 (Stevens, J., dissenting).

143. Abrams, "Relationships of Representation," 1418.

144. Pamela Karlan, "The Rights to Vote: Some Pessimism About Formalism," 71 *Texas Law Review* 1705, 1726 (1993).

145. Pamela Karlan, "All Over the Map: The Supreme Court's Voting Rights Trilogy," 1993 *Supreme Court Review* 245, 254.

146. *Growe* v. *Emison*, 113 S.Ct. 1075 (1993).

147. Ibid., 1083.

148. Ibid., 1085. One of the parties offered law review articles as evidence of racial bloc voting. Law review articles describing racial bloc voting are not a substitute for searching analysis.

149. *Voinovich* v. *Quilter*, 113 S.Ct. 1149 (1993).

150. The concept of influence districts is advocated by Guinier, "Groups, Representation, and Race-Conscious Districting: A Case of the Emperor's Clothes," 71 *Texas Law Review* 1589, 1624, 1633 (1993); and Abrams, "Relationships of Representation," 1435.

151. *Voinovich* v. *Quilter*, 1155.

152. Ibid., 1156–58.

153. Carol Swain, *Black Faces, Black Interests*, 207–8. She claims that we may be at the limits of creating new single member, majority-minority districts. Blacks must look to other strategies, such as coalition building, to increase their numbers in Congress. At the time this was written, there were thirty-six black Representatives from majority-minority districts and three black Representatives from districts that do not have a black majority.

154. Aleinikoff and Issacharoff, "Race and Redistricting," 589.

155. Ibid., 590. Aleinikoff and Issacharoff assert that there were four such cases prior to the 1990 round of redistricting: *Garza* v. *County of Los Angeles,* 918 F.2d 763 (9th Cir. 1990); *White* v. *Daniel,* 909 F.2d 99 (4th Cir. 1990); *Armour* v. *Ohio,* 895 F.2d 1078 (6th Cir. 1990); and *Washington* v. *Tensas Parish Sch. Bd.* 819 F.2d 609 (5th Cir. 1987).

CHAPTER 4: *SHAW* v. *RENO*: WHAT IT MEANS, DOES NOT MEAN, AND WHY

1. *Shaw* v. *Reno*, 125 L.Ed.2d 511 (1993).

2. Todd Purdum, "President Gives Fervent Support to Fighting Bias," *New York Times*, 20 July 1995, A1, defending affirmative action in general.

3. If the state can make such a case, it can withstand strict scrutiny. This became a major issue in subsequent cases.

4. This refers to the 14th and 15th Amendments to the United States Constitution.

5. *Wesberry* v. *Sanders*, 376 U.S. 1 (1964); *Reynolds* v. *Sims*, 377 U.S. 533 (1964); *Gomillion* v. *Lightfoot*, 364 U.S. 339 (1960); *Smith* v. *Allwright*, 321 U.S. 649 (1944); and *Terry* v. *Adams*, 345 U.S. 461 (1953).

6. *United Jewish Organizations of Williamsburg, Inc.* v. *Carey*, 430 U.S. 144 (1977).

7. *South Carolina* v. *Katzenbach*, 383 U.S. 301 (1966).

8. *Presley* v. *Etowah County Commission*, 112 S.Ct. 820 (1992).

9. *Miller* v. *Johnson*, 132 L.Ed.2d 762 (1995).

10. Steven A. Holmes, *New York Times*, "White House to Suspend a Program for Minorities," 8 March 1996, A1, A10.

11. *Los Angeles County* v. *Garza*, 918 F.2d 763 (9th Cir. 1990), *cert. denied*, 111 S.Ct. 681 (1991).

12. *Clinton* v. *Jeffers*, 730 F.Supp. 196, 198 (D.C.E.Ark. 1990), *affirmed*, 111 S.Ct. 662 (1991).

13. See *Growe* v. *Emison*, 113 S.Ct. 1075 (1993) and *Voinovich* v. *Quilter*, 113 S.Ct. 1149 (1993).

14. The covered jurisdictions are predominantly in the South and have large black or Hispanic minorities. The states covered in their entirety are Alabama, Alaska, Georgia, Louisiana, Mississippi, South Carolina, and Virginia. In addition, portions of North Carolina, Arizona, Hawaii, and Idaho are covered.

15. John Dunne, "Remarks," in "Redistricting in the 1990s: The New York Example," 14 *Cardozo Law Review* 1127, 1128–29 (1993).

16. 42 USC sec. 1973.

17. With structural discrimination, we do not recognize intent. There is no smoking gun. It often goes unrecognized unless attention is brought to its consequences, such as disparate results among groups.

18. T. Alexander Aleinikoff and Samuel Issacharoff, "Race and Redistricting: Drawing Constitutional Lines After *Shaw* v. *Reno*," 92 *Michigan Law Review* 588, 639 (1993).

19. Consider the case of *Voinovich* v. *Quilter* (see n.13 above).

20. In Chapter 3, I discussed how Congress amended the VRA in 1982 to eliminate the requirement that plaintiffs allege and prove purposive discrimination.

21. Thernstrom stressed the political power play by blacks, other interested civil rights activists, and the Democratic Party. The VRA was strengthened despite the fact that it accomplished much of what it had been created for in 1965.

22. *Morse* v. *Republican Party of Virginia*, 1996 U.S. LEXIS 2164. A $35 to $45 registration fee for the Virginia Republican convention was interpreted to be a poll tax in violation of the VRA.

23. This was true because each minority accounted for over 5 percent of the population, voted as a bloc and could form a viable majority-minority district. A 5 percent threshold is required to trigger Section 2.

24. Richard Pildes and Richard Niemi, "Expressive Harms, 'Bizarre Districts,' and Voting Rights: Evaluating Election-District Appearances After *Shaw* v. *Reno*," 92 *Michigan Law Review* 483, 550 (1993), citing Michael Barone and Grant Ujifusa, *The Almanac of American Politics 1994*, ed. Eleanor Evans, 1250–51, 1275–76 (New York: Dutton, 1993).

25. See *Voinovich* v. *Quilter*, 113 S.Ct. at 1157; *Chisom* v. *Roemer*, 111 S.Ct. 2354, 2376 (1991) (Kennedy, J., dissenting).

26. Aleinikoff and Issacharoff, "Race and Redistricting," 639; *Shaw* v. *Reno*, 113 S.Ct. 2816, 2831 (1993).

27. Pildes and Niemi, "Expressive Harms," 488.

28. Those states affected by Section 5 were required to preclear their reapportionment plan with either the Justice Department or the district court for the District of Columbia.

29. One of the reasons the 12th Congressional District in North Carolina looked so odd was that North Carolina Democrats attempted both to save their seats and to create majority-minority districts. There was a way to create two relatively compact majority-minority districts in North Carolina, but this would have meant the loss of at least one Democratic seat.

30. C. Vann Woodward, *Reunion and Relations: The Compromise of 1877 and the End of Reconstruction*, 2d ed. (Garden City, N.Y.: Doubleday, 1956), 45, 229–30, 232–33; and J. Morgan Kousser, *The Shaping of Southern Politics: Suffrage Restriction and the Establishment of the One-Party South* (New Haven: Yale University Press, 1974), 1–265.

31. Aleinikoff and Issacharoff, "Race and Redistricting," 590–91.

32. See Katherine Butler, "Reapportionment, the Courts and the Voting Rights Act: A Resegregation of the Political Process?" 56 *University of Colorado Law Review* 58 (1984); Andrew Kull, *The Color-Blind Constitution* (Cambridge, Mass.: Harvard University Press, 1992); and Abigail Thernstrom, *Whose Votes Count?* (Cambridge, Mass.: Harvard University Press, 1987).

33. Pildes and Niemi, "Expressive Harms," 561.

34. The black legislative coalition was a powerful player in the Democratic Party and lobbied for two, not one, majority-minority districts. Ibid., 489.

35. Daniel Polsby and Robert Popper, "Ugly: An Inquiry into the Problem of Racial Gerrymandering Under the Voting Rights Act," 92 *Michigan Law Review* 652, 661 (1992).

36. Pildes and Niemi, "Expressive Harms," 566.

37. Aleinikoff and Issacharoff, "Race and Redistricting," 591.

38. *Voinovich* v. *Quilter*, 113 S.Ct. 1149 (1993); and *Growe* v. *Emison*, 113 S.Ct. 1075 (1993).

39. Carol Swain, *Black Faces, Black Interests* (Cambridge, Mass.: Harvard University Press, 1993), 207.

40. Joan Biskupic, "White Voters Challenge Black-Majority Map," *Washington Post*, 20 April 1993, A4.

41. As mentioned earlier in this chapter, litigants can seek Section 5 approval in the form of preclearance from the Attorney General or declaratory judgment from the federal district court of the District of Columbia. Most litigants prefer to seek preclearance. Pildes and Niemi, "Expressive Harms," 490, n.30, citing Drew S. Days III, "Section 5 and the Role of the Justice Department," in Bernard Grofman and Chandler Davidson, eds., *Controversies in Minority Voting* (Washington, D.C.: Brookings Institution, 1992), 53, 53 n.2.

42. *Shaw* v. *Reno*, 113 S.Ct. 2816, 2823 (1993). At this stage of the litigation, the plaintiffs were procedurally the appellants.

43. Ibid., 2824 (internal cites omitted). The majority in *Shaw I* did not articulate a "right" to participate in a "color-blind" election, though it did use the rhetoric of "color-blind," procedural neutrality to cast its decision.

44. Ibid.

45. Here we may substitute "artificial" for "contorted." Of course, for there to be a contortion, some contrivance must be at work.

46. Hannah Pitkin, *The Concept of Representation* (Berkeley: University of California Press, 1967), 66–67.

47. Pildes and Niemi, "Expressive Harms," 502.

48. Polsby and Popper, "Ugly," citing "I-85 No Route to Congress," *Raleigh News & Observer*, 13 January 1992, A8. Also, Bernard Grofman, "Would Vince Lombardi Have Been Right if He Said, 'When It Comes to Redistricting, Race Isn't Everything, It's the Only Thing'?" 14 *Cardozo Law Review* 1237, 1261 (1993).

49. Pildes and Niemi, "Expressive Harms," 493.

50. Ibid.

51. Ibid. "Vote dilution and district appearance claims share no common conceptual elements."

52. Consider the assertion of various totalitarian regimes this century, such as the USSR, China, or Nazi Germany. Legitimacy was constituted in the total concentration of political power in the state. Dissent was minuscule or nonexistent because the state left no room for such activities.

53. This is why the changing debate over the legality and fairness of political representation in the United States is so necessary and, at times, vociferous. We might argue that political representation is always unfair to some parties because there is room for differing standards of fairness.

54. As noted previously, whites are not a protected group under the VRA, and therefore could not invoke the protections of the VRA because they suffered vote dilution.

55. Pildes and Niemi, "Expressive Harms," 494.

56. Ibid., 494.

57. Recall that the plaintiffs in *UJO* unsuccessfully articulated a constitutional vote dilution claim.

58. *Shaw* v. *Reno*, 125 L.Ed.2d at 523.

59. Ibid., 525. This stance echoed her dissent in *Metro Broadcasting*, in which she noted, "The right to equal protection of the laws is a personal right. . . . securing to each individual an immunity from treatment predicated simply on membership in a particular racial or ethnic group." *Metro Broadcasting, Inc.* v. *FCC*, 497 U.S. 547 (1990) (O'Connor, J., dissenting). Contrast this with the reasoning put forth by Patricia Williams in her law review article, which stresses that the "property interests of large numbers of white individuals are understood to be in irreconcilable tension with the collective dispossession of large numbers of people of color." Patricia J. Williams, "*Metro Broadcasting, Inc.* v. *FCC:* Regrouping in Singular Times," 104 *Harvard Law Review* 525 (1990).

60. *Shaw* v. *Reno*, 125 L.Ed.2d at 529, citing *Wright* v. *Rockefeller*, 376 U.S. 52, 66–67 (1964) (Douglas, J., dissenting).

61. Ibid., 525, citing *Hirabayashi* v. *U.S.,* 320 U.S. 81, 100 (1943).

62. Pildes and Niemi, "Expressive Harms," 500.

63. Ibid., 503.

64. Andrew Kull argues that the apotheosis of color-blind jurisprudence occurred in the early 1960's. See *Goss* v. *Bd. of Ed. of Knoxville*, 373 U.S. 683, 687–88 (1963); *Abington* v. *Schempp*, 374 U.S. 203, 317 (1963) (Stewart, J., dissenting); and *Bell* v. *Maryland*, 378 U.S. 226, 287–88 (1964) (Goldberg, J., concurring), all advocating a color-blind jurisprudence. Cited in Andrew Kull, *The Color-Blind Constitution*, 156–66. These decisions mirror Harlan's dissent in *Plessy*, where he declared "Our Constitution is color-blind, and neither knows nor tolerates classes among citizens." *Plessy* v. *Ferguson*,

163 U.S. 537, 559 (1896), cited in Kull, *The Color-Blind Constitution*, 123.

65. The politically liberal Justice Stevens, writing for the majority in *Morse* v. *Republican Party of Virginia*, 1996 U.S. LEXIS 2164, recalls the liberal rhetoric he used with such effectiveness over fifteen years earlier when dissenting in *Fullilove* v. *Klutznick*, 448 U.S. 448 (1980). In *Shaw I*, Justice Stevens in dissent articulated a race-conscious communitarian narrative with which to defend the 12th Congressional District in particular and majority-minority districting in general.

66. *Shaw* v. *Reno*, 125 L.Ed.2d at 526. O'Connor's view seems to draw heavily on Hayek's theory of equality and merit. Hayek felt it was essential that people of different races be treated equally under the law despite the fact this would lead to unequal results. To do otherwise would restrain individual liberty and undermine notions of merit. Friedrich Hayek, *The Constitution of Liberty* (Chicago: University of Chicago Press, 1960).

67. Polsby and Popper, "Ugly," 663.

68. *Shaw* v. *Reno*, 125 L.Ed.2d at 529.

69. Ibid, 530. An article in the *New York Times* hints at a growing weariness with race-based politics. Voters are more concerned with who can make their cities work and "will take them in whatever shapes, sizes and colors they come in." Politicians who exploit racial animosity have grown tiresome. Voters are more likely to respond to politicians who focus on economic issues and seem to have workable plans. Peter Applebome, "Results Hint at New Indifference to Race," *New York Times*, 4 November 1993, A11.

70. This is one of the metademocratic critiques made by Lani Guinier in *The Tyranny of the Majority* (New York: Free Press, 1994) and by John Hart Ely in *Democracy and Distrust* (Cambridge, Mass.: Harvard University Press, 1980).

71. Justices White, Stevens, Souter, and Blackmun dissented.

72. The results may be roughly the same, but consider the different goals of the Republican Party and the black parties in *Shaw I*. The Republican Party was not overly concerned with assuring the direct representation of blacks in North Carolina. They wanted to create majority-minority districts and thereby weaken the electoral base of Democrats in nearby districts. This strategy would in the end create more black and more Republican officeholders. Black officeholders in North Carolina are not ordinarily Republicans. Nonetheless, the creation of majority-minority districts sometimes means the sacrifice of a white Democratic incumbent. So blacks and Democrats may be at cross-purposes. The attempt to reconcile black demands for more majority-minority districts and Democratic concerns to protect incumbents resulted in the bizarrely shaped North Carolina 12th Congressional District.

73. Pildes and Niemi, "Expressive Harms," 501.

74. *Shaw* v. *Reno*, 125 L.Ed.2d at 538 (White, J., dissenting).

75. Not only is North Carolina a state with a segregationist history, but the nonretrogression principle of Section 5 of the VRA mandates that race be considered in all aspects of its reapportionment process.

76. *Shaw* v. *Reno*, 125 L.Ed.2d at 540 (White, J., dissenting).

77. Such a low threshold of measuring political empowerment is not to be applied to blacks and other minorities under Section 2.

78. See Jürgen Habermas, *Between Facts and Norms: Contributions to a Discourse Theory of Law and Democracy*, trans., William Rehg (Cambridge, Mass.: MIT Press, 1996), chs. 4–6.

79. *Shaw* v. *Reno*, 125 L.Ed.2d at 548 (White, J., dissenting).

80. Ibid., 125 L.Ed.2d at 548 (Blackmun, J., dissenting).

81. Ibid., 125 L.Ed.2d at 549 (Stevens, J., dissenting).

82. See Richard Rorty, *Contingency, Irony and Solidarity* (Cambridge: Cambridge University Press, 1989) and *Philosophy and the Mirror of Nature* (Princeton: Princeton University Press, 1979), on shaping the perceptions of what we see.

83. *Shaw* v. *Reno*, 125 L.Ed.2d at 549 (Stevens, J., dissenting). I do not mean to assert that Stevens's political preference drove his estimation of *Shaw I* to the exclusion of *stare decisis*. Rather, case precedent and Stevens's politics are part of the same practice that begets his *ratio decidendi*.

84. Ibid., 125 L.Ed.2d at 550 (Stevens, J., dissenting).

85. *Fullilove* v. *Klutznick*, 100 S.Ct. 2758, 2783–84 (1980) (Stevens, J., dissenting). Justice Stewart also attacked the government's vague use of race in *Fullilove* as a means to treat groups of people differently. *Fullilove*, 100 S.Ct. at 2797, citing *Plessy* v. *Ferguson*, 163 U.S. 537, 539 (1896) (Harlan, J., dissenting). See *University of California Regents* v. *Bakke*, 438 U.S. 265, 408–21 (Stevens, J., concurring in the judgment in part and dissenting in part), expressing Stevens's uneasiness with state use of racial classification to distribute resources.

86. Communal voting patterns may or may not conflate with racial bloc voting. This was the case in *Shaw I* where it was presumed that blacks would vote for blacks and that the majority would vote so as to frustrate the election of a black candidate. The history of elections in North Carolina demonstrated that this was the case.

87. See Abigail Thernstrom, "More Notes from a Political Thicket," 44 *Emory Law Journal* 911, 933–35 (1995); Jeffrey Hamilton, "Comment: Deeper into the Political Thicket: Racial and Political Gerrymandering and the Supreme Court," 43 *Emory Law Journal* 1519, 1547–48 (1994). This is the view held by those who believe direct (and actual) representation hinges on speaking in an authentic voice.

88. *Shaw* v. *Reno*, 125 L.Ed.2d at 552 (Souter, J., dissenting).

89. See *Johnson* v. *DeGrandy*, 129 L.Ed.2d 775 (1994).

90. That is, there is insight in blindness, but not of the kind we purposefully eschew. Rather, it is insight into that which we do not know how to see or even to desire to see.

91. Even if race is the primary issue in contention, the justices also account for the political background in order to situate race.

92. *City of Cleburne* v. *Cleburne Living Centers, Inc.*, 473 U.S. 432, 455, 459 (1985) (Marshall, J., concurring in the judgment in part and dissenting in part) and *Plessy* v. *Ferguson*, 163 U.S. 537 (1896).

93. *Shaw* v. *Reno*, 125 L.Ed.2d at 552 (Souter, J., dissenting).

94. Roberto Unger, "Critical Legal Studies," 96 *Harvard Law Review* 561, 602 (1982).

95. Mari Matsuda, "Public Response to Racist Speech: Considering the Victim's Story," 87 *Michigan Law Review* 2320 (1989).

96. This is true insofar as democracy conflates with communal claims to political representation.

97. W. Cole Durham, Jr., "Rhetorical Resonance and Constitutional Vision," 14 *Cardozo Law Review* 893, 902 (1993).

98. Ibid., 894, 897.

99. The district court held that the districting plan did meet the exacting standards of strict scrutiny, and that decision was appealed.

100. This is a misplaced belief and not borne out in Court opinions. The Court put limits on the VRA.

101. *Holder* v. *Hall*, 129 L.Ed.2d 687 (1994).

102. Ibid., 692–93.

103. Ibid., 693–96.

104. Ibid., 700 (O'Connor, J., concurring in part, concurring in judgment).

105. See *Chisom* v. *Roemer*, 111 S.Ct. 2354 (1991) (Scalia, J., dissenting).

106. It is ironic that judges complain they are ill equipped to engage in political theory when Supreme Court justices are some of the most accomplished practitioners of political theory. Of course, they sometimes must, in the name of judicial restraint, avow that they are not practicing political theory but are merely interpreting and applying the law.

107. In fact, Thomas cites Frankfurter: "to choose among competing bases of representation—ultimately, really, among competing theories of political philosophy." *Holder*, L.Ed.2d at 705 (Thomas, J., concurring in part, concurring in judgment), citing *Baker* v. *Carr*, 369 U.S. 186, 300 (Frankfurter, J., dissenting). On the other hand, Chief Justice John Marshall had no difficulty articulating political theory where he saw the chance, and it is as a justice who articulated a strong theory of judicial review that Marshall is best remembered.

108. Professor Girardeau Spann questions the likelihood that the Supreme Court will act in a counter-majoritarian fashion in the face of opposition by the majority. This is a warning for those who look to the Supreme Court to defend consistently the representational rights of minorities. Spann, *Race Against the Court: The Supreme Court and Minorities in Contemporary America* (New York: New York University Press, 1993).

109. *Holder*, 129 L.Ed.2d at 702, 703 (Thomas, J., concurring in part, concurring in judgment).

110. Or, he is all too enmeshed in its practice.

111. "Far more pernicious has been the Court's willingness to accept the underlying premise that must inform every minority vote dilution claim: the assumption that the group asserting dilution is not merely a racial or ethnic group, but a group having distinct political interests as well. . . . We have given credence to the view that race defines political interest . . . and must have their own 'minority preferred' representatives holding seats in elected bodies if they are to be considered represented at all. . . . Whenever similarities in political preferences along racial lines exist, we proclaim that the cause of the correlation is irrelevant, but we effectively rely on the fact of the correlation to assume that racial groups have unique political interests. . . . We assume racial groups are political groups and direct federal courts to assure that minorities get their fair share." *Holder*, 129 L.Ed.2d at 709–10 (Thomas, J., concurring in part, concurring in judgment).

112. Ibid., 711.

113. Ibid., 715, 716, 724, 734.

114. Ibid., 129 L.Ed.2d at 741 (Blackmun, J., dissenting).

115. *Johnson* v. *DeGrandy*, 129 L.Ed.2d 775 (1994).

116. Ibid., 775–76.

117. Ibid., 784.

118. Ibid., 786, n.6.

119. It was reasonable for the district court to find vote dilution in the absence of the maximizing majority-minority districts. This was the plaintiffs' position along with the Justice Department and the NAACP. Apparently Souter did not feel the same. There is simply no textual support for either side in the VRA. However, Justice O'Connor in *Voinovich* v. *Quilter*, in 1993, did reject the necessity of creating of black influence districts as a means to maximize black political power. Protecting the ability to elect the candidate of one's choice did not necessitate the maximization of black interest districts in Ohio. *Voinovich* v. *Quilter*, 113 S.Ct. at 1155–56.

120. *DeGrandy*, 129 L.Ed.2d at 794.

121. Swain, *Black Faces, Black Interests*, 72–73.

122. *DeGrandy*, 129 L.Ed.2d at 796.

123. Ibid., 801 (Kennedy, J., concurring in part and in judgment), citing *Metro Broadcasting, Inc.* v. *FCC*, 497 U.S. 547, 636 (1990) (Kennedy, J., dissenting).

124. Ibid., 802, citing *City of Richmond* v. *J. A. Croson Co.*, 488 U.S. 469, 518 (1989) (Kennedy, J., concurring in part and concurring in judgment).

125. Ibid., 802–3 (Kennedy, J., concurring in part and in judgment), citing *Wright* v. *Rockefeller*, 376 U.S. 52, 67 (1964) (Douglas, J., joined by Goldberg, J., dissenting).

126. *Miller* v. *Johnson*, 132 L.Ed.2d 762, 1995 U.S. LEXIS 4462, *5.

127. A second 1995 case put forth a *Shaw I* claim. This case was not decided on the merits, instead the Court sidestepped the legality of majority-minority districts by denying the plaintiffs' claim due to lack of standing. *United States* v. *Hays*, 1995 U.S. LEXIS 4464, involved a claim that Louisiana's congressional redistricting racially gerrymandered in violation of the Equal Protection Clause. The preclearance provisions of the VRA that required the state to submit redistricting plans to the Justice Department before they were put into effect covered Louisiana. Louisiana submitted a plan for preclearance that contained one majority-minority district. The Justice Department refused this plan and demanded a two majority-minority districts. This was done, and Louisiana submitted a plan for eight districts including two majority-minority districts. The Supreme Court managed to avoid consideration of the merits of the Louisiana plan. Appellants' generalized grievance against state action was not enough. Citizens challenging the Louisiana redistricting plan had to show that they were personally injured by a racial classification used in the districting plan. Because the white plaintiffs no longer resided in one of the majority-minority districts, they could not show that they suffered individualized harm, and as a result lacked standing to sue.

128. In other words, if the plaintiffs could make out an equal protection claim, the redistricting plan would be subject to strict scrutiny.

129. *Miller* v. *Johnson*, 1995 U.S. LEXIS at *8.

130. Ibid., *12–13.

131. Ibid., *13–14.

132. Ibid., *15–16.

133. Ibid., *17–18. At this point in the litigation the white plaintiffs were appellees.

134. Ibid., *22, citing *Metro Broadcasting, Inc.* v. *FCC*, 497 U.S. 547, 602 (1990).

135. Ibid., *23. Racial classifications should be read broadly to include "language minorities" delimited under the VRA.

136. This is particularly true with respect to the 1982 amendments to Section 2 of the VRA.

137. *Miller* v. *Johnson*, 1995 U.S. LEXIS at 24–25.

138. This is especially the case when the racial rhetoric stresses separateness.

139. I refer to Justice Kennedy as a philosophical liberal as opposed to a political liberal. Certainly Kennedy's politics can be described as politically conservative.

140. *Miller* v. *Johnson*, 1995 U.S. LEXIS at *27–29. Kennedy was uncomfortable with racial classifications, in particular, because they circumvented individual identification.

141. Ibid., *30.

142. Traditional or natural communities appeared not to bother Kennedy because they did not bear the stigma of state sponsorship.

143. *Miller* v. *Johnson*, 1995 U.S. LEXIS at *30.

144. Ibid., *33.

145. Ibid., *38.

146. Ibid., *42.

147. Ibid., *49.

148. Ibid., *51.

149. Ibid., *14–15.
150. Ibid., *41.
151. Ibid., *49.
152. Ibid., *53–54 (Stevens, J., dissenting).
153. Ibid., *58.
154. Ibid., *62 (Ginsburg, J., dissenting).
155. Ibid., *66.
156. Ibid., *66–68.
157. Ibid., *70.
158. Ibid., *70–71.
159. Ibid., *78.
160. Ibid., *82–83.
161. Ibid., *83.
162. Ibid., *85.
163. Ibid., *86.
164. *Morse* v. *Republican Party of Virginia*, 1996 U.S. LEXIS 2164, *10.
165. Ibid., *16.
166. Ibid., *15.
167. Ibid., *24.
168. Ibid., *64.
169. Ibid., *89 (Scalia, J., dissenting).
170. Ibid., *90–95.
171. Ibid., *95.
172. Ibid., *140 (Thomas, J., dissenting).
173. Ibid., *162.
174. *Shaw* v. *Hunt*, 1996 U.S. LEXIS 3880 (often referred to by members of the Court as *Shaw II*) and *Bush* v. *Vera*, 1996 U.S. LEXIS 3882 (a consolidation of three districting cases in Texas).
175. *Shaw II*, 1996 U.S. LEXIS 3880 at *5, 8.
176. This is the *Miller* standard.
177. *Shaw II*, 1996 U.S. LEXIS 3880 at *12.
178. Ibid., *16.
179. Ibid., *18–20.
180. The Court did not decide whether avoiding Section 2 liability was a compelling state interest. Rather, it decided that, *arguendo*, even if it were, North Carolina did not narrowly tailor its interests to meet that interest when it drew District 12. Ibid., *21–26.
181. Ibid., *25.
182. Ibid., *31.
183. Ibid., *33 (Stevens, J., dissenting).
184. Ibid., *35–37.
185. Ibid., *43–44.
186. Ibid., *88.
187. One district was majority Hispanic and two were majority black.
188. *Bush*, 1996 U.S. LEXIS 3882 at *31.
189. Ibid., *32–33 (internal citations omitted).
190. Ibid., *36–39.
191. Ibid., *42.
192. Ibid., *46–47.
193. Ibid., *49–50.
194. Ibid., *51–52.
195. Ibid., *53. Only one of the three districts was covered by Section 5.

196. Ibid., *94 (Stevens, J., dissenting).

197. Ibid., *103–6.

198. Ibid., *115–17. Moreover, Justice Stevens would not have subjected the three majority-minority districts in question to strict scrutiny in the first place.

199. Ibid., *132.

200. These oddly shaped white districts would in all likelihood not be subject to a *Shaw I* claim nor have to pass muster under the *Miller* standard because considerations of race are not so apparent to the majority when it is the majority who benefits.

201. *Bush* v. *Vera*, *134.

202. Ibid., *142–43.

203. Ibid., *146 (Souter, J., dissenting).

204. Ibid., *151–52.

205. Ibid., *161.

206. Ibid., *165.

207. *Abrams* v. *Johnson*, 1997 WL 331802 (U.S.).

208. Ibid., *2.

209. Ibid., *3.

210. Ibid., *3.

211. Ibid., *6.

212. Ibid., *7.

213. Ibid., *8.

214. Ibid., *9–10.

215. Ibid., *11–12.

216. Ibid., *16–17.

217. Ibid., *18 (Breyer, J., dissenting).

218. Ibid., *20.

219. Ibid., *21.

220. Ibid., *26.

221. Majority-minority districts are still created in practice at the federal, state, and local levels. The propriety of their creation in a fact-specific, particular instance remains in doubt. For a recent example of minority-districting meeting with judicial approval see *Stabler* v. *County of Thurston, Nebraska*, 1997 LEXIS 33753 (8th Cir. 1997). The 11th Circuit Court of Appeals upheld a district court that ordered the creation of a third majority-minority County Board district but rejected the creation of additional majority-minority districts for the School Board and Village Board. The minority in question was Native Americans.

CHAPTER 5: LIBERALISM, COMMUNITARIANISM, AND FAIR REPRESENTATION

1. Michael Sandel, "Review of John Rawls, *Political Liberalism* (New York: Columbia University Press, 1993)," 107 *Harvard Law Review* 1765, 1766–67 (1994). Discusses the communitarian criticism of the priority of the right over the good. For Rawls and Kant, "principles of justice that specify our rights do not depend for their justification on any particular conception of the good life. This presupposes a rights discourse abstracted from debate over the good."

2. The common law, the development of legal doctrine through the interplay of judicial opinions, is a hermeneutic exercise. The interpretation of a particular law is dependent on interpreting previous interpretations or decisions. The result, another decision, is itself open to further interpretation.

3. Linda Greenhouse, "High Court Voids Race-Based Plans for Redistricting," *New*

York Times, 14 June 1996, A1, A2. Elaine Jones of the NAACP-LDF said "the noose is tightening" with respect to chances to increase the number of black Representatives.

4. We may go even further and ask whose voice authentically represents the group. By "authentically," I use as a concept explicitly avoided in voice scholarship to highlight the strong claim to authorization made by group members who depend, in large part, on their physical group membership to authorize their voice. See Randall Kennedy, "Racial Critiques of Legal Academia," 102 *Harvard Law Review* 1745, 1749 (1989); Henry Louis Gates, Jr., "Authenticity, or the Lesson of Little Tree," *New York Times Book Review*, 24 November 1991, 1; and Arthur Austin, "Deconstructing Voice Scholarship," 30 *Houston Law Review* 1671, 1673–75 (1993) for critical appraisals of authenticity and voice scholarship.

5. Lani Guinier describes this as "Black Electoral Success Theory." She argues it is time to move beyond this conception of representation to attack winner-take-all majority rule. See Guinier, *Tyranny of the Majority* (New York: Free Press, 1994), 54–69.

6. Group members tell authentic stories. Nongroup members cannot tell authentic stories. The difference between the two is bound up in group membership. One of the purposes of telling stories is to establish authenticity. Establishing a perspective, which is authentic, does this. In this way, storytelling demarcates group membership. The production and reception of authenticity and of group membership are resolved by the story.

7. I use "associations" and "communal groups" to refer to Tönnies's concepts of *Gesellschaft* and *Gemeinschaft*. Communal groups are something one is born into. One is part of a family group or an ethnicity. Associations entail joining something. The individual, because of her interests, may decide to be a member of the group. See Ferdinand Tönnies, *Community and Association,* trans. Charles Loomis (London: Routledge and Kegan Paul, 1955).

8. See Benedict Anderson, *Imagined Communities* (London: Verso, 1991); Ernst Gellner, *Nations and Nationalism* (Ithaca, N.Y.: Cornell University Press, 1983); and Marie de Lepervanche and Gil Bottomley, eds., *The Cultural Construction of Race* (Sydney: University of Sydney Press, 1988) for discussions on the construction and transformation of group identity.

9. See Kimberle Crenshaw for discussion of multiple and intersecting group solidarities. Crenshaw, "Demarginalizing the Intersection of Race and Sex," 1989 *University of Chicago Legal Forum* 139, 139–52.

10. I differentiate between legal and political discourse because although the former is a subset of the latter, the specialized training and knowledge of "terms of art" necessary to converse fluently in legal discourse need not constitute general political discourse.

11. I use the term "liberals" to describe those who subscribe to the core tenets of liberal theory. I do not use liberalism this context to denote political liberals as opposed to political conservatives. For influential and comprehensive looks at the argument between liberals and communitarians, see Michael Sandel, ed., *Liberalism and Its Critics* (New York: New York University Press, 1984); and Stephen Mulhall and Adam Swift, *Liberals and Communitarians* (Cambridge, Mass.: Blackwell, 1992).

12. Isaiah Berlin, "Two Concepts of Liberty," in Michael Sandel, ed., *Liberalism and Its Critics*, 22–23.

13. Friedrich Hayek, "Equality, Value and Merit," in *Liberalism and Its Critics,* 80.

14. Sandel, "Review of *Political Liberalism*," 1768.

15. Hayek, "Equality, Value, and Merit," 83.

16. Leon Trakman, *Reasoning with the Charter* (Toronto: Butterworths, 1991), 84–88.

17. T. Alexander Alienikoff and Samuel Issacharoff, "Race and Redistricting: Drawing Constitutional Lines After *Shaw* v. *Reno,*" 92 *Michigan Law Review* 588, 600 (1993).

18. Michael Sandel, "The Procedural Republic and the Unencumbered Self," *Political Theory* 12 (1984): 81–96.

19. Pamela S. Karlan, "Maps and Misreadings: The Rule of Geographic Compactness in Racial Vote Dilution Litigation," 24 *Harvard Civil Rights–Civil Liberties Law Review* 173, 191, 214–15 (1989).

20. Justice Thomas implores the majority not to disregard the associational rights of Republicans in *Morse* v. *Republican Party of Virginia,* 1996 U.S. LEXIS 2164, as does Justice Ginsburg in *Abrams* v. *Johnson,* 1997 WL 331802. Justices Kennedy and Breyer acknowledged a claim by the black communities in Georgia to increased representation. However, they disagreed over what constituted a traditional or real community of interest for purposes of complying with the VRA.

21. Charles Taylor, "Hegel: History and Politics," in Sandel, ed., *Liberalism and Its Critics,* 197.

22. Bernard Yack, "Liberalism and Its Communitarian Critics: Does Liberal Practice 'Live Down' to Liberal Theory?" in C. Reynolds, ed., *Community in America: The Challenges of "Habits of the Heart"* (Berkeley: University of California Press, 1988), 156–59; and Yack, *The Problems of a Political Animal: Community, Justice and Conflict in Aristotelian Thought* (Berkeley: University of California Press, 1993), 46.

23. I did not intend this to be an exhaustive list of communal solidarities. For instance, Judy Scales Trent argues that being a black woman is a completely distinct category that the law has been reluctant to acknowledge. Judy Scales Trent, "Black Women and the Constitution: Finding Our Place, Asserting Our Rights," 24 *Harvard Civil Rights–Civil Liberties Law Review* 1, 9–13 (1989).

24. See Bernard Yack, "Liberalism and Its Communitarian Critics," 158–61.

25. See Robert Bellah, et al., *Habits of the Heart* (Berkeley: University of California Press, 1985).

26. W. Cole Durham, Jr., "Rhetorical Resonance and Constitutional Vision," 14 *Cardozo Law Review* 893, 894–97 (1993) describes the rhetorical power of law to include and to exclude. It is constitutive practice. Alisdair MacIntyre, *After Virtue: A Study in Moral Theory* (Notre Dame, Ind.: University of Notre Dame Press, 1984), is nostalgic for interconnectedness and community.

27. This is more properly termed a politico-legal question. For instance, it is not the case that race is somehow simply out there and the law simply encodes race as a salient category. The recognition of race and language minorities in the VRA makes these categories more important in the area of fair representation than they otherwise would have been. Recently there has been a trend among institutional players in voting rights litigation to assume a guardian ethic. Because they are not politicians, the guardians are "more concerned with fixing the results than with improving the politics that gives rise to the results." Timothy G. O'Rourke, "The 1982 Amendments and the Voting Rights Paradox," in Bernard Grofman and Chandler Davidson, eds., *Controversies in Minority Voting* (Washington, D.C.: Brookings Institution, 1992), 113. The VRA was termed "one of the most effective federal instruments of social legislation in the modern era of American reform" in *Controversies in Minority Voting,* 177. The same estimation is found in Chandler Davidson and Bernard Grofman, eds., *Quiet Revolution in the South* (Princeton: Princeton University Press, 1994), 386.

28. This is true if our rhetoric continues to employ the public/private opposition. No doubt we will continue to do so. The convention is strong. So strong that it appears natural to speak of public opposing private in the sense that the divide is somewhere out

there waiting to be found and described.

29. Alienikoff and Issacharoff, "Race and Redistricting," 603.

30. Aristotle, *Politica,* trans., Benjamin Jowett, in *The Basic Works of Aristotle*, ed. Richard McKeon (New York: Random House, 1941), chs. 4–12; Plato, *The Republic*, trans., Richard Sterling and William Scott (New York: W. W. Norton, 1985). In book III, Plato imparts the myth of the metals wherein men of reason, the gold men, ought to govern society.

31. See Aristotle, *The Nichomachean Ethics* in *Introduction to Aristotle*, ed. Richard McKeon (New York: Random House, 1947), book II, ch. 4; *The Nichomachean Ethics* in *The Basic Works of Aristotle;* and *Politica*, book VI.

32. Plato, *The Republic*, book IV. These were the Guardians or philosopher kings.

33. See *Bowers* v. *Hardwick*, 478 U.S. 186 (1986) (sexual orientation), and *San Antonio Independent School District* v. *Rodriguez*, 411 U.S. 1 (1973) (wealth). Neutrality of the law may be compromised in cases involving insular and discrete minorities who suffered from historical disadvantage. The law may be applied specially to advantage these groups through the process of strict scrutiny that requires the government to substantiate a higher burden in order to sustain the deviation from neutrality. It must reflect a compelling state interest that could not be accomplished through less burdensome means.

34. Duncan Kennedy proclaims his own vision of a guardian class (Harvard-trained lawyers) acting for the benefit of society. These are "progressive, left-leaning lawyers" who challenge (and constitute) the dominant socio-economic system that Kennedy finds so oppressive. They define the good as if it were something outside of their own making. This class of people, touched by *arete,* disclaim political motive as they circumscribe the political good. Duncan Kennedy, "Rebels from Principle: Changing the Corporate Law Firm from Within," 36 *Harvard Law School Bulletin* (Fall 1981) in Deborah Rhode, ed., *Professional Responsibility* (Boston: Little, Brown, 1994), 98–100.

35. 5th and 14th Amendments to the United States Constitution.

36. Aristotle, *Politica*, books VI and VII. Political justice describes attaining the interest of the political community.

37. Yack, *The Problems of a Political Animal*, 50.

38. Ibid., 26.

39. Ibid., 27, 29.

40. "Shared identity refers to common elements in the way in which a group of individuals identify themselves. Collective identity . . . refers to the association of one's own identity with a collective will." Ibid., 31.

41. Among others, Derrick Bell, *Faces at the Bottom of the Well: The Permanence of Racism* (New York: Basic Books, 1992); Jerome M. Culp, Jr., "Toward a Black Legal Scholarship: Race and Original Understandings," 41 *Duke Law Journal* 39 (1991); and Culp, "You Can Take Them to Water but You Can't Make Them Drink: Black Legal Scholarship and White Legal Scholars," 1992 *University of Illinois Law Review* 1021.

42. For examples of identity politics or voice scholarship, see Charles R. Lawrence III, "The Id, the Ego, and Equal Protection: Reckoning with Unconscious Racism," 39 *Stanford Law Review* 317 (1987); D. Marvin Jones, "Darkness Made Visible: Law, Metaphor, and the Racial Self," 82 *Georgetown Law Journal* 437 (1993); Ian F. Haney Lopez, "The Social Construction of Race: Some Observations on Illusion, Fabrication, and Choice," 29 *Harvard Civil Rights–Civil Liberties Law Review* 1 (1994); Jerome M. Culp, Jr., "Voice, Perspective, Truth, and Justice: Race and the Mountain in the Legal Academy," 38 *Loyola Law Review* 61 (1992); and Angela Harris, "The Jurisprudence of Reconstruction," 82 *California Law Review* 741 (1994).

43. Yack, *The Problems of a Political Animal*, 32.

44. Pamela S. Karlan, "Maps and Misreadings," 176 (1989).

45. The term "race communitarian" refers to those "race-crits" or critical race theorists and others who share communitarian assumptions about the communal nature of political and social life but who elevate race to the paramount interest around which communities coalesce. Race communitarians adopt a specific conception of the good, which influences how they conceive of rights. The good may be defined as a political structure in which racial groups do not dominate one another but where racial differences are celebrated and promoted. Race communitarianism is one variant of political communitarianism, but it may be the most important variant in our consideration of fair representation, given the importance of race in elections. Critical race theory emerged as an influential branch of legal scholarship. Its adherents exhorted traditional legal scholarship to center areas of the law that have been slighted or ignored. See Richard Delgado and Jean Stefanic, " 'Critical Race Theory': An Annotated Bibliography," 79 *Virginia Law Review* 461 (1993).

46. Trent, "Black Women and the Constitution," 10 (1989) and M. M. Slaughter, "The Multicultural Self," 14 *Cardozo Law Review* 885, 890–91 (1993).

47. Pamela Karlan, "All Over the Map: The Supreme Court's Voting Rights Trilogy," 1993 *Supreme Court Review* 245, 247, 249. Voting rights reflect "a constellation of concepts." When we speak of influencing policy-making, "voting loses its purely individual character." Karlan advances what might be called race-conscious communitarianism. Her notion of group emphasizes racial solidarity. Race becomes the salient political consideration for the group and the issue around which membership, representation, and solidarity are determined. Karlan advocates the civic inclusion model whereby legislatures reflect demography rather than geography. She argues for racial diversity in the legislature and the interest of the state in promoting minority group political efficacy. Karlan, "Maps and Misreadings, 191, 214–15.

48. Cass Sunstein, *The Partial Constitution* (Cambridge, Mass.: Harvard University Press), 76–79.

49. For purposes of standing, usually an individual who has suffered a discrete and insular wrong must bring the claim in court. Failing to adhere to the doctrine of standing may result in the Supreme Court's refusal to consider the merits of a case. See *United States* v. *Hays*, 515 U.S. 737 (1995).

50. Many communitarians writing on politics and the law tend to be left progressive. There are exceptions such as law professor Mary Ann Glendon who is sometimes attacked for her politics. See Sanford Levinson, "Book Review: Mary Ann Glendon, *A Nation Under Lawyers: How the Crisis in the Legal Profession Is Transforming American Society*," 45 *Journal of Legal Education* 143 (1995).

51. See Chapter 1, discussing Burke's theory of representation and discussion of the national interest apart from corporate or partial interests.

52. Political membership entailed allegiance not only to the state but also to the party. For example, Hitler and Mussolini depended on fascist parties, Mao and Stalin on Communist parties, and Robespierre on the Jacobins. Rigidly policed party membership diminished individual autonomy, in the form of developing political ideas, to morbidly scrawny proportions.

53. Nonetheless, Guinier claims that "Congress did not create race as a category; Congress simply acknowledged its political salience." This is a chicken-or-egg assertion. Despite Guinier's disclaimer, it is folly to deny that making race the basis for affirmative political representation increases its value as a politico-legal category. See Guinier, "[E]racing Democracy: The Voting Rights Cases," 108 *Harvard Law Review* 109, 129 (1994).

54. Pierre Bourdieu, *Outline of a Theory of Practice* (Cambridge: Cambridge University Press, 1977), 164–65, describes how classificatory systems naturalize their arbitrariness. Some issues are perceived to be legal categories and some are not.

55. For instance, no one seriously proposes restricting the franchise so as to exclude women. It would be unjust; it would be wrong. Indeed, it is so wrong that it is hard to describe how it could be correct.

56. This does not mean that the types of claims or causes of action will not change. In fact, new causes of action may even be seen as detrimental to minority claims for representation. For instance, when the Supreme Court considers the district's shape or the predominant use of race when districting as a cause of action, the Court may create a legal climate less hospitable for minorities bringing suits to secure fair representation. Although recent cases narrowed the scope of the VRA, it has not been found unconstitutional.

57. This is largely a result of Section 2 of the VRA as amended in 1982. Abigail Thernstrom, *Whose Votes Count?* (Cambridge, Mass.: Harvard University Press, 1987), 226–39. The Court struck down a Georgia districting plan on the grounds that race was the predominant factor used to create a third majority-black district. *Miller* v. *Johnson*, 132 L.Ed.2d 762 (1995). Two years later, the Court found a second Georgia majority-minority district to be unconstitutional leaving Georgia with one majority-minority district. *Abrams* v. *Johnson*, 1997 WL 331802.

58. See *Shaw* v. *Hunt*, 1996 U.S. LEXIS 3880 and *Bush* v. *Vera*, 1996 U.S. LEXIS 3882. On the other hand, the use of single member, majority-minority districts to remedy vote dilution continues. *Stabler* v. *Thurston County, Nebraska*, 1997 LEXIS 33753 (8th Cir. 1997); and *Cannon* v. *Durham County Board of Elections*, 1997 LEXIS 31794 (9th Cir. 1997).

59. Guinier's alarm with the Court's recent series of VRA opinions appears overwrought. She argues that the Court undermines enforcement of the VRA. Instead, I argue, the Court decided cases in ways she found politically disagreeable. The VRA, as Guinier points out ironically, is in a process of revision whereby new arguments are accepted and old arguments are rejected. See Guinier, "[E]racing Democracy" 114, 136–37.

60. "Words are intelligible only within the assumption of some context of intentional production, some already in place predecision as to what kind of person, with what kind of purposes, in relation to what specific goals in a particular situation or writing." Stanley Fish, "Don't Know Much About the Middle Ages: Posner on Law and Literature," in Fish, *Doing What Comes Naturally* (Durham, N.C.: Duke University Press, 1989), 295.

61. Karlan, "Maps and Misreadings," 191.

62. Lani Guinier, "[E]racing Democracy," 125, citing Iris Marion Young, "Polity and Group Difference: A Critique of the Ideal of Universal Citizenship," 99 *Ethics* 250, 261, 273 (1989); and Wendy Brown-Scott, "The Communitarian State: Lawlessness or Law Reform for African Americans?" 107 *Harvard Law Review* 1209, 1217–18 (1994).

63. Brown-Scott, "The Communitarian State," 1217, arguing for modifying communitarianism through race consciousness. Communitarianism that fails to account for structural subordination of African Americans replicates structures of privilege enjoyed by the majority. Adeno Addis also prescribes a race-conscious communitarian state sensitive to imbalances of power among ethnic minorities. Addis, "Individualism, Communitarianism, and the Rights of Ethnic Minorities," 67 *Notre Dame Law Review* 615, 648–58 (1991).

64. Karlan, "Maps and Misreadings," 180, 213–15.

65. Girardeau Spann, *Race Against the Court: The Supreme Court and Minorities in*

Contemporary America (New York: New York University Press, 1993); Gerald Rosenberg, *The Hollow Hope: Can Courts Bring About Social Change?* (Chicago: University of Chicago Press, 1991).

66. This is the case in determining whether protected groups under Section 2 of the VRA have a meaningful opportunity to elect candidates of their choice. This is the results test.

67. Lani Guinier, "The Representation of Minority Interests: The Question of Single-Member Districts," 14 *Cardozo Law Review*, 1135, 1155–56 (1993).

68. Hannah Pitkin, *The Concept of Representation* (Berkeley: University of California Press, 1967), 66. No description self-explicates.

69. For instance, some communitarians may oppose, and some may support, different forms of group preferences and affirmative action programs.

70. See Michael Walzer, *Spheres of Justice: A Defense of Pluralism and Equality* (New York: Basic Books, 1983), 84–91; Michael Sandel, *Liberalism and the Limits of Justice* (Cambridge: Cambridge University Press, 1982); and Sandel, "Review of John Rawls, *Political Liberalism*," 1767. Communities can be created or manufactured in the sense that they are a result of, and not prior to, social practices.

71. Sandel, "Review of John Rawls, *Political Liberalism*," 1766.

72. Depending on their permanence and means of authorization, we might view factions as temporary and in accord with Madisonian principles of representation.

73. See *San Antonio Independent School District* v. *Rodriguez*, 411 U.S. 1, 28 (1973). The Court looks not only at the immutability of group characteristics but also at whether the group has suffered a history of political powerlessness or oppression. The determination of a suspect class, one entitled to the highest level of judicial protection, is a legal determination. It is not indicative of a natural ordering.

74. This type of group is similar to what Tönnies identified as a *Gemeinschaft* or community as opposed to a *Gesellschaft* or association.

75. Contemporary society is comparatively more dynamic than, for example, the antebellum United States. The neutral application of the rule of law did not apply, even on its face, to women and blacks in that period. Looking backward, contemporary society promises a more level playing field for its citizens. Nonetheless, there is neither political nor legal equality. It is difficult to imagine what that would look like if we were also to accommodate all forms of difference. But neither is this a society where people are treated differently by the law solely because of their social status. One attempt to formulate a theory of accommodating difference within legal practices and institutions is Martha Minow, *Making All the Difference* (Ithaca, N.Y.: Cornell University Press, 1990).

76. Groups can wield political power even if their members are not in political office. Elections are often won through coalition building. In addition, groups can exercise political power by extra-governmental means such as the media.

77. Moreover, such a view fails to capture the nuances of what Kimberle Crenshaw refers to as "intersectionality" whereby different individual traits, such as sex and race, combine to place a person in a wholly different politico-legal space than if we limited our view to one or the other. Crenshaw, "Demarginalizing the Intersection of Race and Sex," 139.

78. Thernstrom, *Whose Votes Count?* 146, 160, 172, 174.

79. Guinier generally approves of using race as a proxy for group interests but is afraid reliance on the single member district will continue to obstruct other types of interest group formation. Guinier, *Tyranny of the Majority*, 119–37.

80. Madison argued that the threat of permanent, self-interested factions was in enmity with a stable republic. He acknowledged the inevitability of factions in politics where there is political liberty. He conceived of the individual as having shifting,

multiple attachments that pass into and out of political discourse. Madison, "Federalist No. 10" and "Federalist No. 15" in Alexander Hamilton, John Jay, and James Madison, *The Federalist*, intro. by Edward Mead Earle (New York: Modern Library, 1960) 56–57.

81. Justice Thomas criticizes the trend to reduce interest group politics to racial group politics in the context of making a vote dilution argument under Section 2 of the VRA. *Holder* v. *Hall*, 129 L.Ed.2d 687, 708–14 (1994) (Thomas, J., joined by Scalia, J., concurring in judgment). Justice Kennedy criticizes the assumption that racial politics delimit the political viewpoints or solidarities of minority voters. *Johnson* v. *DeGrandy*, 129 L.Ed.2d 775, 801–3 (1994) (Kennedy, J., concurring in part and in judgment).

82. In *Nineteen Eighty-four* and *Animal Farm*, George Orwell described peculiarly enveloping versions of community. Orwell, *Nineteen Eighty-four* (New York: New American Library, 1983); Orwell, *Animal Farm* (London: Secker & Warburg, 1987). *Animal Farm* is a thinly veiled satire of the Stalinist USSR. *Nineteen Eighty-four* is another trenchant lampoon of political totalitarianism.

83. Charles Taylor argues that liberalism is a "fighting creed," and as such should not try to attain to something it is not: cultural neutrality. Consistent with this theme, Taylor advocates a concept of liberalism explicating a substantive as well as a procedural notion of justice. Charles Taylor, "The Politics of Recognition," in Amy Gutmann, ed., *Multiculturalism: Examining the Politics of Recognition* (Princeton: Princeton University Press, 1994), 62–63.

84. Iris Marion Young, *Justice and the Politics of Difference* (Princeton: Princeton University Press, 1990), 100.

85. In short, Young criticizes those who derive a theoretical perspective from a universalized notion of reason. Liberals are not alone in their inability to account for the politics of difference. According to Young, civic republicanism fails because it reproduces a homogeneous standard of citizenship. It fails to take into account particularities that may require different discourses of citizenship. Ibid., 117. For example by such a standard, Jürgen Habermas's theory of political community and, correspondingly, political action purportedly makes use of an uncritical, from a politics of diversity standpoint, and universalist notion of rationality. This ideal of rationality forecloses those discourses that do not retain all or part of its assumptions. From this view, Habermas's notion of undisturbed communication silences rather· than promotes civic life. Habermas, *The Theory of Communicative Competence, Vol. 2: Lifeworld and System* (Boston: Beacon Press, 1987). Obviously, this line of critique could be expanded to include others besides Habermas. Also see Benjamin Barber, *Strong Democracy* (Berkeley: University of California Press, 1984).

86. Mary Ann Glendon, *Rights Talk* (Toronto: Macmillan, 1991), 47, 59.

87. See *Allen* v. *State Board of Elections*, 393 U.S. 544 (1969) and *Holder* v. *Hall* and *Johnson* v. *DeGrandy* in 1994.

88. See *Davis* v. *Bandemeer* (political parties), *UJO* v. *Carey* (Hasidic religious community), *Morse* v. *Republican Party of Virginia* (political party), *Johnson* v. *DeGrandy* (racial and language minorities), and *Abrams* v. *Johnson* (racial minority).

89. See Miriam Galston, "Taking Aristotle Seriously: Republican-Oriented Legal Theory and the Moral Foundation of Deliberative Democracy," 82 *California Law Review* 329 (1994), for a discussion on the use and misuse of Aristotle by contemporary legal and political commentators.

90. Yack, *The Problems of a Political Animal*, 47.

91. Ibid., 32–33.

92. Ibid., 48.

93. Ibid., 48–49.

94. To say that political justice is a rhetorical exercise does not mean it is merely

rhetorical in the sense that there is a concept of political justice, that is somehow more real and not rhetorical. To label political justice as a rhetorical exercise is simply to describe a practice that involves an interpretive community debating the terms of obligation members owe to each another. Derrida is often misinterpreted when he describes justice as deconstruction. Some legal theorists take this to mean that if the formula of deconstruction is applied to a particular problem, justice can be distilled. But for Derrida, deconstruction is neither a method nor a theory. It describes a highly personal style of interacting with a text or series of texts. It is not a map to get from A to B, nor is it an emancipatory political strategy. Jacques Derrida, "Vor dem Gesetz," in Derek Attridge, ed., Avital Ronell, trans., *Acts of Literature* (New York: Routledge, 1992), 184–86. For an imaginative, dissimilar characterization of Derrida and deconstruction see Drucilla Cornell, "The Philosophy of the Limit: Systems Theory and Feminist Legal Reform," in David Gray Carlson, Drucilla Cornell, and Michael Rosenfeld, eds., *Deconstruction and the Possibility of Justice* (New York: Routledge, 1992); Cornell, *Transformations: Recollective Imagination and Sexual Difference* (New York: Routledge, 1993).

95. Yack, *The Problems of a Political Animal*, 40–41, 57.

96. Ibid., 55–56.

97. Litigation does not constitute deliberation. However, it is an important part of a contentious process surrounding reapportionment jurisprudence that has become even more heated. Indeed, this describes the nonstop institutional litigation surrounding the VRA. Attempts to secure favorable interpretations of fair representation in terms of the 14th and 15th Amendments to the United States Constitution and the VRA are attempts to define a standard of political justice. The VRA is characterized by repeat players who engage in public law litigation: "a term coined to describe judicially managed restructuring of social, political and economic institutions." Gregory Caldeira, "Litigation, Lobbying and the Voting Rights Act," in Grofman and Davidson, eds., *Controversies in Minority Voting*, 238, 242.

98. Yack, *The Problems of a Political Animal*, 60.

99. Ibid., 62.

100. Ibid., 62. Burke considered reasoned debate the central feature of the representative function. See Pitkin's discussion of Burke's theory of representation and the centrality of deliberation in *The Concept of Representation*, 181, citing Edmund Burke, *Burke's Politics*, Ross Hoffman and Paul Levack, eds. (New York: Alfred Knopf, 1949), 227.

101. Young, *Justice and the Politics of Difference*, 67–69.

102. In particular, Cass Sunstein's discussion of an anticaste principle linked to a consideration of race and sex discrimination. It is axiomatic that very few of us are for race and sex discrimination. However, voicing criticisms of Sunstein's anticaste principle does not make us proponents of inequality. There is a multitude of gradations between Sunstein's position and procedural neutrality. Sunstein, *The Partial Constitution*, 339.

103. Yack, *The Problems of a Political Animal*, 70–71. Henry Louis Gates, Jr. describes the concern to protect political orthodoxy by race crits. Henry Louis Gates, Jr., "Let Them Talk," *The New Republic*, 20–27 September 1993, 43–49 reviewing Matsuda, Lawrence, Delgado, and Crenshaw, *Words That Wound: Critical Race Theory, Assaultive Speech and the First Amendment* (Boulder, Colo.: Westview Press, 1993).

104. H. N. Hirsch, "The Threnody of Liberalism," 14 *Political Theory* 423 (1986). See MacIntyre, *After Virtue*, and Bellah, et al., *Habits of the Heart* for representative attacks on liberal practice and the longing or nostalgia for community.

105. The VRA originally protected blacks from disenfranchisement in parts of the

South. Chandler Davidson, "The Voting Rights Act: A Brief History," in Grofman and Davidson, eds., *Controversies in Minority Voting*, 17, 24; and Hugh Davis Graham, "Voting Rights and the American Regulatory State," in Grofman and Davidson, eds., *Controversies in Minority Voting*, 177, 188.

106. "Many of society's hardest questions take the form of constitutional arguments by groups of marginal persons who seek for their members some legal right. The issues raised by such groups cannot be resolved by invoking community sentiment, for these groups challenge too deeply the liberal understanding of membership. It is precisely because these groups are demanding more than the community or polity wishes to grant them that these controversies exist in the first place. Any renewal of community sentiment will accomplish nothing for these groups." Hirsch, "The Threnody of Liberalism," 424.

107. The race-conscious communitarian reduction of reason to a particular voice informed by reason and speech is open to the philosophical communitarian criticism of universalized reason inherent in liberal theory.

108. Kathryn Abrams, "Relationships of Representation in Voting Rights Act Jurisprudence," 71 *Texas Law Review* 1409, 1417–18 (1995) critiquing *Presley* v. *Etowah County Commission*, 112 S.Ct. 820 (1992).

109. Derrick Bell and Patricia Williams find inadequate the legal response to institutional and intentional racism. To some extent they exhort us to listen to excluded groups. On the other hand, both are law professors and use the categories of the law to convince us of the veracity of their arguments. Both are extremely persuasive writers. There is some schizophrenia that characterizes voice scholarship. On the one hand, it asserts the existence of a racial or ethnic community. On the other hand, it employs liberal practice and categories, such as equal protection and strict scrutiny, to assert the legal distinctiveness of racial communities within the liberal state. See Derrick Bell, *And We Are Not Saved: The Elusive Quest for Racial Justice* (New York: Basic Books, 1987); and Patricia Williams, "Spirit-Murdering the Messenger: The Discourse of Fingerpointing as the Law's Response to Racism," 42 *University of Miami Law Review* 127 (1987).

110. "Those who offer community as a solution to the problem of alienation in liberal society are bringing politics into the realm of the social and the personal; they are mixing public and private in an essentially Aristotelian and antiliberal manner. Hirsch, "The Threnody of Liberalism," 425.

111. Young, *Justice and the Politics of Difference*, 120.

112. Graham, "Voting Rights and the American Regulatory State," 177–78; and Bruce Cain, "Voting Rights and Democratic Theory: Toward a Color-Blind Society?" in Grofman and Davidson, eds., *Controversies in Minority Voting*, 261–62, 277.

113. H. N. Hirsch, "The Threnody of Liberalism," 426.

114. Ibid., 429–31, citing Alisdair MacIntyre (nostalgic notion of moral identity attached to small ethno-religious communities) and Michael Walzer (draws on premodern small-scale communities whose members share a strong notion of belonging and consensus). Drucilla Cornell posits transformation of the political and legal community. Transformation is differentiated from evolutionary change, which tends to conserve the *status quo*. Cornell conceives of legal changes transforming the boundaries of the legal and political toward a more inclusive conception of the good. She posits a politico-legal order sensitive to the plaints of the excluded and the one in which the Other is embraced. Cornell, *Transformations*, 1–44.

115. I find this peculiar because these criticisms are made within liberal practices and institutions that allow for vigorous criticisms and respond to them. More accurately, communitarians and civic republicans criticize the politics of the rule of law. Cass

Sunstein, *The Partial Constitution,* 341–44; and Mary Ann Glendon, *Rights Talk*, 73–75.

116. The rule of law is opposed to a legal regime that treats people differently according to their status.

117. This may or may not occur on the minority group's terms. This depends, largely, on the fact situation involved—if the issue is, for example, a redistricting plan that attempts to create majority-minority districts.

118. In fact, contemporary communitarians and civic republicans may seek to repair deficiencies in the rule of law by fortifying it with the recognition of group inequalities. Glendon, *Rights Talk*; Sunstein, *The Partial Constitution* and *After the Rights Revolution* (Cambridge, Mass.: Harvard University Press, 1990); and Minow, *Making All the Difference.*

119. "The impartiality of the law—the substitution of explicit and general rules for discrete decisions based upon that status or circumstances of particular individuals—is after all one of the greatest achievements of liberalism, and one of its principal methods of guaranteeing fairness. But this quality of fixedness has become according to Tribe an iron cage from which we must escape." Hirsch, "The Threnody of Liberalism," 432.

120. The "rule-of-law" was an integral part of the rhetoric used by civil rights activists in such areas as school desegregation, fair housing, and voting rights. It is ironic that we are now told that one of the tools used to end *de jure* discrimination masks our understanding of *de facto* discrimination. In the area of representation, consider how important legal institutions, by definition reflexive of the majority, are in the promotion of minority access to the ballot and ensuring electoral success. MALDEF and the NAACP-LDF are consistently effective litigators. They use the rule of law to promote the recognition and protection of entire groups of people not only in representation but also in other areas of law, such as education, housing, and employment. The organizations that comprise the voting rights bar are repeat players; they have institutional and strategic advantages. Gregory Caldeira, "Litigation, Lobbying and the Voting Rights Act," 238–43.

121. Of course in some sense it is true that we are treated differently because of our social status. For instance, if someone is black, he may be sentenced more harshly than if he were white. Likewise, a poor man may receive less effective representation in a criminal case than a rich man, if for no other reason than that a court-appointed lawyer is not afforded the resources to engage expert witnesses to challenge the state's evidence, as a lawyer for a rich man would be able to do. On the other hand, rich and poor, black and white, are all charged under the same penal code. Each, according to the law, is afforded the same rights and protections from prosecution. The state must prove the same elements of a particular offense and establish the same standard of guilt no matter what the social status of the defendant.

122. For a thorough examination of the Indian experience see Marc Galanter, "Compensatory Discrimination in Political Representation: A Preliminary Assessment of India's Thirty-Year Experience with Reserved Seats in Legislatures," *Economic and Political Weekly,* 14, no. 7–8 (1979): 437–40. Recent concern over the differential treatment among religious groups has worried constitutionalists, as Hindu nationalism appears to be on the ascendant. John F. Burns, "With the Way to Power Open, Hindu Nationalists Falter," *New York Times,* 13 March 1998, A5, and Burns, "Sonia Gandhi Consolidates Her Control of India Party," *New York Times,* 17 March 1998, A6. Michael Walzer criticizes the notion of using quotas to determine the representation of minorities in the United States. "The effect would be to repress every sort of cultural specificity, turning ethnic identity into an administrative classification." Walzer, *What It Means to Be an American* (New York: Marsilio, 1992), 72–74.

123. Walker identifies the difficulty of assigning rights to ethnic groups in the

United States. They have fluctuating populations. Imposing rigid distinctions may not accurately describe the various solidarities that characterize society. Walzer, *What It Means to Be an American*, 70–71.

124. "Both homogeneity and moral education can be politically dangerous: by encouraging the exclusion of outsiders; by encouraging indoctrination or irrationalism; and by compromising privacy and autonomy. It is no accident. . . . that causes liberalism to have no strong theory of community." Hirsch, "The Threnody of Liberalism," 435.

125. Ibid., 438.

126. "Racial or religious ghettos, whether imposed by the majority or chosen freely by members of the group are perhaps the most visible form of exclusion. Political history teaches us nothing if not that the avoidance of others—of strangers—is not always a pleasant experience for those who are excluded." Ibid., 435.

127. Ibid., 437–38.

128. James Madison, "Federalist No. 10," 53–62; and Alexander Hamilton, "Federalist No. 9," 47–52. Bernard Yack suggests that Aristotle and Madison may share some agreement regarding combating the adverse effects of factionalism. Yack, *The Problems of a Political Animal*, 74, n.46.

129. Hirsch, "The Threnody of Liberalism," 440; John P. Kaminski and Richard Leffler, eds., *Federalists and Antifederalists: The Debate over the Ratification of the Constitution* (Madison, Wis.: Madison House, 1989), 4–18.

130. "The Court can tackle various issues, from apportionment to affirmative action. The Court can touch a moral chord, spark a political debate, and suggest possible answers to difficult questions. But a court cannot force human beings to change their definition of their own community if they do not wish to—for what is implicated in this definition of their community is their understanding of their own selves." Hirsch, "The Threnody of Liberalism," 442.

131. Consider how the Court changed its views regarding the parameters of fair representation. Regard for justice demands that the Court formulate an ideal of fair representation, but changing fact patterns, time, amendments to the VRA, and different justices give us a remarkably changing ideal.

132. Hirsch, "The Threnody of Liberalism," 443–44.

133. Kimberle Crenshaw in Mari Matsuda, Charles Lawrence, Richard Delgado, and Kimberle Crenshaw, *Words that Wound: Critical Race Theory, Assaultive Speech and the First Amendment*; Slaughter, "The Multicultural Self," 887–90 (1993); and Trent, "Black Women and the Constitution," 9–10.

134. Yack, *The Problems of a Political Animal*, 82.

135. Ibid., 83.

136. "Liberalism, even at its most permissive, is a hard politics because it offers so few emotional rewards; the liberal state is not a home for its citizens; it lacks warmth and intimacy. Contemporary dissatisfaction takes the form of a yearning for political community, passionate affirmation, explicit patriotism." Walzer, *What It Means to Be an American*, 96, 91.

137. Leon Trakman, *Reasoning with the Charter*, 52.

138. "Classifications are human impositions, or at least culturally based decisions on what to stress among a plethora of viable alternatives. Classifications are therefore theories of order, not simple records of nature. . . . More important, since classifications are actively imposed, not passively imbibed, they shape our thoughts and deeds in ways that we scarcely perceive because we view our categories as 'obvious' and 'natural'." Stephen Jay Gould, "Taxonomy as Politics," *Dissent*, 37 (Winter 1990): 73.

Bibliography

JOURNAL AND NEWSPAPER ARTICLES

Abrams, Kathryn. "Relationships of Representation in Voting Rights Act Jurisprudence." 71 *Texas Law Review* 1409 (1995).

Addis, Adeno. "Individualism, Communitarianism, and the Rights of Ethnic Minorities." 67 *Notre Dame Law Review* 615 (1991).

Aleinikoff, T. Alexander, and Issacharoff, Samuel. "Race and Redistricting: Drawing Constitutional Lines After *Shaw* v. *Reno*." 92 *Michigan Law Review* 588 (1993).

Alexander, Larry. "Lost in the Political Thicket." 41 *Florida Law Review* 563 (1989).

Applebome, Peter. "Results Hint at New Indifference to Race." *New York Times.* 4 November 1993, A11.

Austin, Arthur. "Deconstructing Voice Scholarship." 30 *Houston Law Review* 1671 (1993).

Barnes, Robin D. "Race Consciousness: The Thematic Content of Racial Distinctiveness in Critical Race Scholarship." 103 *Harvard Law Review* 1864 (1990).

Biskupic, Joan. "White Voters Challenge Black-Majority Map." *Washington Post.* 20 April 1993, A4.

Brown-Scott, Wendy. "The Communitarian State: Lawlessness or Law Reform for African Americans?" 107 *Harvard Law Review* 1209 (1994).

Burns, John F. "Sonia Gandhi Consolidates Her Control of India Party." *New York Times.* 17 March 1998, A6.

———. "With the Way to Power Open, Hindu Nationalists Falter." *New York Times.* 13 March 1998, A5.

Butler, Katherine. "Reapportionment, the Courts and the Voting Rights Act: A Resegregation of the Political Process?" 56 *University of Colorado Law Review* 58 (1984).

Butler, Katherine, and Murray, Richard. "Minority Vote Dilution Suits and the Problem of Two Minority Groups: Can a 'Rainbow Coalition' Claim the Protection of the Voting Rights Act?" 21 *Pacific Law Journal* 619 (1990).

Calmore, John. "Critical Race Theory, Archie Shepp and Fire Music: Securing an Authentic Intellectual Life in a Multicultural World." 65 *Southern California Law Review* 2129 (1992).

――――. "Exploring the Significance of Race and Class in Representing the Black Poor." 61 *Oregon Law Review* 201 (1982).

"Court Ruling Upsets Plans for Elections." *New York Times.* 7 April 1998, A15.

Crenshaw, Kimberle. "Demarginalizing the Intersection of Race and Sex." 1989 *University of Chicago Legal Forum* 139.

Culp, Jerome M., Jr. "Voice, Perspective, Truth, and Justice: Race and the Mountain in the Legal Academy." 38 *Loyola Law Review* 61 (1992).

――――. "You Can Take Them to Water but You Can't Make Them Drink: Black Legal Scholarship and White Legal Scholars." 1992 *University of Illinois Law Review* 1021.

――――. "Toward a Black Legal Scholarship: Race and Original Understandings." 41 *Duke Law Journal* 39 (1991).

Delgado, Richard. "Rodrigo's Third Chronicle: Care, Competition, and the Redemptive Tragedy of Race." 81 *California Law Review* 387 (1993).

Delgado, Richard, and Stefanic, Jean. "'Critical Race Theory': An Annotated Bibliography." 79 *Virginia Law Review* 461 (1993).

Dunne, John. "Remarks." In "Redistricting in the 1990s: The New York Experience." 14 *Cardozo Law Review* 1119 (1993).

Durham, W. Cole, Jr. "Rhetorical Resonance and Constitutional Vision." 14 *Cardozo Law Review* 893 (1993).

Evans, Monica. "Stealing Away: Black Women, Outlaw Culture and the Rhetoric of Rights." 28 *Harvard Civil Rights–Civil Liberties Law Review* 263 (1993).

Galanter, Marc. "Compensatory Discrimination in Political Representation: A Preliminary Assessment of India's Thirty-Year Experience with Reserved Seats in Legislatures." *Economic and Political Weekly.* 14, no. 7–8 (1979).

――――. "Why the Haves Come Out Ahead: Speculations on the Limits of Legal Change." 9 *Law and Society Review* 95 (1974).

Galston, Miriam. "Taking Aristotle Seriously: Republican-Oriented Legal Theory and the Moral Foundation of Deliberative Democracy." 82 *California Law Review* 329 (1994).

Gates, Henry Louis, Jr. "Let Them Talk." *The New Republic.* 20–27 September 1993, 43–49.

――――. "Authenticity, or the Lesson of Little Tree." *New York Times Book Review.* 24 November 1991, 1.

Goldberg, Stephanie B. "The Law, a New Theory Holds, Has a White Voice." *New York Times.* 17 July 1992.

Gould, Stephen Jay. "Taxonomy as Politics." *Dissent* 37 (Winter 1990): 73–78.

Greenhouse, Linda. "High Court Voids Race-Based Plans for Redistricting." *New York Times.* 14 June 1996, A1.

Grofman, Bernard. "Would Vince Lombardi Have Been Right If He Said: 'When It Comes to Redistricting, Race Isn't Everything, It's the Only Thing'?" 14 *Cardozo Law Review* 1237 (1993).

Grofman, Bernard, Griffin, Robert, and Glazer, Amihai. "The Effect of Black Population on Electing Democrats and Liberals to the House of Representatives." 17 *Legislative Studies Quarterly* 365 (1992).

Guinier, Lani. "[E]racing Democracy: The Voting Rights Cases." 108 *Harvard Law Review* 109 (1994).

————. "Groups, Representation, and Race-Conscious Districting: A Case of the Emperor's Clothes." 71 *Texas Law Review* 1589 (1993).

————. "The Representation of Minority Interests: The Question of Single-Member Districts." 14 *Cardozo Law Review* 1135 (1993).

————. "No Two Seats: The Elusive Quest for Political Equality." 77 *Virginia Law Review* 1413 (1991).

Hamilton, Jeffrey. "Comment: Deeper into the Political Thicket: Racial and Political Gerrymandering and the Supreme Court." 43 *Emory Law Journal* 1519 (1994).

Harris, Angela. "The Jurisprudence of Reconstruction." 82 *California Law Review* 741 (1994).

Hayden, Grant. "Note: Some Implications of Arrow's Theorem for Voting Rights." 47 *Stanford Law Review* 295 (1995).

Hirsch, H. N. "The Threnody of Liberalism." *Political Theory* 14 (1986): 423–49.

Holmes, Steven A. "Plans for the 2000 Census Are Challenged on 2 Fronts." *New York Times.* 6 June 1996, A14.

————. "White House to Suspend a Program for Minorities." *New York Times.* 8 March 1996, A1.

"I-85 No Route to Congress." *Raleigh News & Observer.* 13 January 1992, A8.

Issacharoff, Samuel. "Judging Politics: The Elusive Quest for Judicial Review of Political Fairness." 71 *Texas Law Review* 1643 (1993).

————. "Polarized Voting and the Political Process: The Transformation of Voting Rights Jurisprudence." 90 *Michigan Law Review* 1833 (1992).

Jones, D. Marvin. "Darkness Made Visible: Law, Metaphor, and the Racial Self." 82 *Georgetown Law Journal* 437 (1993).

Kairys, David. "Conference: The Supreme Court, Racial Politics, and the Right to Vote: *Shaw* v. *Reno* and the Future of the Voting Rights Act." 44 *American University Law Review* 1 (1994).

Karlan, Pamela S. "End of the Second Reconstruction? Voting Rights and the Court." *The Nation.* 23 May 1994, Vol. 258, no. 20, 698; 1994 WL 13444560.

————. "All Over the Map: The Supreme Court's Voting Rights Trilogy." 1993 *Supreme Court Review* 245.

————. "The Rights to Vote: Some Pessimism About Formalism." 71 *Texas Law Review* 1705 (1993).

————. "Maps and Misreadings: The Rule of Geographic Compactness in Racial Vote Dilution Litigation." 24 *Harvard Civil Rights–Civil Liberties Law Review* 173 (1989).

Karlan, Pamela S., and Levinson, Daryl. "Why Is Voting Different?" 84 *California Law Review* 1201 (1996).

Kennedy, Randall. "Racial Critiques of Legal Academia." 102 *Harvard Law Review* 1745 (1989).

Kovacich, Joanne. "The Impact of Law and Policy on the Social Construction of 'Culture.'" Paper presented at the *Law and Society Association* annual conference (1994).

Lawrence, Charles R., III. "The Id, the Ego, and Equal Protection: Reckoning with Unconscious Racism." 39 *Stanford Law Review* 317 (1987).

Levinson, Sanford. "Book Review: Mary Ann Glendon, *A Nation Under Lawyers: How the Crisis in the Legal Profession Is Transforming American Society.*" 45 *Journal of Legal Education* 143 (1995).

Lopez, Ian F. Haney. "The Social Construction of Race: Some Observations on Illusion, Fabrication, and Choice." 29 *Harvard Civil Rights–Civil Liberties Law Review* 1 (1994).

Loury, Glenn C. "The Conservative Line on Race." *Harper's.* November 1997, 144–54.

Matsuda, Mari. "Public Response to Racist Speech: Considering the Victim's Story." 87 *Michigan Law Review* 2320 (1989).

McCloskey, Robert G. "The Supreme Court, 1961 Term—Foreword: The Reapportionment Case." 76 *Harvard Law Review* 54 (1962).

Michelman, Frank. "Law's Republic." 97 *Yale Law Journal* 1493 (1988).

Pildes, Richard. "The Politics of Race. Review of *Quiet Revolution in the South*, edited by Chandler Davidson and Bernard Grofman." 108 *Harvard Law Review* 1359 (1995).

Pildes, Richard, and Niemi, Richard. "Expressive Harms, 'Bizarre Districts,' and Voting Rights: Evaluating Election-District Appearances After *Shaw* v. *Reno.*" 92 *Michigan Law Review* 483 (1993).

Polsby, Daniel D., and Popper, Robert D. "Ugly: An Inquiry into the Problem of Racial Gerrymandering Under the Voting Rights Act." 92 *Michigan Law Review* 652 (1993).

Purdum, Todd. "President Gives Fervent Support to Fighting Bias." *New York Times.* 20 July 1995, A1.

Rohter, Larry. "A Black-Hispanic Struggle over Florida Redistricting." *New York Times.* 30 May 1992, A6.

Sandel, Michael. "Review of John Rawls, *Political Liberalism.*" 107 *Harvard Law Review* 1765 (1994).

———. "The Procedural Republic and the Unencumbered Self." *Political Theory* 12 (1984): 81–96.

Slaughter, M. M. "The Multicultural Self." 14 *Cardozo Law Review* 885 (1993).

Stark, Barbara. "Postmodern Rhetoric, Economic Rights and an International Text: 'A Miracle for Breakfast.' " 33 *Virginia Journal of International Law* 433 (1993).

Starks, Samuel. "Note: Understanding Government Affirmative Action and *Metro Broadcasting, Inc.*" 41 *Duke Law Journal* 933 (1992).

Taibi, Anthony D. "Symposium on Race Consciousness and Legal Scholarship: Race Consciousness, Communitarianism, and Banking Regulation." 1992 *University of Illinois Law Review* 1103.

Tatalovich, Anne. "Rhetoric or Reality: Casting an Empirical Eye on the Tort Reform Debate." Vol. 7, no. 1, in *Researching Law: An American Bar Foundation Update* (Winter 1996).

Thernstrom, Abigail. "More Notes from a Political Thicket." 44 *Emory Law Journal* 911 (1995).

Trent, Judy Scales. "Black Women and the Constitution: Finding Our Place, Asserting Our Rights." 24 *Harvard Civil Rights–Civil Liberties Law Review* 1 (1989).

Unger, Roberto. "Critical Legal Studies." 96 *Harvard Law Review* 561 (1982).

West, Robin. "Toward a First Amendment Jurisprudence of Respect: A Comment on George Fletcher's 'Constitutional Identity'." 14 *Cardozo Law Review* 759 (1993).

———. "The Supreme Court, 1989 Term—Foreword: Taking Freedom Seriously." 104 *Harvard Law Review* 43 (1990).

White, Lucie E. "The Legacy of *Goldberg* v. *Kelly*: A Twenty Year Perspective: *Goldberg* v. *Kelly* on the Paradox of Lawyering for the Poor." 56 *Brooklyn Law Review* 861 (1990).

Williams, Patricia J. "*Metro Broadcasting, Inc.* v. *FCC*: Regrouping in Singular Times." 104 *Harvard Law Review* 525 (1990).

———. "Alchemical Notes: Reconstructing Ideals from Deconstructed Rights." 22 *Harvard Civil Rights–Civil Liberties Law Review* 401 (1987).

————. "Spirit-Murdering the Messenger: The Discourse of Fingerpointing as the Law's Response to Racism." 42 *University of Miami Law Review* 127 (1987).

Yanos, Alexander. "Note: Reconciling the Right to Vote with the Voting Rights Act." 92 *Columbia Law Review* 1810 (1991).

Young, Iris Marion. "Polity and Group Difference: A Critique of the Ideal of Universal Citizenship." 99 *Ethics* 250 (1989).

BOOKS, CHAPTERS, AND MONOGRAPHS

Adams, John. *The Works of John Adams.* Edited by Charles Francis Adams. Boston: Little, Brown, 1956.

————. *The Political Writings of John Adams.* Edited by George A. Peek, Jr. New York: Liberal Arts Press, 1954.

Amy, Douglas. *Real Choices/Real Voices.* New York: Columbia University Press, 1993.

Anderson, Benedict. *Imagined Communities.* London: Verso, 1991.

Appiah, K. Anthony. "Identity, Authenticity, Survival." In *Multiculturalism: Examining the Politics of Recognition.* Edited by Amy Gutmann. Princeton: Princeton University Press, 1994.

Aristotle. *Introduction to Aristotle.* Edited by Richard McKeon. New York: Modern Library, 1947.

————. *The Nichomachean Ethics.* Translated by Benjamin Jowett. In *The Basic Works of Aristotle.* Edited by Richard McKeon. New York: Random House, 1941.

————. *Politica.* Translated by Benjamin Jowett. In *The Basic Works of Aristotle.* Edited by Richard McKeon. New York: Random House, 1941.

Barber, Benjamin. *Strong Democracy.* Berkeley: University of California Press, 1984.

Barone, Michael, and Ujifusa, Grant. *The Almanac of American Politics 1994.* Edited by Eleanor Evans. New York: Dutton, 1993.

Bell, Derrick. *Faces at the Bottom of the Well: The Permanence of Racism.* New York: Basic Books, 1992.

————. *And We Are Not Saved: The Elusive Quest for Racial Justice.* New York: Basic Books, 1987.

Bellah, Robert, Madsen, Richard, Sullivan, William M., Swidler, Ann, and Tipton, Steven. *Habits of the Heart.* Berkeley: University of California Press, 1985.

Berlin, Isaiah. "Two Concepts of Liberty." In *Liberalism and Its Critics.* Edited by Michael Sandel. New York: New York University Press, 1984.

————. "Equality." In *Concepts and Categories.* Edited by Henry Harvey. New York: Viking Press, 1979.

Bickel, Alexander. *The Morality of Consent.* New Haven: Yale University Press, 1975.

————. *The Supreme Court and the Idea of Progress.* New York: Harper and Row, 1970.

Birch, A. H. *Representation.* New York: Praeger, 1971.

Bourdieu, Pierre. *Outline of a Theory of Practice.* Cambridge: Cambridge University Press, 1977.

Burke, Edmund. *Edmund Burke on Government, Politics and Society.* Edited by B. W. Hill. New York: International Publications Service, 1976.

————. *Burke's Politics.* Edited by Ross Hoffman and Paul Levack. New York: Alfred Knopf, 1949.

Burke, Kenneth. *Language as Symbolic Action.* Berkeley: University of California Press, 1968.

————. *A Rhetoric of Motives.* New York: George Braziller, 1955.

Cain, Bruce. "Voting Rights and Democratic Theory: Toward a Color-Blind Society?" In *Controversies in Minority Voting*. Edited by Bernard Grofman and Chandler Davidson. Washington, D.C.: Brookings Institution, 1992.

Caldeira, Gregory. "Litigation, Lobbying and the Voting Rights Act." In *Controversies in Minority Voting*. Edited by Bernard Grofman and Chandler Davidson. Washington, D.C.: Brookings Institution, 1992.

Canavan, Francis. *The Political Reason of Edmund Burke*. Durham, N.C.: Duke University Press, 1960.

Cornell, Drucilla. *Transformations: Recollective Imagination and Sexual Difference*. New York: Routledge, 1993.

———. "The Philosophy of the Limit: Systems Theory and Feminist Legal Reform." In *Deconstruction and the Possibility of Justice*. Edited by David Gray Carlson, Drucilla Cornell, and Michael Rosenfeld. New York: Routledge, 1992.

Davidson, Chandler. "The Voting Rights Act: A Brief History." In *Controversies in Minority Voting*. Edited by Bernard Grofman and Chandler Davidson. Washington, D.C.: Brookings Institution, 1992.

Davidson, Chandler, and Grofman, Bernard, eds. *Quiet Revolution in the South*. Princeton: Princeton University Press, 1994.

Derrida, Jacques. *Specters of Marx*. New York: Routledge, 1994.

———. "Force of the Law: The Mystical Foundation of Authority." In *Deconstruction and the Possibility of Justice*. Edited by David Gray Carlson, Drucilla Cornell, and Michael Rosenfeld. New York: Routledge, 1992.

———. "Vor dem Gesetz." In *Acts of Literature*. Translated by Avital Ronell. Edited by Derek Attridge. New York: Routledge, 1992.

Eagleton, Terry. *The Ideology of the Aesthetic*. Cambridge, Mass.: Blackwell, 1990.

———. *Literary Theory: An Introduction*. Minneapolis: University of Minnesota Press, 1983.

Ely, John Hart. *Democracy and Distrust*. Cambridge, Mass.: Harvard University Press, 1980.

Fish, Stanley. *Doing What Comes Naturally*. Durham, N.C.: Duke University Press, 1989.

Foucault, Michel. *The Order of Things*. New York: Random House, 1970.

Galston, William. *Goods, Virtues and Diversity in the Liberal State*. Cambridge: Cambridge University Press, 1992.

Gellner, Ernst. *Nations and Nationalism*. Ithaca, N.Y.: Cornell University Press, 1983.

Gillette, William. *The Right to Vote*. Baltimore: Johns Hopkins University Press, 1969.

Glazer, Nathan. "The United States." In *The Protection of Ethnic Minorities: Comparative Perspectives*. Edited by Robert G. Wirsing. New York: Pergamon Press, 1981.

Glendon, Mary Ann. *Rights Talk*. Toronto: Macmillan, 1991.

Graham, Hugh Davis. "Voting Rights and the American Regulatory State." In *Controversies in Minority Voting*. Edited by Bernard Grofman and Chandler Davidson. Washington, D.C.: Brookings Institution, 1992.

Grossman, Joel B., and Wells, Richard. *Constitutional Law and Judicial Policy Making*, 3d ed. New York: Longman, 1989.

Guinier, Lani. *The Tyranny of the Majority*. New York: Free Press, 1994.

Gutmann, Amy. "Introduction." In *Multiculturalism: Examining the Politics of Recognition*. Edited by Amy Gutmann. Princeton: Princeton University Press, 1994.

Habermas, Jürgen. *Between Facts and Norms: Contributions to a Discourse Theory of Law and Democracy.* Translated by William Rehg. Cambridge, Mass.: MIT Press, 1996.

———. *The Theory of Communicative Competence Vol. 2: Lifeworld and System.* Boston: Beacon Press, 1987.

Hamilton, Alexander. "The Federalist No. 9." In Alexander Hamilton, John Jay, and James Madison, *The Federalist.* Introduction by Edward Mead Earle. New York: Modern Library, 1960.

Hayek, Friedrich. "Equality, Value and Merit." In *Liberalism and Its Critics.* Edited by Michael Sandel. New York: New York University Press, 1984.

———. *The Constitution of Liberty.* Chicago: University of Chicago Press, 1960.

Hochschild, Jennifer. *What Is Fair? American Beliefs About Distributive Justice.* Cambridge, Mass.: Harvard University Press, 1981.

Kaminski, John P., and Leffler, Richard, eds. *Federalists and Antifederalists: The Debate over the Ratification of the Constitution.* Madison, Wis.: Madison House, 1989.

Kennedy, Duncan. "Rebels from Principle: Changing the Corporate Law Firm from Within," from 36 *Harvard Law School Bulletin* (Fall 1981). In *Professional Responsibility.* Edited by Deborah Rhode. Boston: Little, Brown, 1994.

Kousser, J. Morgan. *The Shaping of Southern Politics: Suffrage Restriction and the Establishment of the One-Party South, 1880–1910.* New Haven: Yale University Press, 1974.

Kull, Andrew. *The Color-Blind Constitution.* Cambridge, Mass.: Harvard University Press, 1992.

Lepervanche, Marie de, and Bottomley, Gil, eds. *The Cultural Construction of Race.* Sydney: University of Sydney Press, 1988.

Machiavelli, Niccolo. *The Prince and the Discourses.* Translated by Luigi Ricci. New York: Random House, 1940.

MacIntyre, Alisdair. *After Virtue: A Study in Moral Theory.* Notre Dame: University of Notre Dame Press, 1984.

Madison, James. "The Federalist Nos. 10, 15 & 48." In Alexander Hamilton, John Jay, and James Madison, *The Federalist.* Introduction by Edward Mead Earle. New York: Modern Library, 1960.

Matsuda, Mari, Lawrence, Charles, Delgado, Richard, and Crenshaw, Kimberle. *Words That Wound: Critical Race Theory, Assaultive Speech and the First Amendment.* Boulder, Colo.: Westview Press, 1993.

May, Larry. *The Morality of Groups: Collective Responsibility, Group-Based Harm, and Corporate Rights.* Notre Dame: University of Notre Dame Press, 1987.

Minow, Martha. *Making All the Difference.* Ithaca, N.Y.: Cornell University Press, 1990.

Mulhall, Stephen, and Swift, Adam. *Liberals and Communitarians.* Cambridge, Mass.: Blackwell, 1992.

New Expanded Webster's Dictionary. Taunton, Mass.: World Book Marketing, 1989.

O'Rourke, Timothy G. "The 1982 Amendments and the Voting Rights Paradox." In *Controversies in Minority Voting.* Edited by Bernard Grofman and Chandler Davidson. Washington, D.C.: Brookings Institution, 1992.

Orwell, George. *Animal Farm.* London: Secker & Warburg, 1987.

———. *Nineteen Eighty-four.* New York: New American Library, 1983.

Pitkin, Hannah. *Wittgenstein and Justice.* Berkeley: University of California Press, 1972.

———. *The Concept of Representation.* Berkeley: University of California Press, 1967.

Plato. *The Republic.* Translated by Richard Sterling and William Scott. New York: W. W. Norton, 1985.

Rawls, John. *A Theory of Justice.* Cambridge, Mass.: Harvard University Press, 1971.

Rhode, Deborah, ed. *Professional Responsibility.* Boston: Little, Brown, 1994.

Rogin, Michael. *Ronald Reagan, the Movie, and Other Episodes in Political Demonology.* Berkeley: University of California Press, 1987.

Rorty, Richard. *Contingency, Irony and Solidarity.* Cambridge: Cambridge University Press, 1989.

————. *Philosophy and the Mirror of Nature.* Princeton: Princeton University Press, 1979.

Rosenberg, Gerald N. *The Hollow Hope: Can Courts Bring About Social Change?* Chicago: University of Chicago Press, 1991.

Sandel, Michael. *Liberalism and the Limits of Justice.* Cambridge: Cambridge University Press, 1982.

————, ed. *Liberalism and Its Critics.* New York: New York University Press, 1984.

Spann, Girardeau. *Race Against the Court: The Supreme Court and Minorities in Contemporary America.* New York: New York University Press, 1993.

Sunstein, Cass. *The Partial Constitution.* Cambridge, Mass.: Harvard University Press, 1993.

————. *After the Rights Revolution.* Cambridge, Mass.: Harvard University Press, 1990.

Swain, Carol. *Black Faces, Black Interests.* Cambridge, Mass.: Harvard University Press, 1993.

Taagepera, Rein, and Shugart, Matthew Soberg. *Seats and Votes: The Effects and Determinants of Electoral Systems.* New Haven: Yale University Press, 1989.

Taylor, Charles. "The Politics of Recognition." In *Multiculturalism: Examining the Politics of Recognition.* Edited by Amy Gutmann. Princeton: Princeton University Press, 1994.

————. "Hegel: History and Politics." In *Liberalism and Its Critics.* Edited by Michael Sandel. New York: New York University Press, 1984.

Thernstrom, Abigail. *Whose Votes Count?* Cambridge, Mass.: Harvard University Press, 1987.

Thernstrom, Stephan, and Thernstrom, Abigail. *America in Black and White: One Nation, Indivisible.* New York: Simon & Schuster, 1997.

Thornton, Margaret. *The Liberal Promise: Anti-Discrimination Legislation in Australia.* Oxford: Oxford University Press, 1990.

Tocqueville, Alexis, de. *Democracy in America.* Edited by Richard D. Heffner. New York: Mentor Books, 1956.

Tönnies, Ferdinand. *Community and Association.* Translated by Charles Loomis. London: Routledge and Kegan Paul, 1955.

Trakman, Leon. *Reasoning with the Charter.* Toronto: Butterworths, 1991.

United States Department of Labor, Office of Policy Planning and Research. *The Negro Family: The Case for National Action.* Washington, D.C.: U.S. Government Printing Office, March 1965.

Walzer, Michael. *What It Means to Be an American.* New York: Marsilio, 1992.

————. *Spheres of Justice: A Defense of Pluralism and Equality.* New York: Basic Books, 1983.

Webster's New Universal Unabridged Dictionary. New York: Barnes & Noble, 1989.

Williams, Melissa. "Voice, Trust and Memory: Marginalized Groups and the Failings of Liberal Representation." Ph.D. diss., Harvard University, 1993.

Wolin, Sheldon S. *Politics and Vision.* Boston and Toronto: Little, Brown, 1960.

Woodward, C. Vann. *Reunion and Relations: The Compromise of 1877 and the End of Reconstruction,* 2d ed. Garden City, N.Y.: Doubleday, 1956.
Yack, Bernard. *The Problems of a Political Animal: Community, Justice and Conflict in Aristotelian Thought.* Berkeley: University of California Press, 1993.
———. "Liberalism and Its Communitarian Critics: Does Liberal Practice 'Live Down' to Liberal Theory?" In *Community in America: The Challenges of "Habits of the Heart."* Edited by C. Reynolds. Berkeley: University of California Press, 1988.
Young, Iris Marion. *Justice and the Politics of Difference.* Princeton: Princeton University Press, 1990.

CASES

Abington v. *Schempp,* 374 U.S. 203 (1963).
Abrams v. *Johnson,* 1997 WL 331802.
Adarand v. *Pena,* 515 U.S. 200 (1995).
Allen v. *State Board of Elections,* 393 U.S. 544 (1969).
Armour v. *Ohio,* 895 F.2d 1078 (6th Cir. 1990).
Asian Americans for Equality v. *Koch,* 129 Misc.2d 67, 492 N.Y.S.2d 837 (1985).
B. C. Foreman v. *Dallas County,* 117 S.Ct. 2357 (1997).
Baker v. *Carr,* 369 U.S. 186 (1962).
Beer v. *United States,* 425 U.S. 130 (1976).
Bell v. *Maryland,* 378 U.S. 226 (1964).
Bowers v. *Hardwick,* 478 U.S. 186 (1986).
Bush v. *Vera,* 1996 U.S. LEXIS 3882.
Cannon v. *Durham County Board of Elections,* 1997 LEXIS 31794 (9th Cir. 1997).
Chisom v. *Roemer,* 111 S.Ct. 2354 (1991).
City of Cleburne v. *Cleburne Living Centers, Inc.,* 473 U.S. 432 (1985).
City of Monroe v. *United States,* 1997 U.S.LEXIS 6898.
City of Richmond v. *J. A. Croson Co.,* 488 U.S. 469, 109 S.Ct. 706 (1989).
City of Richmond v. *United States,* 422. U.S. 358 (1975).
Clinton v. *Jeffers,* 730 F.Supp. 196 (D.C.E.Ark. 1990), *affirmed,* 111 S.Ct. 662 (1991).
Colgrove v. *Green,* 328 U.S. 549 (1946).
Davis v. *Bandemeer,* 478 U.S. 109 (1986).
Dillard v. *Baldwin County Board of Education,* 686 F.Supp. 1459 (M.D. Ala. 1988).
Dupree v. *Moore,* 65 U.S.L.W. 3374 (1996).
Fortson v. *Dorsey,* 379 U.S. 433 (1965).
Frontiero v. *Richardson,* 411 U.S. 677 (1971).
Fullilove v. *Klutznick,* 448 U.S. 448, 65 L.Ed.2d 902, 100 S.Ct. 2758 (1980).
Garza v. *County of Los Angeles,* 918 F.2d 763 (9th Cir. 1990).
Gomillion v. *Lightfoot,* 364 U.S. 339 (1960).
Goss v. *Bd. of Ed. of Knoxville,* 373 U.S. 683 (1963).
Gray v. *Sanders,* 372 U.S. 368 (1963).
Growe v. *Emison,* 113 S.Ct. 1075 (1993).
Hirabayashi v. *U.S.,* 320 U.S. 81 (1943).
Holder v. *Hall,* 512 U.S. 874, 129 L.Ed.2d 687, 114 S.Ct. 2581 (1994).
Hopwood v. *Texas,* 84 F.3d 720 (1996).
Houston Lawyers' Assn. v. *Attorney General of Texas,* 111 S.Ct. 2376 (1991).
Jacobellis v. *Ohio,* 378 U.S. 184 (1964).
Johnson v. *DeGrandy,* 129 L.Ed.2d 775 (1994).
Karcher v. *Daggett,* 462 U.S. 725 (1983).
Lopez v. *Monterey County,* 1996 U.S. LEXIS 6826.

Los Angeles County v. *Garza*, 918 F.2d 763 (9th Cir. 1990), *cert. denied* 111 S.Ct. 681 (1991).
Metro Broadcasting, Inc. v. *FCC*, 497 U.S. 547 (1990).
Miller v. *Johnson*, 132 L.Ed.2d 762, 1995 U.S.LEXIS 4462.
Mobile v. *Bolden*, 446 U.S. 55 (1980).
Morse v. *Republican Party of Virginia*, 1996 U.S.LEXIS 2164.
Piscataway v. *Taxman*, 91 F.3d 1547, 117 S.Ct. 2506 (1997).
Plessy v. *Ferguson*, 163 U.S. 537 (1896).
Presley v. *Etowah County Commission*, 112 S.Ct. 820 (1992).
Reno v. *Bossier Parish School Board*, 117 S.Ct. 1491 (1997).
Reynolds v. *Sims*, 377 U.S. 53384 S.Ct. 1362 (1964).
Rogers v. *Lodge*, 458 U.S. 613 (1982).
San Antonio Independent School District v. *Rodriguez*, 411 U.S. 1 (1973).
Shaw v. *Barr (Reno)*, No. 92-357, "Appellants' Brief on the Merits" (1992).
Shaw v. *Hunt*, 1996 U.S. LEXIS 3880 (*Shaw II*).
Shaw v. *Hunt*, 861 F. Supp. 408 (E.D.N.C. 1994).
Shaw v. *Reno*, 125 L.Ed.2d 511, 113 S.Ct. 2816 (1993) (*Shaw I*).
Smith v. *Allwright*, 321 U.S. 649 (1944).
South Carolina v. *Katzenbach*, 383 U.S. 301 (1966).
Stabler v. *County of Thurston, Nebraska*, 1997 LEXIS 33753 (8th Cir. 1997).
Terry v. *Adams*, 345 U.S. 461 (1953).
Thornburg v. *Gingles*, 478 U.S. 30 (1986).
United Jewish Organizations of Williamsburg, Inc. v. *Carey*, 430 U.S. 144 (1977).
United States v. *Hays*, 515 U.S. 737, 1995 U.S. LEXIS 4464.
United States v. *Jones*, 125 F.3d 1418 (11th Cir. 1997).
University of California Board of Regents v. *Bakke*, 438 U.S. 265 (1978).
Voinovich v. *Quilter*, 113 S.Ct. 1149 (1993).
Washington v. *Tensas Parish Sch. Bd.*, 819 F.2d 609 (5th Cir. 1987).
Wesberry v. *Sanders*, 376 U.S. 1 (1964).
Whitcomb v. *Chavis*, 403 U.S. 124 (1971).
White v. *Daniel*, 909 F.2d 99 (4th Cir. 1990).
White v. *Regester*, 412 U.S. 755 (1973).
Wright v. *Rockefeller*, 376 U.S. 52 (1964).
Young v. *Fordice*, 117 S.Ct. 1228 (1997).

Index

About the Author

CHRISTOPHER M. BURKE is Assistant Attorney General in the State of Wisconsin Department of Justice.

ISBN 0-313-30751-2

9 0 0 0 0 >

EAN

9 780313 307515

HARDCOVER BAR CODE